Bioethics, Human Rights and Health Law:
Principles and Practice

Second Edition

Bioethics, Human Rights and Health Law: Principles and Practice

Second Edition

Ames Dhai and David McQuoid-Mason

JUTA

Bioethics, Human Rights and Health Law: Principles and Practice

First edition 2011
Second edition 2020

Juta and Company (Pty) Ltd
PO Box 14373, Lansdowne, 7779, Cape Town, South Africa
1st Floor, Sunclare Building, 21 Dreyer Street, Claremont 7708

www.juta.co.za

© Juta and Company (Pty) Ltd 2020

ISBN 978 1 48513 072 7

WebPDF 978 1 48513 073 4

Production specialist: Mmakasa Ramoshaba
Editor: Lee-Ann Ashcroft
Proofreader: Wendy Priilaid
Typesetter: Elinye Ithuba
Cover designer: Drag and Drop
Indexer: Lexinfo

Typeset in Adobe Caslon Pro 11/13.5

Dedication

Ames Dhai would like to dedicate this book to her granddaughter Nura who is her inspiration to continue writing and to her husband Faruk for his unstinting support over the years.

David McQuoid-Mason would like to dedicate this book to Fiona Kirkwood and to thank her for her unwavering support over the years.

Table of Contents

Preface

This book is intended to be an introductory guide for healthcare practitioners, legal practitioners, healthcare students and law students who are concerned with the delivery of healthcare services in South Africa. The book emphasises the ethical and legal aspects of healthcare in the country while making passing references to international human rights and ethical standards applicable to healthcare services. As the book is a guide, it does not deal exhaustively with the topics discussed. Instead it aims to give healthcare and legal practitioners some general guidelines which it is hoped will be of practical use to them.

The book is divided into two parts: Part 1 provides an introduction to bioethics, health law and human rights and includes chapters on ethical concepts, theories and principles, the international codes of healthcare ethics, health and human rights and basic health law. Part 2 deals with specific topics such as professionalism and healthcare, the practitioner–patient relationship, consent, confidentiality, medical malpractice and professional negligence, reproductive health, genetics, the use of human tissue, death and dying, HIV and AIDS and the law, resource allocation, healthcare aspects of business ethics, human health and the environment, and the ethics of research.

The revised chapters have been written by the editors / authors, who would like to acknowledge the contributions to the first edition by Donna Knapp van Bogaert, Harriet Etheredge, Jillian Gardner, Peter Cleaton-Jones and Norma Tsotsi.

The idea of the book was conceived by the Steve Biko Centre for Bioethics, University of the Witwatersrand, Johannesburg. This second edition is a joint venture between the School of Clinical Medicine at the Faculty of Health Sciences, University of the Witwatersrand, Johannesburg and the Centre for Socio-Legal Studies, University of KwaZulu-Natal.

Ames Dhai
Visiting Professor
School of Clinical Medicine
Faculty of Health Sciences
University of the Witwatersrand
Johannesburg

David McQuoid-Mason
Professor and Acting Director
Centre for Socio-Legal Studies
University of KwaZulu-Natal
Durban

Specialist Ethicist
Office of the President and CEO of the South African Medical Research Council.

About the authors

Ames Dhai: PhD (Wits), MBCHB (Natal), FCOG (SA), LLM (Natal), PGDipIntResEthics (UCT)

Ames Dhai is a leading authority in Bioethics. She is Visiting Professor of Bioethics and Health Law at the School of Clinical Medicine, Faculty of Health Sciences, University of the Witwatersrand, Johannesburg and Specialist Ethicist at the Office of the President and CEO of the South African Medical Research Council (SAMRC). She is Founder and Past Director of the Steve Biko Centre for Bioethics at the Faculty (2007 – 2019). She is Honorary Professor in the College of Human and Health Sciences, Swansea University, UK. She is Chairperson of the National Bioethics Committee of the UNESCO National Commission, and the SAMRC Bioethics Advisory Panel. She is also a Vice Chairperson of the International Bioethics Committee of UNESCO. She is on the Academy of Science South Africa (ASSAF) Biosafety and Biosecurity Committee and has served on several consensus panels of the ASSAF, including the ASSAF Panel on Gene Therapies and Gene Editing ELSI. She is Editor-in-chief of the South African Journal of Bioethics and Law and Associate Editor of the South African Medical Journal. She is a mediator with international accreditation through the Centre for Effective Dispute Resolution, UK. She can be credited with entrenching bioethics and human rights as an integral aspect of health sciences in SA. Using an academic platform, Professor Dhai has taken a lead in health advocacy and activism locally and internationally and has published extensively in this area.

David McQuoid-Mason: BComm (Natal), LLB (Natal), LLM (London), PhD (Natal), Advocate of the High Court of South Africa

Professor David J McQuoid-Mason is a Professor of Law at the Centre for Socio-Legal Studies, University of KwaZulu-Natal, Durban, a Fellow of the University of KwaZulu-Natal, and a previous holder of Visiting Professorships at Strathclyde University, Scotland and Griffith University, Australia. He is President of the Commonwealth Legal Education Association. He has taught LLM programmes in Law and Medical Practice and HIV/AIDS, Human Rights and the Law; and Medical Law and Ethics at the Nelson R Mandela Medical School. He has run numerous CPD workshops on Medical Law and Ethics throughout the country. He has facilitated at NGO training workshops on Street Law, Human Rights and Democracy in over 60 countries in Africa, Asia, Europe and North America.

Professor McQuoid-Mason teaches and researches in the fields of legal education, access to justice and medical law and ethics, and has published over 150 articles in law and medical journals, 60 chapters in books and 18 books. He has delivered over 150 papers at national conferences and over 200 at international conferences. He was awarded a Special Mention by UNESCO for his work in human rights education; DCLs (honoris causa) by the University of Windsor, Ontario, Canada and the University of Northumbria, United Kingdom, for his access to justice work around the world; and the Advocate of the Year award by Street Law Incorporated for his work in establishing Street Law legal literacy programmes around the world. He is an National Research Foundation A-rated Researcher.

Table of cases

Table of legislation

Introduction to *Bioethics, Human Rights and Health Law: Principles and Practice –* Background

CHAPTER 1

Ethical concepts, theories and principles and their application to healthcare

Ames Dhai and David McQuoid-Mason

By the end of this chapter readers will be able to:

1. Apply the different concepts in bioethics.
2. Understand how differing worldviews impact on patient care.
3. Apply the different theories in ethics to the healthcare context.
4. Understand how value conflicts could arise in the healthcare context.
5. Know how to avoid value conflicts and how to handle ethical dilemmas in the healthcare context.

1.1 Introduction

Philosophy is involved in many areas of human inquiry such as 'the philosophy of mind' and 'the philosophy of science'. Another branch, 'moral philosophy', typically involves applying certain types of analysis and argument in order to develop general criteria for differentiating between right and wrong, and good and evil. Ethics is a division of moral philosophy. Ethics is concerned with the moral choices people make and includes the study of right and wrong actions.[1] In other words, ethics is the study of morality.

Ethics, as a study of morality, involves a careful, systematic reflection on and analysis of actions and behaviour. Morality, as the value dimension of human decision making and behaviour, includes nouns like 'virtue', 'rights' and 'responsibilities' and adjectives like 'good', 'bad', 'right', 'wrong', 'just' and 'unjust'.[2] Bioethics may be defined as an ethical reflection on a vast array of moral issues concerning all living things which arise from the application of biomedical science to human affairs and the whole biosphere. Under its umbrella falls the practice of ethics in healthcare.

---

1   R Veach *Medical Ethics* (1997).
2   See generally, JR Williams *World Medical Association Medical Ethics Manual* (2005).

While ethics is closely related to the law, ethics and law are not identical. However, in many countries ethics is incorporated into some aspects of the law. In South Africa, ethics, especially in the health context, may be found in the Bill of Rights of the Constitution,[3] certain Acts of Parliament (e.g. the National Health Act[4]) and regulatory and policy documents which make provision for healthcare practitioners to be prosecuted should their conduct be unethical. Ethics quite often prescribes higher standards than the law (e.g. the law states that confidentiality dies with the patient, whereas the Health Professions Council of South Africa (HPCSA) ethical rules require the next of kin or the executor of the deceased's estate to consent to any disclosures about a deceased patient being made by the treating physician).[5]

1.2   Worldviews

1.2.1   Self-formulation

What constitutes the core foundational values and beliefs of individuals is embedded in them through their learning and felt experiences from childhood onwards. Childhood is the critical period of social development. It is the beginning of self-formulation.[6] In childhood, self-development is influenced by the teachings of people such as parents, religious and educational instructors, community leaders and peers. What people are taught and how they experience life contribute to their understanding of, for example, who they are, where they fit into society and what values they consider important.

The time and place of a person's birth and development also impact on his or her self-formulation.[7] For example, a male child born in 20th century China has a very different understanding of his value to society from that of a girl child born in 19th century India. Self-formulation is also influenced by a person's particular traits, habits, behavioural and cognitive dispositions – in other words, his or her genes. Another factor that contributes to the formulation of a person's self is his or her physical environment. If people were born and spent their formative years in a place where there was war or civil strife, famine or toxic fumes, these experiences would influence their development and become imprinted in their minds and bodies, or both.

---

3   Constitution of the Republic of South Africa, 1996.
4   61 of 2003.
5   Health Professions Council of South Africa *Ethical and Professional Rules of the Health Professions Council of South Africa* rule 13(2)(c).
6   L Kohlberg *Essays on Moral Development: The Philosophy of Moral Development* vol 1 (1981).
7   DR Shaffer *Social and Personality Development* 5 ed (2005).

1.2.2 Social order and worldview

As people mature, values and beliefs concerning who people are and where they fit into the social order represent their worldview. A person's worldview is his or her theoretical concept of reality, part of his or her social identity.[8] In addition, through others, people acquire role-specific sets of values and beliefs. By role-specific is meant that individuals are taught to accept the roles ascribed to them by a particular society.[9]

For example, females in one society may be taught that subservience to males is the norm, while in another society females may be taught that gender equality is the norm. Whatever the case, because individuals are part of a given society, they are effectively taught their role-specific sets of values in the routine course of their lives.[10] In this way, the social order of a particular society is reproduced.

1.2.3 Familiarities and challenges

People's interactions with the world are shaped by how they see the world in the same way as their perceptions of the world are shaped by their interactions with it. A person's own particular worldviews and ways of life are those with which the person is the most familiar. People are familiar and comfortable with their own worldviews, and as a result they often do not see any reason to examine them carefully or to criticise them.[11] They simply accept them. A person may say, for example: 'I believe the way I believe because I was taught to believe that way. I do not see anything wrong with it. I don't even think about it'. Or, 'People whom I admire taught me to believe the way I do. If I don't believe them, then I don't respect them'. Or, 'This is what my society stands for and I don't see anything wrong with it – so why should I ask questions?'

Statements such as these are problematic, because they simply close any chance of dialogue amongst people.[12] While it is acknowledged that powerful forces shape people and that the values people are taught are important, human beings may still be able to exercise their free will. Ethics requires that people reflect on their own preconceptions. Ethics requires people to confront issues in a broader perspective and to interrogate their familiar ways of thinking within the context of their cultures, traditions and religious beliefs.

---

8   HA Bosma, DJ Delevita and HD Grotevant (eds) *Identity Development: An Interdisciplinary Approach* (1994) 67–80.
9   DJ Benjamin, JJ Choi and A Strickland *Social Identity and Preferences* (2008).
10 JJ Thompson *Ideology and Modern Culture* (1992) 87.
11 S Hampshire, B Williams, T Nagel and R Dworkin *Public and Private Morality* (1991).
12 EF Chatman 'A theory of life in the round' (1999) 5 (3) *J Am Soc Informat Sci* 207–19.

Living in a pluralistic world will present challenges to the preconceived notions that are embedded in the worldviews and ways of life of different segments of South African society. This is because healthcare practitioners living in a pluralist society are necessarily involved with a variety of people with differing beliefs and value systems, (e.g. patients and co-workers who may have different worldviews from theirs).

1.3 Values and value systems

The study of values and value systems is complex. What people value may range from their personal preferences, desires or needs, to things more objective such as truth, beauty and health. Different worldviews encompass sets of values shared by an individual or a group of individuals. The values people hold may share similarities, but they may also conflict. Value conflicts should not necessarily be viewed as undesirable. Rather, they should represent a challenge. Otherwise, if people are bound by the limits of their present boundaries, how can they then grow, develop and realise their true potential?

People can clarify their values by reflecting on their own worldviews. By doing so they may find that some of their values make sense and some do not. Moreover, when people step out of their own 'boxes' they may realise that while there are diverse values embedded in worldviews, they are not all necessarily irreconcilable and there are many ways of understanding the world. Sensitive healthcare practitioners recognise that each situation they face is complex and that differences in worldviews require negotiation – not blanket dismissals.

Values and value systems are also entwined in the roles people play both as individuals and professionals in society. Individuals engage in different roles in society as is appropriate to their circumstances. For example, people may be mothers, friends, artists or healthcare practitioners. Each of these different roles involves some degree of social and psychological interaction. However, they all share a common dimension – they all involve morality. It is the involvement of others in people's lives that grounds moral relationships. As human beings are socially inclined, their actions or inactions will in some way be connected to other humans. Entwined in their choices of actions or inactions are considerations of value (e.g. who or what they value and how they express it).

1.3.1 Healthcare and values

The word 'value' is used and understood in many different ways. Values are often thought of in a hierarchical sense. Applying this to healthcare practice, it might be said that the most cherished value in healthcare is trust, while another important value is compassion.

'Value' may also be regarded as a process of evaluating actions in relation to other moral categories. For example, values and systems of values may be applied in the context of healthcare professional groups or associations. When it is said that trust is of value to healthcare practitioners, its meaning may be expressed in terms of certain principles, standards or qualities that are considered worthwhile, desirable or important to the healthcare profession.

A moral position on an issue is usually based upon a profession's current value system. Values and value ranking both persist and change over time. For example, what was at one time considered as a first principle or highest professional value, such as strong paternalism, does not represent current consensus. Healthcare practitioners have an obligation to remain mindful of their profession's values and organisationally revisit them from time to time.

As mentioned, values in the healthcare professions are based on their current value systems; however, these systems may change as society changes. For instance, the values on which the post-apartheid South African Constitution[13] is based include 'human dignity, the achievement of equality and the advancement of human rights and freedoms, ... [n]on-racialism and non-sexism', and the '[s]upremacy of the Constitution and the rule of law'.[14] This means that while the healthcare professions' value systems in South Africa may impose ethical standards higher than what is required in the Constitution, they can never be lower than, and in conflict with, the Constitution and the law. For example, the HPCSA ethical rule about confidentiality extending after death[15] sets a higher standard than that required in the Constitution and the law. This is because both the Constitution and the HPCSA recognise that when people die their rights die with them, although there may be safeguards about how their bodies are handled.[16]

1.3.2 Value judgements

A person making a value judgement entails that person forming his or her own judgement about value issues, especially when faced with a value conflict. It is on this basis that people are held responsible for their behaviour. People are constantly faced with value conflicts between the various spheres of their lives such as in science, belief systems or religion, family, politics and sexuality.

---

13   Constitution of the Republic of South Africa, 1996.
14   Section 1(a)–(c).
15   Ethical Rules of Conduct for Practitioners registered under the Health Professions Act 56 of 1974 Rule 13(2).
16   DJ McQuoid-Mason 'Disclosing details about the medical treatment of a deceased public figure in a book: Who should have consented to the disclosures in Mandela's Last Days' (2017) 107(12) 1072–1074.

These value conflicts intersect within their own personalities in their social lives and professions.[17]

When people say that they 'have certain values' it means that they make their own judgements about how they should behave or the values they embrace. This could differ according to the values of different groups. Sometimes people articulate their personal values and at other times they do not.

When people reflect upon how they should behave, this may rule out the mere acceptance of the preferred code of behaviour with which they were brought up. If they decide to conform to the worldviews of a group or tradition, they should be able to justify the reasonableness of it. They should not simply conform because it is the general practice.

1.3.3 Personal and professional values

Personal and professional value judgements may take on differing dimensions and may not always coincide. In healthcare practice, this is an important consideration as personal value judgements may directly influence the ways in which patients are treated because of conflicts between healthcare practitioners in their roles as professionals and their patients who express different values. A major consideration is whether healthcare practitioners should act in accordance with their own personal values or adapt their behaviour to be in keeping with the values of their profession.

If healthcare practitioners allow their personal values to override other considerations to the prejudice of their patients because their values differ, such conduct would be a breach of their professional responsibility. Healthcare practitioners are obliged to move beyond their personal value systems where these may prejudice their patients. It must be recognised that some patients may have worldviews different from those of their healthcare providers. Healthcare ethics requires that healthcare practitioners frame their personal and professional values differently. Healthcare professionals are required to regard the wellbeing of their patients as their primary value. In conflicting situations, professional values must inform the behaviour of healthcare providers towards their patients.

A lesson in this respect can be learnt from the general principles regarding the limitations on patient autonomy where healthcare practitioners are requested by their patients to engage in unethical or illegal practices. A good example is the Michael Jackson case, where the singer requested his doctor give him a Propofol anaesthetic at home to help him sleep, when this anaesthetic should only be administered in a hospital environment. When Jackson died as a result,

---

17   *Max Weber Essays in Sociology* (1919); cf HH Gerth and C Wright Mills (eds) *Max Weber Essays in Sociology* (1984).

the doctor could not, amongst other excuses, argue that he was respecting Jackson's autonomy because Jackson had consented. The doctor was found guilty of culpable homicide.[18]

1.4   Cultural relativism

One of the values embedded in professional practice by healthcare providers is the alleviation of pain and suffering. Therefore, if a health practitioner is requested by a father to scarify his three-year-old son's face deeply without anaesthesia because it is his cultural tradition, there is conflict between the value system of the patient and the professional value of alleviating pain and suffering. Does respecting different worldviews mean that the practitioner should perform any action or procedure that the patient requests – even if it conflicts with the values of the particular practitioner's profession? To answer this question, it is necessary to have a brief understanding of the term 'cultural relativism'.

Cultural relativism claims that there is no absolute universal truth – be it ethical, moral or cultural. It is argued that since there is no way to judge what is right or wrong or good or bad between different cultures, all cultural beliefs and values are ethnocentric.[19] In other words, cultural relativism could be viewed as the belief that no ethical principles are universal and that they must yield to cultural differences. Cultural relativists claim that their traditions must be non-critically accepted by all those outside their culture.

A major flaw in the idea of cultural relativism is identified in the nature of culture itself – culture is not static and all cultures change through time. What is a particular practice or tradition within a specific culture today may not be the same in ten years' time.[20] For example, it is said that the Zulu King Shaka abolished circumcision for Zulu men nearly 200 years ago, but the current Zulu King Goodwill Zwelithini has reintroduced circumcision to reduce the incidence of HIV infection.[21] Furthermore, judging a particular tradition within a culture today as deficient or harmful is not the same as disrespecting the whole culture. In practice, cultural relativism often provides justifications for the infliction of harm and the violation of basic human rights. Some of the groups most commonly harmed by claims of cultural relativism are those who are marginalised and vulnerable such as women, children and the elderly.

---

18   DJ McQuoid-Mason 'Michael Jackson and the limits of patient autonomy' (2012) 5(1) *SAJBL* 11–14.
19   E Gellner *Relativism and the Social Sciences* (1985).
20   K Gyekye *Tradition and Modernity Philosophical Reflections on the African Experience* (1997).
21   DJ McQuoid-Mason 'Is the mass circumcision drive in KwaZulu-Natal involving neonates and children less than 16 years of age legal? What should doctors do?' (2013) 103(5) *SAMJ* 283–284.

1.4.1   *Cultural relativism: How should healthcare practitioners respond?*

In the case of the three-year-old boy mentioned above,[22] assume that the healthcare practitioner understands that the father does not intend to cause his child harm because his request is made to express a treasured cultural tradition. Tolerance as a value is well recognised in the context of healthcare practice. Tolerance means that health practitioners should accept circumstances which give rise to traditions other than their own and should indicate their willingness to live peacefully within a pluralist society. However, this does not make the participation by the healthcare practitioner in the scarification of the boy right or good. The health practitioner's professional value judgement should be that the request of the father, because it consists of the infliction of unnecessary physical suffering to the child, cannot be allowed. Blanket compliance to all traditional practices can be dangerous. The question to be answered when confronted with such dilemmas is 'whether the practice promotes or hinders the welfare of the people whose lives are affected by it'.[23] In other words, who is harmed and who is helped? While justice and fairness require that people respect different values and treat all cultural groups as equal, this is quite different from saying that all those outside their culture must non-critically accept their traditions – particularly when they cause harm to marginalised and vulnerable groups.[24]

Positive steps that healthcare practitioners can take in circumstances similar to those involving the three-year-old boy are to use the consultation as an opportunity for patient education and the sharing of ideas. Education of patients is a professional value and an important role of healthcare professionals. Healthcare professionals are obliged to transcend cultural boundaries, never to intentionally cause harm, and always to avoid the perpetuation of suffering and injustice. The consultation could be the starting point for this.

In this respect, healthcare practitioners in South Africa are assisted by the Constitution, which states that while people 'belonging to a cultural … community may not be denied the right to enjoy their culture' and 'to form, join and maintain cultural … associations and other organs of civil society',[25] they 'may not be exercised in a manner inconsistent with any provision of the Bill of Rights'.[26] In short, the healthcare practitioner in the situation regarding scarification of the young boy, may during the counselling session explain to the boy's father that his or her hands are tied by the Constitution, and that if the father wishes to challenge the decision of the healthcare practitioner the father will have to go to court.

---

22   See above para 1.4.
23   J Rachels *The Elements of Moral Philosophy* 2 ed (1993) 29.
24   R Macklin *Against Relativism: Cultural Diversity and the Search for Ethical Universals in Medicine* (1999).
25   Section 31(1)(*a–b*).
26   Section 31(2).

1.5 Kantian deontology

Immanuel Kant was the first philosopher to put the concept of duty at the centre of ethics. Deontology is a rule-based theory (*deon* being the Greek word for 'duty'). Rule-based theories say, for example, 'do this', 'don't do that' or 'that is your duty'. Common examples of where duties are expressed in rules are the biblical 'Ten Commandments', and the professional ethical guidelines and codes of conduct.

Kant believed that all humans are rational beings. This means that people should not act only out of instinct or pure emotion, but should rather make rational or reasoned choices. Because humans can reason, each human being is a holder of intrinsic dignity. Kant does not focus on producing some societal good – he is concerned with how people act, their motives and intentions (i.e. the action). How we act is based on 'a maxim'.

1.5.1 Kant: Maxims and the categorical imperatives

A maxim is a general action-guiding principle always to act in a prescribed way whenever the case arises.[27] Kant has argued that ethical reasoning is based on the ideal of people living by principles that, at least, could take the form of sets of rules – what he calls moral laws. Kant expresses moral law in the form of categorical imperatives. Categorical imperatives are absolute commands of reason that permit no exceptions and have no concern with practical benefit or pleasure. Kant formulated three versions of the categorical imperative:

(a) Act in a manner as if the maxim of your action were to become by your will a universal law of nature

(b) Act in a manner so as to treat humanity, whether in your own person or that of any other person, never solely as a means but always also as an end

(c) Act in a manner as if you were by your maxims in every case a legislating member in the universal kingdom of ends.[28]

Kant's categorical imperative has three components:

(a) It is a maxim – a general action-guiding principle.

(b) It is a universal law – a principle that applies always, under all circumstances, everywhere, and for everyone.

(c) It requires the will to act accordingly – this is an appeal to a person's moral conscience.[29]

---

27   I Kant *Grounding for the Metaphysics of Morals* (1785); JW Ellington (trans) *Grounding for the Metaphysics of Morals* 3 ed (1993) 32–36.

28   I Kant *Grounding for the Metaphysics of Morals* (1993) 30.

29   Ibid. 42–48.

In other words, when considering whether their actions are right or wrong, people should ask the following questions:

(a)   What is the maxim that guides my action?

(b)   Can I apply my maxim to all people everywhere under any circumstances?

(c)   Is my maxim consistent?

If these three required components are fulfilled, then how the person acts is ethical and is right. An act is morally right if, and only if, a person can consistently will that the maxim supporting the action should apply always and everywhere.

According to deontology, what is right or wrong is a matter of doing one's duty. In other words, people have a moral duty to do the things that are right and not to do things that are wrong. Kant states that rational persons have dignity insofar as they are capable of moral action,[30] and those who have this capacity are said to be autonomous. Kantian dignity requires people to respect not only their own dignity but also the dignity of others.[31] Kant's idea of dignity excludes those who lack the capacity for autonomous action. Some examples of individuals who do not have the capacity to act autonomously are infants, people in persistent vegetative states and those who are severely mentally challenged.

Kant also argues that, as a human being, everyone has intrinsic value. The value of a person's moral status is vital in that it determines his or her moral obligations to others. Adult rational human beings are considered to be moral agents with moral agency. Many ideas in bioethics may be derived from the works of Kant, of which his principle of respect for the dignity of persons remains paramount as an expression of the intrinsic value, dignity and worth of human life. Under Kant's umbrella of respect for persons, other current bioethical mandates may be derived such as confidentiality, promise keeping, informed consent, truth telling and the notion of human rights. These are all applicable to the practitioner–patient relationship.

1.6   Consequentialism

The consequentialist set of theories is based on the consequences of people's actions. They are sometimes called 'teleological' theories, from the Greek word *telos*, meaning 'goal'. Consequentialism holds that morality should guide an individual's conduct in such a way that the outcome is the best, and what is considered right or wrong depends on the consequences of acts (i.e. the ends justify the means). It follows that the more good consequences are produced,

---

30   I Kant *Groundwork for the Metaphysics of Morals* vol 4 (1911) 435.

31   I Kant *Groundwork for the Metaphysics of Morals* (1785) TK Abbott (trans); cf Lara Denis (ed) *Groundwork for the Metaphysics of Morals* (2005).

the better the act. Consequentialism is drawn upon when making decisions that involve trade-offs (e.g. should resources be used for liver transplants that would benefit a few or for mass vaccinations that would benefit many more?). It is this set of theories that, in the main, informs public health policy.

1.6.1 Utilitarianism

Utilitarianism is a well-known form of consequentialism and is commonly referred to as 'the greatest happiness for the greatest number'.[32] Right or wrong is a function of the consequences of people's actions. Individuals should act in a way that they produce the greatest possible balance of utility (good, happiness or pleasure) over bad for everyone affected by their actions.[33] Impartiality is an important aspect of utilitarianism. The pleasures and pains of all sentient beings ought to be taken equally into account when decisions are made. The classical utilitarian calculus does not permit any favouritism or privilege based on mutual feelings, family relationships, shared nationalities and the like.[34] There is therefore an attempt to reach a truly objective means of judging the morality (usefulness) of all behaviour, without exception.[35]

1.7 Communitarianism

Communitarian means pertaining to or characteristic of a community. It is the perspective that recognises both individual human dignity and the social dimension of being human.[36] Communal means relating to or benefiting a community. Communalism is a political theory advocating a society in which all property is publicly owned and each person is paid and works according to his or her needs and ability. It is a model of political organisation that stresses ties of affection, kinship and a sense of common purpose and tradition.[37] The meaning of community varies from referring to a political state to smaller communities, institutions and to the family.[38]

---

32   HP Kainz *Benthamite Social Utility as a Strictly Objective Norm* (1998); M Häyry *Liberal Utilitanarianism and Applied Ethics* (1994) 9.
33   WH Shaw *Social and Personal Ethics: Classical Theories* (1993) 54.
34   M Häyry *Liberal Utilitarianism and Applied Ethics* (1994) 3–10.
35   HP Kainz *Benthamite Social Utility as a Strictly Objective Norm* (1988).
36   A Etzioni 'Introduction' in E Etzioni (ed) *The Essential Communitarian Reader* (1998) ix–xxxix.
37   S Blackburn *Oxford Dictionary of Philosophy* (1966).
38   K Gyekye *Tradition and Modernity: Philosophical Reflections on the African Experience* (1997).

1.7.1 Communitarianism and ethics

In communitarianism, the individual is embedded in a context of social relationships and interdependence, and is never just an insulated person.[39] Social values, such as peace, harmony, stability, generosity, solidarity, compassion, mutual reciprocity, social well-being and sympathy, are promoted in this way of viewing the world and challenge the individualist liberal concept of a common good. The focus here is that of emphasising awareness about and commitment to responsibilities to other members of the community.[40]

1.7.2 African communitarianism

Communalism has been and is still (partially) the structure of traditional African society where its socio-economic life is based on the principle of common ownership.[41] African communalism is expressed in Joseph Mbiti's coinage of the African worldview: 'I am because we are; and since we are, therefore I am'. In other words, 'I exist because the community exists'.[42] This is what is commonly meant by the term 'Ubuntu'.

A person's sensitivity to the interests and well-being of the community is considered a primary value. Individual rights are viewed as having equal status with responsibilities. The view on responsibilities to others is rooted in the consideration of their needs rather than their rights. Rights are given attention, but equal attention is given to other values of the community that, in certain cases, may be regarded as overriding. The individual is both autonomous and a communal being. It is recognised that besides being a social being by nature, the individual also possesses rationality, moral sense, capacity for virtue and capacity for free choice. This has the advantage of keeping the individual's ability to take a distanced view of the practices and the values promoted by one's community.[43] By autonomy being interpreted in this relational way, interconnectedness, interrelatedness and interdependence of dignity, rights and responsibilities of all people are highlighted.[44] Consequently, an entitlement of respect for all human beings is created.

---

39   TL Beauchamp and JF Childress *Principles of Biomedical Ethics* 4 ed (1997).
40   E Etzioni (ed) *The Essential Communitarian Reader* (1998) 72–79.
41   K Wiredu 'How not to Compare African Thought with Western Thought' in EC Eze (ed) *African Philosophy: An Anthology* (2000) 193–199.
42   Ibid.
43   K Gyekye *Tradition and Modernity: Philosophical Reflections on the African Experience* (1997).
44   J Mfutso-Bengo and F Masiye 'Toward an African Ubuntuology Bioethics in Malawi in the Context of Globalization' in C Myser (ed) *Bioethics around the Globe* (2001) 152–163.

Following centuries of suppression by colonialism, and in South Africa by decades of apartheid, there is now a resurgence of African indigenous values.[45] Both academic and professional circles in Africa are leaning more to African values for the practice of ethics and since 1994, Ubuntu has been systematically drawn upon by the courts when arriving at judgments.[46]

An important ethical consideration inherent in Ubuntu is that of an appreciation of the survival of the community. Ubuntu translates into humanness. It includes values of compassion, caring, justice/law, righteousness, harmony and balance. Therefore, the fundamental basis of an African approach towards ethics is the Ubuntu standard - which reflects living in solidarity with other people and humanness grounded in social life. Participating and getting involved in the life world of 'the Other' without a standpoint of superiority is necessary for ethical conduct in this context.[47] This has particular bearing on the practitioner–patient relationship.

1.7.3 Communitarianism and healthcare

The concepts of public health and distributive justice or a collective duty to take care of all citizens, and to provide equal access to healthcare, ensure the involvement of the family in decision making and a shared consensus about public policies are expressions of the worldview of communitarianism. The appeal of communitarianism is that it sounds more satisfactory and humane to live in an organic community than to be alienated in an aggregate of autonomous individuals.

1.8 Virtue ethics

The focus of virtue ethics is on the character of the virtuous individual and on the inner traits, dispositions and motives that qualify the person as being virtuous. It is concerned with what sort of person is good or virtuous and what sort of life people ought to live, and it dates back to Aristotle (384–322 BCE), during the Ancient Greek era. This model of ethics suggests that the proper understanding of what is right in human action is a matter of sensitivity and fine discernment incorporated into good habits of moral thought, desire and action, rather than general rules and principles. It thinks primarily in terms of noble or ignoble, admirable or deplorable, good or bad, in preference to what is obligatory

---

45   A Dhai 'Understanding ethics with specific reference to health research' in *Health Research Ethics. Safeguarding the interests of health research participants* (2019) 2–30.
46   TW Bennet *'Ubuntu*: the Concept and its Value' *Ubuntu: An African Jurisprudence* (2018) 24–59.
47   N Mkhize *'Ubuntu-Botho* Approach to Ethics: An Invitation to Dialogue' in N Nortje, A Hoffman and JC De Jongh (eds) *African Perspectives on Ethics for Healthcare Professionals* (2018) 25–48.

or permissible or wrong according to the rules or norms. Universal principles that allow for no exceptions – such as Kant's categorical imperative – are eschewed.[48] There are many character traits that are considered as virtues such as benevolence, fairness, reasonableness, civility, friendliness, self-confidence, compassion, generosity, self-control, honesty, self-discipline, cooperativeness, industriousness, self-reliance, courage, justice, tactfulness, courteousness, loyalty, thoughtfulness, dependability and moderation.[49]

1.8.1   Virtue ethics and healthcare

Consideration of the character of individuals making healthcare decisions has led to the resurgence of interest in the ethics of their moral character (i.e. virtue ethics), because society views healthcare practitioners as moral agents with special commitments and responsibilities.[50] Healthcare practitioners need to approach their work as a patient-centred profession in which they pursue both technical and personal excellence. Some of the virtues practitioners should seek to attain are compassion, trustworthiness and personal integrity.[51]

1.9   The ethics of care

The ethics of care takes its roots in the work of Gilligan[52] and differs from other theories of ethics in that its focus is not directed on the macro organisation of society (as in utilitarianism), but on a micro level which will influence the macro level. Care, not duty, is central to morality in the ethics of care which is closely aligned to virtue ethics.

Major proponents of the ethics of care agree that there has been a historic disconnection between ethical theories as conceived in the masculine sense of impersonal justice and a feminine approach to ethics in which care, a sense of responsibility and obligation to others are recognised. In the latter, true objectivity consists in recognising how emotional involvement in making moral judgements is not only proper but necessary in order to identify exactly what action is carried out.[53]

One of the difficulties in realising an ethics of care approach lies in the very organisation of modern society. In competitive markets where self-gain is

---

48   B Williams *Ethics and the Limits of Philosophy* (1985) 55.

49   J Rachels *The Elements of Moral Philosophy* (2003).

50   ED Pellegrino *The Virtues in Medical Practice* (1993).

51   ED Pellegrino 'The internal morality of clinical medicine: A paradigm for the ethics of the helping and healing professions' (2001) 26(6) *J Med and Phil* 559–579.

52   C Gilligan *A Different Voice: Psychological Theory and Women's Development* (1982).

53   V Held *The Ethics of Care* (2005).

predominant, the social environment is not conducive to stepping out of this reality to reflect on caring relationships.[54]

Care ethics identifies the importance of promoting a social environment that is not based on marketplace competition or contracts between rational, self-interested economic agents,[55] but on family relations. Care ethics points out that everyone is in essence dependent on others.[56]

1.10 The 'four principles'

Beauchamp and Childress[57] provide a principle-based framework for resolving ethical problems which trouble healthcare practitioners that is sometimes referred to as the 'four principles'. Through a process of balancing the principles of autonomy, non-maleficence, beneficence and justice, they argue that healthcare dilemmas may often be resolved.[58] Duties flow from principles that are prima facie and can be overruled by some other stronger moral consideration. Each principle is binding unless it clashes with an equal or stronger obligation[59] thereby resulting in a moral dilemma.

The principles have to be interpreted in terms of existing social practices and particular contexts, and the ways in which they will be balanced may differ between contexts. For example, the principle of autonomy in an individualistic Western liberal perspective will differ significantly from that of some non-Western cultures in which the idea of decision taking is placed within a community.

1.10.1 The principle of respect for autonomy

Beauchamp and Childress relate respect for autonomy to individual autonomous choice and decision making by patients.[60] This principle takes into consideration self-determination and is the basis of informed consent and respecting confidentiality in healthcare practice. It acknowledges the right of individuals to hold views, make choices and take actions based on their values and beliefs. This principle comprises both negative and positive obligations. The negative obligation entails that there should be no controlling influences by others for an action to be truly autonomous. The positive obligation requires that autonomous

---

54   C Gilligan 'Moral Orientation and Moral Development' in E Feder Kittay and DT Meyers (eds) *Women and Moral Theory* (1987) 19–33.

55   M Friedman 'Feminism in ethics: Conceptions of autonomy' in M Fricker and J Hornsby (eds) *The Cambridge Companion to Feminism in Philosophy* (2000) 205–211.

56   MA Slote *The Ethics of Care and Empathy* (2007).

57   TL Beauchamp and JF Childress *Principles of Biomedical Ethics* (1979).

58   Ibid.

59   TL Beauchamp and JF Childress *Principles of Biomedical Ethics* 3 ed (1994) 33–36.

60   Ibid. 58–103.

decision making needs to be facilitated by treating the individual with respect when sharing information and assisting them to understand.[61] This is of particular importance during the informed consent process.

1.10.2 The principle of non-maleficence

In healthcare practice, non-maleficence is defined as the principle of intentionally not inflicting harm. This principle is usually explained using the terms 'harm' and 'injury'. Injury could, on the one hand, be harm, but on the other it could refer to injustice, violation or wrong. Non-maleficence requires that needless risk of harm is to be avoided, and when risk is inevitable it should be minimised as far as is reasonably possible.[62]

1.10.3 The principle of beneficence

Beneficence means doing good for others and promoting others' interests and well-being. It is different from benevolence, wishing good for others. In healthcare practice this principle requires practitioners to act in the best interests of their patients and to aim at promoting their positive welfare. The duty of beneficence is inherent in the role of the practitioner. It is insufficient simply to avoid harmful acts, and positive steps must be taken to assist others. However, obligations of extreme sacrifice and altruism are not obligations emanating from beneficence.[63]

1.10.4 The principle of justice

The principle of justice in healthcare refers mainly to distributive justice and the fair allocation of scarce healthcare resources. Whereas the principles of autonomy, beneficence and non-maleficence focus on how we ought to treat individuals, the principle of justice considers whether the individual is properly treated when considered within the larger picture. It assists in determining whether the benefits and burdens are distributed fairly in society. Justice requires that equals are to be treated equally and that the distribution of burdens and benefits should be fair. Exploiting the vulnerabilities of patients is one of the ways in which justice as fairness is violated in the healthcare context.[64]

---

61   TL Beauchamp and JF Childress *Principles of Biomedical Ethics* 3 ed (1994) 58–103.
62   Ibid.
63   Ibid.
64   Ibid.

These principles are consistent with the International Bill of Rights,[65] the African Charter of Human and People's Rights,[66] the South African Constitution[67] and the South African Patients' Rights Charter.[68]

1.11   The harm principle

The utilitarian John Stuart Mill[69] articulates what is commonly called the harm principle, as follows:

> The only purpose for which power can be rightfully exercised over any member of a civilized community, against his will, is to prevent harm to others. His own good, either physical or moral, is not a sufficient warrant. He cannot rightfully be compelled to do or forbear because it will be better for him to do so, because it will make him happier, because, in the opinion of others, to do so would be wise or even right.

If individuals are causing harm only to themselves, others may not interfere. Only actions that violate others' rights and harm others' welfare are grounds for legal and social censure. However, those actions that harm only the perpetrator of the harmful action warrant no grounds for interference.

1.12   Paternalism

When healthcare practitioners act in what they consider as being in the best interests of their patients even though such action is not consistent with their patients' beliefs and desires, the practitioners are conducting themselves paternalistically. Paternalism ensues when a practitioner disregards a rational patient's autonomous decision-making ability. It is a form of disrespect and abuse of the patient's dignity.

---

65 Consisting of the United Nations Universal Declaration of Human Rights (1948), the United Nations Covenant on Civil and Political Rights (1966) and the United Nations Covenant on Economic, Social and Cultural Rights (1966).
66 Organization of African Unity African Charter of Human and Peoples Rights (1981).
67 Constitution of the Republic of South Africa, 1996.
68 Department of National Health Patients' Rights Charter: https://www.safmh.org.za/documents/policies-and-legislations/Patient%20Rights%20Charter.pdf (accessed on 2 June 2020); generally, see below para 3.4.
69 JS Mill *On Liberty* (1958).

Some questions on what the healthcare practitioner should do

A pregnant woman consults a healthcare practitioner to terminate her pregnancy. She satisfies the legal requirements for a termination of pregnancy. On religious grounds the practitioner does not believe in abortion. How should the practitioner reconcile her worldview with that of her patient?

CHAPTER 2

Codes of healthcare ethics

Ames Dhai

By the end of this chapter readers will be able to:

1. List the important international and national codes of medical ethics and the bodies responsible for their authorship and enforcement.
2. Explain the content for the more relevant ethical guidelines.
3. Appreciate the benefits of adhering to international and local ethical guidelines in healthcare practice.
4. Explain some of the contents of the Health Professions Council of South Africa (HPCSA) ethics guideline booklets.
5. Appreciate the steps involved in analysing an ethical dilemma in the healthcare context.

2.1   Introduction

There are at least two ways to approach a bioethical inquiry. One is ethics formulated as professional codes of conduct that seek to provide guidance to practitioners when ethical dilemmas are encountered and the other is the process of resolving dilemmas through philosophical reasoning. Codes serve as a source of moral authority, and are used among professionals and laypersons to set standards for ethical conduct, to define new ethical issues, and to support one position or another in ethical discourse.[1] Ethical codes in healthcare set down norms to regulate the interactions between patients and their practitioners, and practitioners and their colleagues, thereby providing a framework and guidelines for morality in healthcare and health practice. Healthcare practitioners and students in training are expected to internalise the shared values of the profession that they enter. In most countries, healthcare practitioners are self-regulated, hence ethical codes are necessary to allow for a realisation of the claim by health practitioners that they are capable of disciplining themselves in all areas, especially when faced with challenges.

---

1   ED Pellegrino 'Codes, virtue, and professionalism' in J Sugarman and D Sulmasy (eds) *Methods in Medical Ethics* 2 ed (2010) 91–107.

Professional codes in healthcare are as old as antiquity, and despite the Hippocratic Oath[2] being over 2 500 years old, the principles have survived the test of time and have been included in modern versions of the oath internationally by the World Medical Association[3] (WMA) and the International Council of Nurses[4] (ICN), and nationally by statutory councils including the Health Professions Council of South Africa[5] (HPCSA) and the South African Nursing Council[6] (SANC). Moreover, Health Science Faculties and Medical Schools in South Africa have developed their own versions of the Hippocratic Oath.[7] Therefore, the Hippocratic tradition is seen even now as the most fundamental underpinning of the moral values shared by healthcare practitioners.

That the healthcare practitioner's primary duty is to act in the patient's best interest and to avoid harm is widely accepted by all practitioners. This is echoed in the Declaration of Geneva[8] (a modern-day version of the Hippocratic Oath, see below) and the Florence Nightingale Pledge. In 1893, the Florence Nightingale Pledge was taken for the first time by nurses in the United States. It has since been adopted by the nursing profession in many countries. In South Africa it has been adapted into the South African Nursing Council Code of Ethics for Nursing Practitioners, and is the oath taken by nurses at graduation.

The wide acceptance by practitioners to benefit and not harm patients is the most enduring legacy of the Hippocratic Oath. However, the Nuremberg Trials exposed the fact that not all practitioners abided by the Hippocratic legacy. Professional conscience and responsibility had to be revisited. The body set up to do this was the World Medical Association (WMA). While the codes and guidelines emanating from the WMA are specific to medical practice, their scope is wide enough to apply to all the different categories of health practice.

In South Africa, the HPCSA, a statutory body in terms of the Health Professions Act,[9] is responsible for setting the standards for the ethical and professional conduct of practitioners registered with the council. The vision and motto of the HPCSA is to protect the public and guide the professions.[10] Almost every profession we can conceive of is advised by international codes of ethics.

---

2   'The Hippocratic Oath' in TA Mappes and D DeGrazia (eds) *Biomedical Ethics* 5 ed (2001) 66.

3   World Medical Association: https://www.wma.net/ (accessed on 23 March 2020).

4   International Council of Nurses: http://www.icn.ch/ (accessed on 23 March 2020).

5   Health Professions Council of South Africa: http//www.hpcsa.co.za/ (accessed on 23 March 2020).

6   South African Nursing Council: http//www.sanc.co.za (accessed on 23 March 2020).

7   A Dhai 'The Life Esidimeni tragedy: Moral pathology and an ethical crisis' (2018) 108(5) *SAMJ* 382–385.

8   World Medical Association Declaration of Geneva: https://www.wma.net/policies-post/wma-declaration-of-geneva/ (accessed on 23 March 2020).

9   Act 56 of 1974.

10   See footnote 5 above.

These codes are designed as a guide for good moral practice of one's profession. Healthcare professionals are no exception.

The World Medical Association was established after World War II, mainly in reaction to reports of atrocities involving physicians. Today it is considered the global representative body for physicians, overarching 114 national medical associations with a combined membership of over seven million physicians.[11] Although the WMA takes the lead in formulating ethical codes for medical practice, it is the responsibility of medical associations from individual countries to adapt WMA guidelines and formulate guidelines specific to their own circumstances. In South Africa, medical practitioners look to the HPCSA and the South African Medical Association (SAMA) for ethical guidance. At general assemblies of the WMA, ethical codes are ratified and updated, thus WMA guidelines are usually current and address pertinent contemporary ethical issues.

Ethical guidelines are not usually legal documents, thus their implementation depends much upon the moral orientation and motivation of individual healthcare professionals. In order to be the 'best' healthcare practitioner possible, it is essential not only to practise within the limits of the law, but also to hold higher ethical standards. These standards are dictated by ethical guidelines and codes of conduct.

2.2   The Nuremberg Code

Arguably the first 'modern' code of medical ethics, the Nuremberg Code was ratified after World War II, in August 1947.[12] The code was drafted by the American judges who presided over the famous Nuremberg Trials of Nazi war criminals (some of whom were doctors and scientists), who had committed atrocities during the war. For example, doctors had conducted cruel research on human subjects without their informed consent, conducted mass sterilisation of the mentally and physically disabled and participated in the development of scientific methods of mass killing using gas. The Nuremberg Code was the first international instrument to address the autonomy of the patient in the researcher–patient relationship.

The Nuremberg Code states, quite unequivocally, that 'the voluntary consent of the human subject is absolutely essential'.[13] Furthermore, the duty and

---

11   See footnote 3 above.
12   Brown University *The Nuremberg Code: Wartime Experiments on the Inmates of Nazi Concentration Camps* (2000):   cf   http://www.brown.edu/Courses/Bio_160/Projects2000/Ethics/THENUREMBURGCODE.html (accessed on 9 July 2009).
13   Nuremberg Tribunal *The Nuremberg Code* (1948): http://ohsr.od.nih.gov/guidelines/nuremberg.html (accessed on 9 July 2009).

responsibility for acquiring this high standard of consent rests in the hands of all those who conduct research amongst human volunteers. During the course of the research, volunteers should be at liberty to leave at any time, without detriment to their health and healthcare.[14] Similarly, researchers must be prepared to terminate health research involving human volunteers if there is good scientific and medical evidence that continuing the research would result in the 'injury, disability or death of the human subject'.[15]

2.3   The World Medical Association Ethical Guidelines

A synopsis of some relevant declarations and oaths emanating from the World Medical Association follows below.

2.3.1   *World Medical Association's Declaration of Geneva*

The World Medical Association's Declaration of Geneva is a document that details the ethical duties and obligations of physicians towards their patients.[16]

Physicians must pledge to dedicate their lives to the service of humanity and ensure that the health and well-being of their patients will be their first consideration. They also need to respect the autonomy and dignity of their patients; respect patient confidentiality even after the patient has died; maintain the utmost respect for human life; practise their profession with conscience and dignity and according to good medical practice; and foster the honour and noble traditions of the medical profession. Physicians will need to give to their teachers, colleagues and students the respect and gratitude that is their due and share their medical knowledge for the benefit of patients and the advancement of healthcare.

Medical knowledge cannot be used to violate human rights and civil liberties even under threat. Physicians are not to permit considerations of age, disease or disability, creed, ethnic origin, gender, nationality, political affiliation, race, sexual orientation, social standing or any other factor to intervene between their duty and their patients. Duty to self is also recognised in the declaration. Physicians are required to attend to their own health, well-being and abilities so that care of the highest standard can be provided.[17]

The Declaration of Geneva is an updated modern version of the Hippocratic Oath, which succinctly summarises the undertakings of one who is to be admitted to the medical profession.[18]

---

14   Nuremberg War Crimes Tribunal *The Nuremberg Code* (1948) s 9.
15   Ibid.
16   See footnote 8 above.
17   See footnote 8 above.
18   See footnote 8 above.

Declaration of Geneva: The Physician's Pledge[19]

AS A MEMBER OF THE MEDICAL PROFESSION:

I SOLEMNLY PLEDGE to dedicate my life to the service of humanity;

THE HEALTH AND WELL-BEING OF MY PATIENT will be my first consideration;

I WILL RESPECT the autonomy and dignity of my patient;

I WILL MAINTAIN the utmost respect for human life;

I WILL NOT PERMIT considerations of age, disease or disability, creed, ethnic origin, gender, nationality, political affiliation, race, sexual orientation, social standing or any other factor to intervene between my duty and my patient;

I WILL RESPECT the secrets that are confided in me, even after the patient has died;

I WILL PRACTISE my profession with conscience and dignity and in accordance with good medical practice;

I WILL FOSTER the honour and noble traditions of the medical profession;

I WILL GIVE to my teachers, colleagues, and students the respect and gratitude that is their due;

I WILL SHARE my medical knowledge for the benefit of the patient and the advancement of healthcare;

I WILL ATTEND TO my own health, well-being, and abilities in order to provide care of the highest standard;

I WILL NOT USE my medical knowledge to violate human rights and civil liberties, even under threat;

I MAKE THESE PROMISES solemnly, freely, and upon my honour.

2.3.2 World Medical Association Declaration of Lisbon on the Rights of the Patient

Just as physicians have the right to practise in their chosen profession, those whom they treat are also afforded certain rights. The World Medical Association's Declaration of Lisbon on the Rights of the Patient (Declaration of Lisbon) stipulates the rights of patients and the ethical principles which dictate these rights.

19　Adopted by the 2nd General Assembly of the World Medical Association, Geneva, Switzerland, September 1948 and amended by the 22nd World Medical Assembly, Sydney, Australia, August 1968 and the 35th World Medical Assembly, Venice, Italy, October 1983 and the 46th WMA General Assembly, Stockholm, Sweden, September 1994 and editorially revised by the 170th WMA Council Session, Divonne-les-Bains, France, May 2005 and the 173rd WMA Council Session, Divonne-les-Bains, France, May 2006 and amended by the 68th WMA General Assembly, Chicago, United States, October 2017: https://www.wma.net/policies-post/wma-declaration-of-geneva/ (accessed on 20 April 2020).

The Declaration of Lisbon states that patients have the following moral rights:

(a) They have the right to medical care of good quality.

(b) They must be treated without favouritism and without discrimination.

(c) They should be afforded continuity of care.

(d) When allocating scarce medical resources, all patients are entitled to a fair selection procedure.[20]

(e) They have the right to freedom of choice, including the right to change practitioners and receive a second opinion.[21]

(f) They have the right to self-determination, including the right to make their own decisions, to refuse certain treatments and also to refuse participation in medical research.[22]

(g) They have the right to information, including the right to know their health status, the treatment options available, the information in their patient files, the right to culturally specific information in the patient's language – as well as the right not to be informed should the patient so choose.[23]

(h) They have the right to confidentiality at all times.[24]

(i) They have the right to be educated about their specific and general health status.[25]

(j) They have the right to dignity.[26]

(k) They have the right to religious assistance from a religious leader of their chosen faith.[27]

In terms of the Declaration of Lisbon, an unconscious patient has the following rights:

(a) The right to a proxy decision maker – preferably one who knows the patient and can gauge the possible preferences of the patient;[28] and

(b) The right to emergency treatment without consent provided it is not contrary to the explicit or implied wishes of the patient.[29]

---

20   World Medical Association *Declaration on the Rights of the Patient* (2005): http://www.wma.net/e/policy/l4.htm (accessed on 23 March 2020) s 1(*a*)–(*f*).

21   Ibid. s 2(*a*) and (*b*).

22   Ibid. s 3(*a*)–(*c*).

23   Ibid. s 7(*a*), (*c*) and (*d*).

24   Ibid. s 8.

25   Ibid. s 9.

26   Ibid. s 10.

27   Ibid. s 11.

28   Ibid. s 4(*a*).

29   Ibid. s 4(*b*). However, it is important to note that doctors always have a duty to save the life of a patient who has attempted suicide (*Declaration of the Rights of the Patient* s 4(*c*)).

A legally incompetent patient has the following rights:

(a) The right to be involved in decision making – even minors without legal capacity have the right to express their views on the treatment offered and to have these views taken into account[30]

(b) The right to confidentiality and if capable of making a rational decision, such decision should be respected[31]

(c) The right to advocacy from his or her physician where a parent or caregiver forbids a treatment which is deemed to be in the best interests of the patient in question – the physician has a duty to challenge such a decision and approach relevant authorities if needs be.[32]

2.3.3 World Medical Association's Declaration of Madrid on Professionally-led Regulation

Something which is almost unique to the medical profession is that practitioners are allowed to be self-regulating and autonomous. Unfortunately, this independence is abused by some practitioners. The World Medical Association's Declaration of Madrid on Professionally-led Regulation (Declaration of Madrid) outlines an ethical code for self-regulation and professional autonomy in the caring professions.

The Declaration of Madrid notes that the cornerstone of professional autonomy is that physicians are allowed to exercise their professional judgement unhindered by others.[33] The World Medical Association believes that physician autonomy helps to ensure quality patient care, thus it should not be compromised.[34] The Declaration of Madrid encourages physicians to engage in a system of self-regulation within their individual countries to help ensure that autonomy is maintained in an ethical manner.[35]

Specific mention is made of the responsibility of physicians to keep abreast of scientific and technological advances in medicine.[36] The challenge posed to physicians in the Declaration of Madrid is that practice should always be ethical and of the highest possible standard.[37]

---

30   World Medical Association *Declaration on the Rights of the Patient* (2005) s 5(*a*).

31   Ibid. s 5(*b*).

32   Ibid. s 5(*c*).

33   World Medical Association *Declaration on Professionally-led Regulation* (2019): https://www.wma.net/policies-post/wma-declaration-of-madrid-on-professionally-led-regulation/ (accessed on 23 March 2020).

34   World Medical Association *Declaration on Professionally-Led Regulation* (2019) Preamble.

35   Ibid. Item 4.

36   Ibid. Items 2, 7.

37   Ibid. Item 8.

It is common knowledge that in some countries, resource shortages make it almost impossible for practitioners to provide the standard of care they would ideally like. This is recognised and accepted. In some situations, ensuring the best interests of the patient might require that the practitioner disobeys the law (e.g. in apartheid South Africa). The Declaration of Madrid urges physicians to do their best for their patients even in difficult situations where there may often be a good deal of professional dissatisfaction.

2.3.4 *World Medical Association's Declaration of Ottawa on Child Health*

In South Africa, a child is considered as anybody who is under 18 years of age.[38] Physicians are reminded that children are a vulnerable group. Thus, special provisions apply to their capacity to give an informed consent when seeking medical treatment.[39]

The World Medical Association's Declaration of Ottawa on Child Health (Declaration of Ottawa) provides an ethical framework for the medical treatment of children.[40] The declaration begins by noting that science has now proven that to reach their potential children need to grow up in a place where they can thrive spiritually, emotionally, mentally, physically and intellectually.[41] Physicians are encouraged to always do what is in the best interests of the child.[42]

The Declaration of Ottawa states that the medical care of children should comply with the following ethical principles:

(a) Children have the right to a safe and secure environment.[43]

(b) Children have the right to be provided with a place where they can have good health and development.[44]

(c) Children have the right to informed consent and self-determination, even if they are not legally allowed to give consent and their views should always be considered in the decision-making process.[45]

(d) Those caring for children are to have special training and skills necessary to enable them to respond appropriately to the medical, physical, emotional and developmental needs of children and their families.[46]

---

38 Children's Act 38 of 2005 s 17.
39 See Children's Act 38 of 2005 ss 129–130.
40 World Medical Association *Declaration on Child Health* (2009); https://www.wma.net/policies-post/wma-declaration-of-ottawa-on-child-health/. (Accessed 23 March 2020).
41 Ibid. Preamble.
42 Ibid. Principle 3a.
43 Ibid. Principle 1.
44 Ibid. Principle 3.
45 Ibid. Principle 3j.
46 Ibid. Principle 3b.

(e) Children have the right to confidentiality of information.[47]

(f) Children have the right to be admitted to hospital if necessary if the care required cannot be provided at home, in the community or at an outpatient facility.[48]

(g) Children have the right to mental healthcare and prompt referral to interventions when problems are identified.[49]

(h) Children are to be provided with rehabilitation services and support within the community.[50]

(i) All children are to be treated with dignity and respect.[51]

(j) Children are to share in the benefits of scientific research relevant to their needs.[52]

Healthcare practitioners are encouraged to use their discretion when dealing with children. Children often lack the ability to express themselves and they are subordinate to parents and guardians upon whom they depend for day-to-day survival.

2.3.5 The World Medical Association's Declaration of Helsinki on Ethical Principles for Medical Research Involving Human Subjects

Research ethics committees in Africa rely on the Declaration of Helsinki on Ethical Priniciples for Medical Research Involving Human Subjects[53] (Declaration of Helsinki) to dictate ethical research decisions. It is thought that the Declaration of Helsinki is by far the most cited research ethics document in central and west Africa. In Europe, the European Parliament has recommended as follows:

> Because the principles laid down in the Declaration of Helsinki provide the highest level of patient protection, they should be implemented and applied to ensure the effective protection of clinical trial participants, especially of those in third countries.[54]

On the other hand, in 2008 the Food and Drug Administration (FDA) of the United States announced that it would not hold drug companies conducting clinical trials to the high ethical standards mandated by the Declaration

---

47 World Medical Association *Declaration on Child Health* (2009) Principle 4e.
48 Ibid. Principle 3f.
49 Ibid. Principle 3d.
50 Ibid. Principle 3h.
51 Ibid. Principle 4b.
52 Ibid. Principle 4d.
53 World Medical Association *Declaration of Helsinki on Ethical Principles for Medical Research Involving Human Subjects* (2013).
54 European Parliament Directorate General for External Policies *Clinical Trials in Developing Countries. How to Protect People against Unethical Practices* (2009) para 3.2; https://www.somo.nl/wp-content/uploads/2009/04/Clinical-Trials-in-Developing-Countries.pdf (accessed on 24 March 2020.

of Helsinki. The reason cited for this was because the Declaration of Helsinki 'favours available treatments over placebos' which the FDA did not prefer in some instances.[55] In South Africa and most other countries, researchers are still required to uphold the Declaration of Helsinki as it promotes the protection of vulnerable populations who are likely to participate in clinical trials and other medical research.

The 13 principles of the Declaration of Helsinki lay the foundation for the rest of the code. Based on the deontological (duty-based) approach, Article 9 of the principles states that physicians who are involved in medical research have a duty to protect the life, health, dignity, integrity, right to self-determination, privacy and confidentiality of personal information of research subjects.[56] This duty extends to patients who take part in clinical trials. The Declaration of Helsinki makes it clear that the goals of medical research can never take precedence over the rights and interests of individual research subjects. It explicitly states that protecting the well-being of vulnerable research participants is essential in such research. Thus the Declaration of Helsinki is primarily concerned with protecting those involved in research and promoting ethical research.

The Declaration of Helsinki makes provision for informed consent in clinical trials, storage and testing of human tissue and other samples, data management, statistical analysis, environmental protection, ethics committee approval and post-trial access.

When it comes to the use of placebos, the Declaration of Helsinki in Article 33 states that in general, the risks, benefits, burdens and effectiveness of a new intervention should be tested against those of the best current proven interventions. In the case where no intervention currently exists, testing against a placebo arm is acceptable. In exceptional circumstances where any scientifically sound methodological reasons exist for the use of a placebo to determine the efficacy or safety of an intervention, one may be used. This is contingent upon the undertaking that patients in the placebo group are not subject to any risk of serious or irreversible harm as a result of the placebo. The Declaration of Helsinki further states: 'Extreme care must be taken to avoid abuse of this option'.

As with all other ethical codes, the Declaration of Helsinki relies upon the moral stance of physicians for its implementation. Fortunately, this is reinforced to a large extent by research ethics committees who often use the Declaration of Helsinki as a guide. In South Africa, protocols which do not conform to the Declaration of Helsinki will go unapproved by research ethics committees.

---

55   J Couzin 'FDA drops Helsinki rules' (2008) 390 *Science* 731; cf http://www.sciencemag.org/cgi/reprint/320/5877/731b.pdf (accessed on 29 June 2009).

56   World Medical Association *Declaration of Helsinki on Ethical Principles for Medical Research Involving Human Subjects* (2013) Principle 9.

2.3.6 The World Medical Association's Declaration of Taipei on Ethical Considerations Regarding Health Databases and Biobanks

On 22 October 2016, the World Medical Association (WMA) approved new ethical guidelines for physicians who were involved in the collection and use of identifiable health data and biological material in health databases and biobanks. These guidelines would help people control the use of their health data by respecting the rights to autonomy, privacy and confidentiality which individuals should be entitled to and as set out in the guidelines. Hence, they would be able to exercise control over the secondary use of their personal data and biological material, both in and beyond research.[57] The guidelines were called the Declaration of Taipei on Ethical Considerations Regarding Health Databases and Biobanks (Declaration of Taipei).[58]

A health database is defined in the declaration as 'a system for collecting, organizing and storing health information', and a biobank as 'a collection of biological materials and associated data'.[59] It describes biological materials as samples obtained from living or deceased individuals which can provide biological, including genetic, information about that individual. The collections in the health databases and biobanks are described as being from individuals and populations. Both health databases and biobanks give rise to similar concerns regarding dignity, autonomy, privacy, confidentiality and discrimination.

The Preamble[60] highlights that the declaration is intended to cover the collection, storage and use of identifiable data and biological material beyond the individual care of patients. While it is in concordance with the Declaration of Helsinki, it also provides additional ethical principles for research. It stresses the importance of research using health databases and biobanks. The impact of this research often results in significant acceleration and improvement in the understanding of health, diseases, and the effectiveness, efficiency, safety and quality of preventive, diagnostic and therapeutic interventions. It appeals to the social contract by stressing that health research represents a common good in the interests of individual patients as well as populations and society. Physicians are cautioned that while their country-level ethical, legal and regulatory norms and standards should be considered, no national or international requirements should reduce or eliminate any of the protections in the Declaration.

---

57 'New *Guidelines* will help people control use of their health data': http://www.wma.net/en/40news/20archives/2016/2016_25/index.html (accessed on 24 March 2020).

58 A Dhai 'The WMA Declaration of Taipei: Human databases and biobanks for the common good' (2016) 9(2) *SAJBL* 50–51.

59 *WMA Declaration of Taipei on Ethical Considerations regarding Health Databases and Biobanks* (2016): http://www.wma.net/en/30publications/10policies/d1/index.html (accessed on 24 March 2020).

60 Ibid.

The ethical principles[61] emphasise that database- and biobank-related activities and research should be of benefit to society and, in particular, public health. Protecting privacy and confidentiality is essential for maintaining trust and integrity, and physicians have both ethical and legal obligations as stewards when it comes to protecting information provided by their patients. While detailed stipulations on information to be shared with individuals are listed where data and materials are stored for multiple and indefinite uses, the type of consent that should be obtained is not specified and neither is any specific type of consent censured. Because of these detailed stipulations, blanket consent will not be a feasible option.

In the event of a clearly identified, serious and immediate threat where the health of the population needs to be protected, and anonymous data will not be practicable, the requirement for consent may be waived conditional to ethics committee clearance. Regarding the justice principle, the declaration specifies that the interests and rights of communities, in particular when vulnerable, will need to be protected, especially with regard to benefit sharing. Exploitation of intellectual property must be safeguarded by ensuring protections for ownership of materials whereby rights and privileges must be considered and contractually defined. A policy addressing intellectual property and covering the rights of all stakeholders needs to be communicated transparently. Health databases and biobanks will require ethics approval by independent ethics committees.

Robust governance[62] mechanisms are necessary to foster trustworthiness and should be designed such that the rights of individuals prevail over the interests of other stakeholders and science; relevant information is made available to the public; there is consultation and engagement with individuals and their communities; and custodians of health databases and biobanks are accessible and responsive to all stakeholders. Several elements regarding governance are laid down, including criteria and procedures for access to and the sharing of health data or biological material including the systematic use of material transfer agreements when necessary and the procedures for re-contacting participants where relevant.

---

61   WMA *Declaration of Taipei on Ethical Considerations regarding Health Databases and Biobanks* (2016) Art 1–7.
62   Ibid.

2.3.7 The World Medical Association's Declaration of Tokyo: Guidelines for Physicians Concerning Torture and Other Cruel, Inhuman or Degrading Treatment or Punishment in Relation to Detention and Imprisonment

The Declaration of Tokyo: Guidelines for Physicians Concerning Torture and Other Cruel, Inhuman or Degrading Treatment or Punishment in Relation to Detention and Imprisonment (Declaration of Tokyo) deals with the treatment of those who are detained in prisons around the world. The Declaration of Tokyo – first ratified in 1975 – has taken on new significance since 11 September 2001 when Britain and the US declared 'war on terror' in Afghanistan, Iraq and other parts of the world in a bid to stamp out terrorism. In the course of this conflict, many have been detained as terrorist suspects and kept in detention for months without being charged. It is trite that sometimes detainees are tortured in order to extract information. In such circumstances, it is of vital importance that physicians take a strong moral stance when it comes to treating prisoners. This can often be difficult as the environment is by definition one of asymmetrical power relationships and intimidation.[63] The Declaration to Tokyo lays out some clear and practically useful guidelines for practitioners in this situation.

The Declaration of Tokyo explicitly states as follows:

> The physician shall not countenance, condone or participate in the practice of torture or other forms of cruel, inhuman or degrading procedures, whatever the offence of which the victim of such procedures is suspected, accused or guilty, and whatever the victim's beliefs or motives, and in all situations, including armed conflict and civil strife.[64]

Furthermore, the Declaration of Tokyo states that it is absolutely unethical for a physician to furnish others with the necessary skills or equipment to carry out such actions. It is recommended that when providing medical assistance to detainees, physicians take the utmost care to maintain confidentiality relating to patient records and medical information. It is also important that they try to prevent the use of medical records and confidential information to aid in interrogation.

The Declaration of Tokyo advises that if a mentally and legally competent prisoner refuses nourishment or medical care, his or her wishes should be respected. The competence of the detainee in question should be confirmed by

---

63   WMA *Declaration of Taipei on Ethical Considerations regarding Health databases and Biobanks* (2016) Art 20–24.

64   WMA *Guidelines for Physicians Concerning Torture and Other Cruel, Inhuman or Degrading Treatment or Punishment in Relation to Detention and Imprisonment* (2016).

at least one other independent physician. As with all such medical decisions, physicians should explain the consequences to the prisoner in question.[65]

Although the Declaration of Tokyo explicitly condemns physicians who assist in torture and inhuman treatment of detainees, some practitioners still seem to do so. Possible reasons for this may be monetary incentives or political intimidation. Accepting such incentives or succumbing to such pressures compromises the first duty of physicians towards their patients. Such conduct amounts to a 'conflict of interest' and should always be avoided.[66]

2.4 International Council of Nurses (ICN) Code of Ethics[67]

An international code of ethics for nurses was first adopted by the International Council of Nurses (ICN) in 1953. It has been revised and reaffirmed at various times since, with the latest revision being in 2012.

The Preamble underscores the fundamental responsibilities of nurses:

(a) To promote health

(b) To prevent illness

(c) To restore health

(d) To alleviate suffering.

It goes on further to state that inherent in nursing is a respect for human rights, including cultural rights, the right to life and choice, to dignity and to be treated with respect. Nursing care is respectful of and unrestricted by considerations of age, colour, creed, culture, disability or illness, gender, sexual orientation, nationality, politics, race or social status. Nurses are to render services to the individual, family and community, and coordinate their services with those of related groups.

Relevant elements of the code are as follows:

The nurse's primary professional responsibility is to people requiring care;

In providing care, the nurse promotes an environment in which the human rights, values, customs and spiritual beliefs of the individual, family, and community are respected;

The nurse ensures that the individual receives accurate, sufficient and timely information in a culturally appropriate manner on which to base consent for care and related treatment;

---

65   World Medical Association *Guidelines for Physicians Concerning Torture and Other Cruel, Inhuman or Degrading Treatment or Punishment in Relation to Detention and Imprisonment* (2016) Art 8.

66   See below Chapter 15 para 15.1.

67   https://www.icn.ch/sites/default/files/inline-files/2012_ICN_Codeofethicsfornurses (accessed on 23 March 2020).

The nurse holds in confidence personal information and uses judgement in sharing this information;

The nurse shares with society the responsibility for initiating and supporting action to meet the health and social needs of the public, in particular those of vulnerable populations;

The nurse advocates for equity and social justice in resource allocation, access to health care and other social and economic services;

The nurse demonstrates professional values such as respectfulness, responsiveness, compassion, trustworthiness and integrity;

The nurse carries personal responsibility and accountability for nursing practice;

The nurse uses judgement regarding individual competence when accepting and delegating responsibility;

The nurse at all times maintains standards of personal conduct which reflect well on the profession;

The nurse is active in developing and sustaining a core of professional values;

The nurse takes appropriate action to safeguard individuals, families and communities when their health is endangered by a co-worker or any other person.

Therefore, nurse practitioners and managers must provide care that respects human rights and is sensitive to the values, customs and beliefs of people. They need to establish standards of care and a work setting that promotes quality care.

Florence Nightingale Pledge[68]

I solemnly pledge myself before God and in the presence of this assembly; To pass my life in purity and to practice my profession faithfully. I will abstain from whatever is deleterious and mischievous and will not take or knowingly administer any harmful drug. I will do all in my power to maintain and elevate the standard of my profession and will hold in confidence all personal matters committed to my keeping and family affairs coming to my knowledge in the practice of my calling. With loyalty will I endeavour to aid the physician in his work, and devote myself to the welfare of those committed to my care.

---

68 https://www.truthaboutnursing.org/press/pioneers/nightingale_pledge.html#gsc.tab=0 (accessed on 23 March 2020).

2.5   Codes of healthcare ethics and South Africa

Many of the healthcare professions in South Africa are governed by the HPCSA,[69] which is a statutory body established by the Health Professions Act as previously stated,[70] and South African Nursing Council, a statutory body established under the Nursing Act.[71] Both councils have published ethical codes and failure to practise according to these ethical codes may be construed as illegal. In such cases, healthcare practitioners may be called before a disciplinary hearing of the councils and, if found guilty, may lose their licence to practise.

Ethical guidelines are an invaluable reference for situations when practitioners are faced with moral dilemmas in which a weighting of options and the formulating of a well-reasoned decision is required. These councils acknowledge that such dilemmas occur frequently in South Africa where practice is constrained by resource and personnel shortages, unmanageable patient loads and the burden of HIV. These circumstances frequently require healthcare professionals to make difficult decisions regarding the allocation of resources and deciding who will receive treatment. Their guidelines are designed to provide practical guidance for such ethical dilemmas.

2.5.1   The South African Nursing Council Code of Ethics for Nursing Practitioners in South Africa[72]

The South African Nursing Council Code of Ethics was promulgated in May 2013. It starts off by stating that ethics is an integral part of the nursing profession and forms the foundation thereof. Its preamble is similar in most respects to the ICN Code of Ethics. It does, however, affirm that it is a binding document and the content must be complied with. It goes on to assert that because it is premised on the principles of respect for life, human dignity and the rights of other persons, its application is to be considered in conjunction with all applicable South African law as well as international policy documents which include, but are not limited to, the Universal Declaration of Human Rights, the ICN Code of Ethics, the Patients' Rights Charter and all other nursing and healthcare policy frameworks providing guidance and direction for responsible practice in nursing (s 1).

---

69   Health Professions Council of South Africa *General Ethical Guidelines for the Health Care Professions*: https://www.hpcsa.co.za/Uploads/Professional_Practice/Ethics_Booklet.pdf (accessed on 3 June 2020).
70   56 of 1974 ss 49, 61(2) and 61A(2).
71   33 of 2005 s 2.
72   https://www.sanc.co.za/aboutpledge.htm (accessed on 23 March 2020).

Section 3 describes some of the core ethical principles that nurses are at all times expected to observe:

Core ethical principles for nurses

(Social) justice – Nurses are at all times expected to act fairly and equitably in situations of competing interests. They should pursue justice and advocate on behalf of vulnerable and disadvantaged patients.

Non-maleficence – This requires a nurse to consciously refrain from doing harm of any nature whatsoever to patients, individuals, groups and communities.

Beneficence – This is a requirement to do good and choose the best option of care under given circumstances and act with kindness at all times. It gives expression to compliance with the 'duty to care' as a professional practice imperative.

Veracity – The nurse is required to act with truthfulness and honesty and to ensure that the information provided to and on behalf of the patient is always in the patient's best interests.

Fidelity – This entails adherence to factual and truthful accounting and balancing that with respecting, protecting and maintaining confidential information pertaining to the delivery of healthcare, including health records of patients.

Altruism – Nurses are at all times to show concern for the welfare and wellbeing of patients.

Autonomy – The autonomy of patients to make their own decisions and choices in matters affecting their health should be respected.

Caring – Nurses are required to demonstrate the art of nurturing by both applying professional competencies and positive emotions that will benefit both nurse and the patient with inner harmony.

The ethical principles have to be upheld at all times in whatever role nursing practitioners fulfil as direct or indirect patient care providers including, amongst others, administrators and policy developers.

Section 4 contains the value statement and declares that the code is based on the belief that nurses have a number of values. Pertinent values are listed below:

South African Nursing Council Value Statement for Nurses

Human life;

Respect, dignity and kindness;

The right to access to quality nursing and healthcare for all;

The provision of accurate and truthful information in accordance with informed consent;

Integrity of persons in their care as well as the image of the profession;

Confidentiality and privacy of personal information and belongings of patients;

A culture of safety and an ethically friendly environment, which includes the protection of patients.

2.5.2 Nurses' Pledge of Service – SA

Below is the oath taken by nursing graduates in South Africa:

South African Nurse's Oath[73]

I solemnly pledge myself to the service of humanity and will endeavour to practice my profession with conscience and with dignity.

I will maintain, by all the means in my power, the honour and noble tradition of my profession.

The total health of my patients will be my first consideration.

I will hold in confidence all personal matters coming to my knowledge.

I will not permit consideration of religion, nationality, race or social standing to intervene between my duty and my patient.

I will maintain the utmost respect for human life.

I make these promises solemnly, freely and upon my honour.

---

73   Nurses' Pledge of Service – SA: http://www.sanc.co.za/aboutpledge.htm (accessed on 24 March 2020).

2.5.3 The Health Professions Council Guidelines for Good Practice in the Health Care Professions

The HPCSA has produced a series of Guidelines for Good Practice in the Health Care Professions booklets.[74] The booklets cover the following:

(a) Booklet 1: *General ethical guidelines for the health care professions*

(b) Booklet 2: *Ethical and professional rules of the Health Professions Council of South Africa*

(c) Booklet 3: *National Patients' Rights Charter*

(d) Booklet 4: *Seeking patients' informed consent: The ethical considerations*

(e) Booklet 5: *Confidentiality: Protecting and providing information*

(f) Booklet 6: *Guidelines for the management of patients with HIV infections or AIDS*

(g) Booklet 7: *Guidelines for the withholding and withdrawing of treatment*

(h) Booklet 8: *Guidelines on reproductive health management*

(i) Booklet 9: *Guidelines on patient records*

(j) Booklet 10: *Guidelines for the practice of telemedicine*

(k) Booklet 11: *Guidelines on overservicing, perverse incentives and related matters*

(l) Booklet 12: *Guidelines for the management of health care waste*

(m) Booklet 13: *General ethical guidelines for health researchers*

(n) Booklet 14: *Guidelines for biotechnology research in South Africa*

(o) Booklet 15: *Research, development and use of chemical, biological and nuclear weapons*

(p) Booklet 16: *Ethical guidelines on social media*

(q) Booklet 17: *Ethical guidelines on palliative care.*

2.5.4 The HPCSA's core ethical values and standards

Registration with the HPCSA confers rights and privileges on practitioners to practise their professions. Correspondingly, practitioners have moral or ethical duties to others and society. Maintaining good professional practice is grounded in core ethical values and standards. Standards are the directives that follow the core values.

---

74 Health Professions Council of South Africa *Ethics Guideline* booklets: *https://www.hpcsa. co.za/?contentId=0&menuSubId=18&actionName=Core%20Operations* (accessed on 24 March 2020).

Some of the core ethical values and standards required of healthcare practitioners are included in the following box:[75]

Core ethical values and standards required of healthcare practitioners

Respect for persons: Practitioners should respect and acknowledge the intrinsic worth, dignity and sense of value of their patients.

Best interests or well-being (non-maleficence): Practitioners should not harm or act against the best interests of patients, even when the interests of the latter conflict with their own self-interest.

Best interest or well-being (beneficence): Practitioners should act in the best interests of patients even when the interests of the latter conflict with their own personal self-interest.

Human rights: Practitioners should recognise and respect the human rights of all individuals.

Autonomy: Practitioners should honour the right of patients to self-determination or to make their own informed choices, and to live their lives by their own beliefs, values and preferences.

Integrity: Practitioners should incorporate these core ethical values and standards as the foundation for their character and practice as responsible healthcare professionals.

Truthfulness: Practitioners should regard truth and truthfulness as the basis of trust in their professional relationships with patients.

Confidentiality: Practitioners should treat personal or private information as confidential in professional relationships with patients – unless overriding reasons confer a moral or legal right to disclosure.

Compassion: Practitioners should be sensitive to, and empathise with, the individual and social needs of their patients and seek to create mechanisms for providing comfort and support where appropriate and possible.

Tolerance: Practitioners should respect the rights of people to have different ethical beliefs as these may arise from deeply held personal, religious or cultural convictions.

Justice: Practitioners should treat all individuals and groups in an impartial, fair and just manner.

Professional competence and self-improvement: Practitioners should continually endeavour to attain the highest level of knowledge and skills required within their area of practice.

Community: Practitioners should strive to contribute to the betterment of society in accordance with their professional abilities and standing in the community.

---

75   See generally, Health Professions Council of South Africa Booklet 1: *General Ethical Guidelines for Health Care Professions* (2016).

2.5.5 The analysis process for ethical reasoning

Sometimes, there may be a clash between the demands of the core ethical values and standards that results in competing demands on practitioners. The dilemmas that ensue can be addressed through ethical reasoning. The Golden Rule is that practitioners should treat their patients in a manner in which they would like themselves to be treated. The HPCSA and the WMA recommend the following steps when analysing ethical issues:

Analysing ethical issues

Step 1. *Formulate the problem:* Determine whether the issue at hand is an ethical one, then ascertain if there is a better way of understanding it.

Step 2. *Gather information:* All the relevant information, including clinical, personal and social data, must be collected.

Step 3. *Consult authoritative sources:* Sources such as the HPCSA guidelines, practitioner associations and respected colleagues should be consulted. Check how practitioners generally deal with such matters.

Step 4. *Consider the different options:* Consider alternative solutions in light of the principles and values they uphold.

Step 5. *Make a moral assessment:* The ethical content of each option should be weighed by asking the following questions:

(a) What are the likely consequences of each option?

(b) What are the most important values, duties and rights involved? Which weighs the heaviest?

(c) What are the weaknesses of the practitioner's individual view concerning the correct option?

(d) How would the practitioner want to be treated under similar circumstances – that is, apply the Golden Rule?

(e) How does the practitioner think that the patient would want to be treated in the particular circumstances?

(f) Discuss your proposed solution with those whom it will affect.

(g) Act on your decision with sensitivity to others affected.

(h) Evaluate your decision and be prepared to act differently in the future.

2.5.6 Why should I practise according to these guidelines?

The HPCSA guidelines are comprehensive and cover almost all matters relating to healthcare practice. South African healthcare practitioners are advised to refer to these guidelines in cases where they are unsure of how to proceed. Given that the guidelines have ethical standing and are very often consistent with the law, it is imperative to practise within the parameters they set.

Many of the ethical guidelines may appear to be aspirational given the shortage of resources in developing countries such as South Africa. However, healthcare practitioners are expected to practise within the ethical framework provided by the HPCSA. Good ethical practice will ensure an enhanced relationship of trust between practitioners, their patients and their colleagues.

Healthcare practitioners are expected to aspire to a 'higher calling' to provide health services to society which often requires self-sacrifice and dedication. Ethical guidelines assist practitioners to achieve such a calling.

Ethical guidelines should also be seen as a form of insurance, because if healthcare professionals follow them, they will be acting in accordance with the requirements of the regulatory authorities and the law. Ethical guidelines may also help to solve complicated medical dilemmas in a fair and morally justifiable manner.

2.6   Duty to patients

From the Hippocratic Oath and Nuremberg Code through to the WMA declarations and modern treatises on bio-weaponry and health databases, the first duty of healthcare practitioners is always towards their patients. International ethical codes and those of the HPCSA place the patient at the very centre of healthcare practice and are consistent with the South African Constitution.[76]

The benefit of healthcare practitioners familiarising themselves with the ethical guidelines of the HPCSA, and of practising in accordance with them, will be to ensure that they conduct themselves in accordance with the 'higher calling' to which their patients and the public expect them to aspire.

Some questions on codes of healthcare ethics

1.   Discuss why ethical codes and guidelines are necessary in the healthcare context.

2.   What is the Golden Rule in the context of healthcare practice? Why?

3.   Explain how the situation should be approached when core ethical values and standards clash, resulting in competing demands on practitioners.

---

76   See below Chapter 3.

Health and human rights

David McQuoid-Mason and Ames Dhai

By the end of this chapter readers will be able to:

1. Explain the relationship between human rights and medical ethics.
2. Explain what human rights are.
3. Explain the difference between civil and political rights, and economic and social rights.
4. Explain how the different ethical principles relate to human rights in international conventions and national legislation and policies.
5. Describe the relationship between the human rights and universal healthcare coverage.

3.1 Introduction

The interplay between human rights and medical ethics is crucial for the proper provision of healthcare in democratic and caring societies. Not only do practitioners have to ensure that their own conduct does not contravene professional ethics and human rights standards, but as advocates of their patients, they have an obligation to protest when the behaviour of others violates these standards. When health is harmed as a consequence of the neglect or abuse of rights, practitioners have a moral duty to act in the best interests of their patients.

Although the primary responsibility for ensuring that human rights are respected lies with governments, practitioners feel a particular responsibility to consider human rights issues in their practices and to mandate their representatives to lobby actively on a wide range of such issues.[1] An example of such a body in South Africa is the South African Medical Association. In the words of the World Medical Association:

---

1   British Medical Association *The Medical Profession and Human Rights* (2001) 14–42.

> Medical practitioners have an ethical duty and a professional responsibility to act in the best interests of their patients ... This duty includes advocating for patients, both as a group (such as advocating on public health issues) and as individuals.[2]

Society accords health practitioners with power and authority with the expectation that they will be altruistic and have special duties and obligations towards the patients that they treat. These duties and obligations confer correlative rights to patients, who are also increasingly seen as having some responsibilities as well. Hence rights and duties can be viewed as two sides of the same coin: on the one side, the moral rights of an individual or population being matched by, on the other side, a concomitant moral duty on the part of someone else. In the healthcare context, practitioners have an ethical obligation to provide assistance in the best interests of their patients, which supports the conclusion that patients have a moral right to that help. At an individual level, these rights and duties are applicable within a limited context – that of a pre-existing practitioner–patient relationship. However, at a population level, the profession's responsibility is perceived as extending to the wider society at large.

3.2 What are human rights?

Human rights are the rights we have by virtue of being human. These are fundamental rights owned by every human being from birth and are comprehensively defined in international human rights instruments and codes.[3] Human rights have been codified into international human rights law and national law in some countries. When human rights have been ratified and acceded to in international agreements or legislated for in national legal systems, they also become legal rights.

Moral rights differ from human rights because they depend on a shared societal perception about what the basic essentials for a civilised existence are. Moral rights may be considered to be claims that individuals are justified in making on others because of a societal background of shared beliefs supporting such claims. Both moral and human rights are distinct from other weaker beliefs about individual entitlement in that they are believed to trump the preferences of others.[4]

---

2   Preamble to the WMA Statement on Patient Advocacy and Confidentiality. Adopted by the 45th World Medical Assembly, Budapest, Hungary, October 1993, revised by the 57th WMA General Assembly, Pilanesberg, South Africa, October 2006 and reaffirmed by the 203rd WMA Council Session, Buenos Aires, Argentina, April 2016 : https://www.wma.net/policies-post/wma-statement-on-patient-advocacy-and-confidentiality/ (accessed on 23 March 2020).

3   See below para 3.4.

4   British Medical Association *The Medical Profession and Human Rights* (2001) 14–42.

It has been said that health practitioners need to know about human rights for the following reasons:

(a) Health policies, programmes, practices and research may inadvertently violate human rights.

(b) Human rights violations may have important adverse effects on the health of individuals and groups.

(c) Promoting human rights is an essential part of efforts to promote and protect public health.[5]

It is clear that the human rights paradigm provides a useful framework within which the health profession may begin to lobby for health promotion and protection.

The United Nations Charter of 1945 is a reflection of the desire to protect human rights following World War II. The objectives of setting down international standards of human rights were twofold:[6]

(a) To provide a means of defending individuals against the abuses of power committed by organs of the state

(b) To promote individuals' opportunities to thrive and develop through measures such as education, healthcare and a safe living environment, i.e. the social determinants of health.

These principles laid the foundation for the International Bill of Rights[7] which was introduced to protect people from a wide range of suffering and deprivation.

3.3   Categories of human rights

Human rights may be broadly divided into civil and political rights, economic and social rights, and environmental and cultural rights. However, it is generally accepted that human rights are universal, inalienable, indivisible and interdependent. Basic beliefs about human rights apply all over to everyone in the same way. Respect for civil and political rights cannot be separated from the enjoyment of social, economic or even cultural rights. However, genuine economic and social development also means that individuals must have political and civil freedoms to participate in the process.[8]

---

5   K Boyd, R Higgs and A Pinching (eds) *The New Dictionary of Medical Ethics* (1997) 126.
6   British Medical Association *The Medical Profession and Human Rights* (2001) 14–42.
7   See below para 3.4.
8   British Medical Association *The Medical Profession and Human Rights* (2001) 14–42.

Initially, human rights were divided into two broad categories as a result of the creation of the two international covenants[9] which, together with the Universal Declaration of Human Rights, constituted the International Bill of Rights. For the purposes of this chapter, the focus will be on civil and political rights, and economic and social rights.

3.3.1 Civil and political rights

The International Covenant on Civil and Political Rights[10] was introduced to guarantee civil and political rights and to protect people from oppression by the state. These rights are also called 'first generation' rights'.[11] They focused on the belief that all citizens are entitled to participation in the political process and freedom from interference by the state, provided that their actions are not harmful to others. Hence these rights conferred upon individuals in society the freedom to act without undue constraint. These rights represent negative freedoms or negative rights.[12] Some examples of negative rights and freedoms are:

(a) the right not to be subjected to medical or scientific experimentation without consent;

(b) the right to freedom from torture; and

(c) the right to freedom from slavery.

3.3.2 Economic and social rights

Economic and social rights, also known as 'second generation' rights, recognise the fact that it takes more than freedom from interference by the state for people to survive and develop. For instance, access to economic and other resources like food, shelter and clean water is necessary for an adequate standard of living. Economic and social rights are positive rights,[13] and represent claims on the state for the provision of basic services.

The single greatest determinant of health is socio-economic status.[14] Some examples of socio-economic rights are:

(a) the right to access healthcare;

(b) the right to social security; and

(c) the right to education.

---

9   United Nations International Covenant on Civil and Political Rights (1966) and the International Covenant on Economic, Social and Cultural Rights (1966).

10   United Nations International Covenant on Civil and Political Rights (1966).

11   British Medical Association *The Medical Profession and Human Rights* (2001) 14–42.

12   See generally, I Berlin *Four Essays on Liberty* (1990).

13   I Berlin *Four Essays on Liberty* (1990); cf International Covenant on Economic, Social and Cultural Rights (1966).

14   British Medical Association *The Medical Profession and Human Rights* (2001) 14–42.

It has been said that moral priority should be given to access to appropriate healthcare. This reflects the belief that health is also a basic human need of much more importance than basic human desires.[15] Where health is not optimal, people will not develop optimally. Ill health or physical disability will diminish one's potential to develop to the best of one's ability.

3.4 The human right to health

Health, our most basic good, is essential for our well-being. This is what makes health a fundamental human right and intricately links it with our understanding of a life in dignity. The right to health contains both freedoms and entitlements, with the former including informed choice and the latter provision of equality of opportunity to allow for everyone to enjoy the highest attainable level of health. The right to health refers to the right to the enjoyment of a variety of goods, facilities, services and conditions necessary for its realisation.[16]

Several international human rights treaties and instruments have given recognition to this right, with its first articulation being in 1946 in the Constitution of the World Health Organization (WHO) whose Preamble includes that:

> the enjoyment of the highest attainable standard of health is one of the fundamental rights of every human being without distinction of race, religion, political belief, economic or social condition.[17]

In 1948, the Universal Declaration of Human Rights (UDHR) included health in the right to an adequate standard of living.[18] Similar to the WHO Constitution, the 1966 International Covenant on Economic, Social and Cultural Rights (ICESCR), widely considered as the central international human rights law in terms of the protection of the right to health, affirms health as being the '… right of everyone to the enjoyment of the highest attainable standard of physical and mental health'.[19]

Regionally the right to health is established in the African Charter on Human and People's Rights, also known as the Banjul Charter[20] and nationally

---

15   British Medical Association *The Medical Profession and Human Rights* (2001) 14–42.

16   United Nations and World Health Organization *The Right to Health* UN Fact Sheet No 31 (2008): http://www.ohchr.org/Documents/Publications/Factsheet31.pdf (accessed on 24 March 2020).

17   Constitution of the World Health Organization (1948): http://apps.who.int/gb/bd/PDF/bd47/EN/constitution-en.pdf?ua=1 (accessed on 24 March 2020).

18   United Nations *Universal Declaration of Human Rights* (1948): http://www.un.org/en/universal-declaration-human-rights/ (accessed on 24 March 2020).

19   United Nations *International Covenant on Economic, Social and Cultural Rights* (1966): https://www.ohchr.org/Documents/ProfessionalInterest/cescr.pdf (accessed on 24 March 2020).

20   Organisation of African Unity African Charter on Human and People's Rights (1981): https://hrnjuganda.org/wp-content/uploads/African-Charter-on-Human-and-Peoples-Rights.pdf (accessed on 24 March 2020).

in section 27 of the Bill of Rights of the Constitution of South Africa.[21] The latter affirms the right of everyone to have access to healthcare services with reproductive healthcare given specific mention. An obligation is placed on the state to achieve progressive realisation of this right within its available resources by instituting reasonable legislative and other measures. Emergency medical treatment may not be refused. Of note, section 28 affirms the right of children (anyone under the age of 18) to basic healthcare services without the limitation of progressive realisation within available resources. The National Health Act[22] and the Patients' Rights Charter[23] are examples of South Africa's response to its constitutional mandate on health. National health insurance (NHI), however, is the direct and most germane response to that directive and towards realising universal health coverage.

South Africa's plans for universal healthcare coverage in the form of the NHI have been in the pipeline for some time. Historically, in 2011, the Green Paper was published for comment.[24] This was followed by a Draft White Paper in 2015 and a White Paper, the National Health Insurance Policy (NHIP) in 2017. The NHIP underpins the establishment of a unified health system in the country based on the principles of social solidarity, progressive universalism, equity and health as a public good and a social investment, thereby underscoring the values of justice, fairness and equity.[25] The NHIP has been critical in informing the National Health Insurance Bill which was released on 18 June 2018 for public comment.[26] Universal healthcare coverage is being promoted globally and is in line with the United Nation's Sustainable Development Goal 3.[27]

Comprehensive quality healthcare services are envisaged as a right of all South Africans as we progress towards universal population coverage, the promise of the NHI. It seems that the reality of limited resources entails that quality is to be limited to being adequate.

---

21   Constitution of the Republic of South Africa, 1996 – Chapter 2: Bill of Rights: https://www.gov.za/documents/constitution/chapter-2-bill-rights (accessed on 24 March 2020).

22   61 of 2003: https://www.gov.za/sites/www.gov.za/files/a61-03.pdf (accessed on 24 March 2020).

23   Republic of South Africa Patients' Rights Charter (1999): http://www.hpcsa.co.za/downloads/conduct_ethics/rules/generic_ethical_rules/booklet_3_patients_rights_charter.pdf (accessed on 24 March 2020).

24   Department of Health Policy on National Health Insurance (2011): http://pmg-assets.s3-website-eu-west-1.amazonaws.com/docs/110812nhi_0.pdf (accessed on 24 March 2020).

25   Department of Health National Health Insurance Policy (2017): https://cdn.mg.co.za/content/documents/2017/06/29/whitepaper-nhi-2017compressed.pdf (accessed on 24 March 2020).

26   Department of Health National Health Insurance Bill (2018): https://www.gov.za/sites/default/files/41725_gon635s.pdf (accessed 24 March 2020).

27   UNDP Sustainable Development Goals (2015): http://www.undp.org/content/dam/undp/library/corporate/brochure/SDGs_Booklet_Web_En.pdf (accessed on 24 March 2020).

3.5 A bioethical framework for reflecting on health and human rights

The bioethical principles of autonomy, beneficence, non-maleficence and justice,[28] which were discussed previously,[29] provide a useful framework for reflecting on aspects of human rights instruments that affect health. Elements of these principles can be found in documents such as the International Bill of Rights, the African Charter of Human and People's Rights (hereafter referred to as the African Charter)[30] and the Bill of Rights in the South African Constitution. As mentioned before, the International Bill of Rights consists of the Universal Declaration of Human Rights (UDHR),[31] the International Covenant on Economic, Social and Cultural Rights (ICESCR)[32] and the International Covenant on Civil and Political Rights (ICCPR).[33] The South African Bill of Rights is found in Chapter 2 of the Constitution.[34] A charter specific to health in South Africa is the Patients' Rights Charter.[35] A number of statutes and the common law also provide protection of patients' rights and will be discussed later.[36]

For the purposes of this chapter, the four bioethical principles will be discussed in relation to:

(a) the International Bill of Rights;
(b) the African Charter;
(c) the South African Constitution; and
(d) the South African Patients' Rights Charter.

3.5.1 Autonomy and human rights

The principle of autonomy recognises the duty of healthcare professionals to respect the freedom of patients to make decisions for themselves.[37] Aspects of autonomy can be found in:

---

28 TL Beauchamp and JF Childress *Principles of Biomedical Ethics* 3 ed (1994) 67–113.
29 See above para 1.10.
30 Organization of African Unity African Charter of Human and People's Rights (1981).
31 United Nations Universal Declaration of Human Rights (1948).
32 United Nations International Covenant on Economic, Social and Cultural Rights (1966).
33 United Nations International Covenant on Civil and Political Rights (1966).
34 Constitution of the Republic of South Africa, 1996.
35 https://www.safmh.org.za/documents/policies-and-legislations/Patient%20Rights%20Charter.pdf (accessed on 4 June 2020).
36 See below Chapter 4. See generally, DJ McQuoid-Mason 'An Introduction to aspects of health law: bioethical principles, human rights and the law' (2008) 1(1) *SAJBL* 1–4.
37 See above para 1.10.

(a) the International Bill of Rights;

(b) the African Charter;

(c) the South African Constitution; and

(d) the South African Patients' Rights Charter.

3.5.1.1 The International Bill of Rights

Autonomy is recognised in the International Bill of Rights in the provisions of:

(a) the UDHR regarding the right to life, liberty and security of the person;[38] privacy;[39] freedom of movement;[40] and the right to freedom of thought, conscience and religion;[41] and

(b) the ICCPR regarding the right to life,[42] liberty and security of the person;[43] liberty of movement;[44] and the right to freedom of thought, conscience and religion.[45]

3.5.1.2 The African Charter

Autonomy is also protected in the African Charter which recognises the right to:

(a) respect for life and the integrity of one's person;[46]

(b) liberty and security of the person;[47]

(c) freedom of conscience and free practice of religion;[48] and

(d) freedom of movement.[49]

3.5.1.3 The South African Constitution

Like in the International Bill of Rights and the African Charter, the principle of autonomy is recognised in the Constitution in the Bill of Rights provisions regarding:

(a) the right to bodily and psychological integrity;[50]

(b) the right to privacy;[51]

---

38   Article 3 of the UDHR.
39   Article 12.
40   Article 13.1.
41   Article 18.
42   Article 6.1 of the ICCPR.
43   Article 9.1.
44   Article 12.1.
45   Articles 18.1 and 18.3.
46   Article 4 of the African Charter.
47   Article 6.
48   Article 8.
49   Article 12.1.
50   Section 12(2) of the Constitution.
51   Section 14.

(c) the right to life[52] (which includes the right of mentally competent patients not to live by refusing treatment);[53]

(d) the right to freedom of movement[54] (e.g. the right of mentally competent patients to voluntarily discharge themselves);[55] and

(e) the right to freedom of religion and belief[56] (e.g. respecting a mentally competent patient's right to refuse medical treatment for him- or herself on religious grounds – but not necessarily to refuse treatment for his or her children in life-threatening situations).[57]

Given that informed consent and confidentiality are cornerstones of medical practice, this section focuses on the right to bodily and psychological integrity and the right to privacy.

Bodily and psychological integrity

According to the Constitution, everyone has the right to bodily and psychological integrity which includes the right:

(a) to make decisions about reproduction; and

(b) to security and control over their body.[58]

In the healthcare setting, this translates to the right to informed decision making which includes informed consent and informed refusal.

Privacy and confidentiality

In terms of the Constitution, everyone has a right to privacy, which includes not having the privacy of their communications infringed.[59] A breach of confidentiality by a medical practitioner or other healthcare professional is clearly an impairment of a patient's right to this privacy. Likewise, the obtaining of information about a person without his or her consent would amount to an invasion of privacy. For example, the failure to obtain a proper consent to test a person's blood after he or she had voluntarily given a blood sample was held to be a violation of the person's constitutional right to privacy.[60]

---

52   Section 11.
53   See s 6(1)(*d*) of the National Health Act 61 of 2003.
54   Section 21(1) of the Constitution.
55   See s 19(*d*) of the National Health Act 61 of 2003.
56   Section 15(1) of the Constitution.
57   *Hay v B* 2003 (3) SA 492 (W).
58   Constitution s 12(2).
59   Section 14.
60   *C v Minister of Correctional Services* 1996 (4) SA 292 (T).

3.5.1.4 The South African Patients' Rights Charter

According to the Patients' Rights Charter,[61] every citizen has the right to participate in the development of health policies and in decision making on matters effecting his or her health.

The charter affirms the right of patients to be given full and accurate information about:

(a) the nature of their illness;

(b) diagnostic procedures;

(c) proposed treatment; and

(d) costs involved for them to make a decision that affects any one of these elements.

The Charter also affirms that a patient may refuse treatment provided such refusal does not endanger the health of others.

Members of medical aid and insurance schemes have the right to information pertaining to their scheme. Patients also have the right to know who the person is that is providing their healthcare.

Information on the availability of health services, and how best to utilise such services, must be made available in a language that is understood by the population.

On the issue of confidentiality and privacy, the charter states that information concerning a person's health may only be disclosed with informed consent, except when required by any law or an order of the court.

3.5.2 Beneficence and human rights

The principle of beneficence recognises the duty on health professionals to do good for their patients.[62] Aspects of beneficence can be found in:

(a) the International Bill of Rights;

(b) the African Charter;

(c) the South African Constitution; and

(d) the South African Patients' Rights Charter.

---

61 https://www.safmh.org.za/documents/policies-and-legislations/Patient%20Rights%20Charter.pdf (accessed on 4 June 2020).

62 TL Beauchamp and JF Childress *Principles of Bioethics* 3 ed (1994) 194–249.

3.5.2.1 The International Bill of Rights

Beneficence is recognised in the International Bill of Rights in the provisions of the UDHR regarding:

(a) the right to social security;[63]
(b) the right to a standard of living adequate for a person's health and well-being and that of his or her family.[64]

The principle is also reflected in the ICSECR which provides for:

(a) the right to an adequate standard of living;[65]
(b) the right of everyone to enjoy the highest attainable standard of physical and mental health by requiring state parties to:

  (i) provide for the reduction of still births and of infant mortality and for the healthy development of the child;
  (ii) improve all aspects of environmental and industrial hygiene;
  (iii) prevent, treat and control epidemic, endemic, occupational and other diseases; and
  (iv) create conditions which assure to everyone medical service and medical attention in the event of sickness.[66]

In terms of the ICSECR, everyone also has the right to receive information.[67]

3.5.2.2 The African Charter

Beneficence is found in the provisions of the African Charter dealing with:

(a) the right to receive information;[68] and
(b) the right to attain the best available state of physical and mental health.[69]

In respect of (b), state parties to the charter are required to take the necessary measures to protect the health of their people and to ensure that they receive medical attention when they are sick.[70] The state must also take care of the family's physical and moral health[71] and take special measures to protect the aged and disabled in keeping with their physical or moral needs.[72]

---

63 Article 22 of the UDHR.
64 Article 25.1.
65 Article 11.1 of the ICSECR.
66 Article 12.1.
67 Article 19.
68 Article 9.1 of the African Charter.
69 Article 16.1.
70 Article 16.2.
71 Article 18.1.
72 Article 18.4.

3.5.2.3 The South African Constitution

Beneficence is recognised in the provisions of the Bill of Rights in the Constitution that state as follows:

(a) Everyone has the right of access to healthcare within available resource[73] (e.g. HIV-positive patients should be provided with access to proper medication if they cannot afford it).

(b) Everyone has the right of access to reproductive healthcare[74] (e.g. the right to obtain a legal termination of pregnancy).[75]

(c) Children have the right to basic healthcare services[76] (e.g. babies born of HIV-positive mothers should be provided with prophylactic treatment).[77]

(d) Everyone has the right of access to information[78] (e.g. the right of access to their health records).

3.5.2.4 The South African Patients' Rights Charter

On the issue of access to healthcare, the Patients' Rights Charter[79] affirms that everyone has the right to healthcare services. These services include:

(a) timely emergency care at any healthcare facility that is open regardless of the patient's ability to pay;

(b) rehabilitation and treatment;

(c) special needs in the case of newborn infants, children, pregnant women, the aged, the disabled, persons in pain, persons living with HIV and AIDS patients;

(d) counselling, without discrimination, coercion or violence, especially in matters pertaining to reproductive health, cancer and AIDS; and

(e) palliative care in the case of incurable or terminal illness.

3.5.3 *Non-maleficence and human rights*

The principle of non-maleficence recognises the duty on health professionals not to harm their patients.[80] Aspects of non-maleficence can be found in:

---

73   Section 27(1)(*a*) of the Constitution.
74   Section 12(2).
75   See Choice on Termination of Pregnancy Act 92 of 1996.
76   Section 28(1)(c) of the Constitution.
77   See *Minister of Health v Treatment Action Campaign (Case 2)* 2002 (5) SA 721 (CC).
78   Section 32(1).
79   https://www.safmh.org.za/documents/policies-and-legislations/Patient%20Rights%20Charter.pdf (accessed on 4 June 2020).
80   TL Beauchamp and JF Childress *Principles of Bioethics* 3 ed (1994) 120–184.

(a)   the International Bill of Rights;

(b)   the African Charter;

(c)   the South African Constitution; and

(d)   the South African Patients' Rights Charter.

3.5.3.1 The International Bill of Rights

Non-maleficence is recognised in the International Bill or Rights in the provisions of the UDHR which state that nobody shall be subjected to:

(a)   cruel, inhuman or degrading treatment;[81] or

(b)   arbitrary interference with their privacy.[82]

Similarly, the ICCPR provides that nobody may be:

(a)   deprived of their liberty;[83]

(b)   subjected to unlawful interference with their privacy;[84]

(c)   subjected to cruel, inhuman or degrading treatment – in particular, nobody may be subjected without their free consent to medical or scientific experimentation;[85] and

(d)   denied the right in community with other members of their group, to enjoy their own culture, to profess and to practise their own religion or to use their own language[86] (e.g. persons belonging to ethnic, religious or language minorities).

3.5.3.2 The African Charter

Examples of non-maleficence in the African Charter are:

(a)   the prohibition of all forms of exploitation and degradation, including cruel, inhuman or degrading treatment;[87]

(b)   the provision that nobody may be illegally deprived of the right to liberty or security of the person.[88]

---

81   Article 5 of the UDHR.
82   Article 12.
83   Article 9 of the ICCPR.
84   Article 17.1.
85   Article 7.
86   Article 27.
87   Article 5 of the African Charter.
88   Article 6.

3.5.3.3 The South African Constitution

(a) The Bill of Rights in the Constitution has similar provisions to the ICCPR and the African Charter regarding non-maleficence and the right of people not to be treated or punished in a cruel, inhuman or degrading manner[89] (e.g. patients left to lie on the floor or shouted at by healthcare practitioners).

(b) Like the ICCPR, the Constitution provides that nobody may be subjected to medical or scientific experiments without their informed consent[90] (e.g. patients must be informed that a health service is for experimental or research purposes).

(c) The Constitution also provides that nobody may be denied the right to practise their religion or culture or to speak their language[91] (i.e. healthcare personnel must communicate with patients in a language they can understand).[92]

(d) The Constitution goes further than the International Bill of Rights by also providing that everyone is entitled to an environment that is not harmful to health or well-being,[93] and that nobody may be refused emergency medical treatment.[94]

(e) Section 10 of the Constitution affirms everyone's right to inherent human dignity and their right to have their dignity respected and protected.

3.5.3.4 The South African Patients' Rights Charter

The Patients' Rights Charter[95] provides as follows:

(a) Healthcare practitioners must display a positive disposition that demonstrates courtesy, human dignity, patience, empathy and tolerance.

(b) No one can be abandoned by a health practitioner or health facility that initially took responsibility for the patient's health (patients are thereby also assured of continuity of care).

---

89   Constitution s 12(1)(*e*).
90   Section 12(2)(*c*).
91   Section 31(1).
92   See also s 6(2) of the National Health Act 61 of 2003.
93   Constitution s 24(*a*).
94   Section 27(3).
95   https://www.safmh.org.za/documents/policies-and-legislations/Patient%20Rights%20Charter.pdf (accessed on 4 June 2020).

3.5.4 *Justice and human rights*

The principle of justice or fairness recognises the duty of health professionals to treat their patients justly and fairly.[96] Aspects of justice or fairness can be found in:

(a) the International Bill of Rights;

(b) the African Charter;

(c) the South African Constitution; and

(d) the South African Patients' Rights Charter.

3.5.4.1 The International Bill of Rights

Justice and fairness are recognised in the International Bill of Rights and the ICCPR.

The provisions of the UDHR state that everyone is born free and equal in dignity and rights[97] and entitled to all the rights and freedoms in the UDHR without distinction of any kind, such as race, colour, sex, language, religion, political or other opinion, national or social origin, property, birth or other status.[98]

The ICCPR provides that:

(a) every child has the right, without any discrimination as to race, colour, sex, language, religion, national or social origin, property or birth, to be protected by his or her family, society and the state;[99]

(b) all persons are equal before the law and are entitled, without any discrimination, to the equal protection of the law. This means that the law should prohibit any discrimination and guarantee to all persons equal and effective protection against discrimination on any ground such as race, colour, sex, language, religion, political or other opinion, national or social origin, property, birth or other status.[100]

3.5.4.2 The African Charter

The African Charter recognises the justice principle by providing as follows:

(a) Everyone shall be entitled to enjoy the rights and freedoms in the charter without distinction of any kind such as race, ethnic group, colour, sex, language, religion, political or any other opinion, national and social origin, fortune, birth or other status.[101]

---

96   TL Beauchamp and JF Childress *Principles of Bioethics* 3 ed (1994) 256–302.

97   Article 1 of the UDHR.

98   Article 2.

99   Article 24.1 of the ICCPR.

100 Article 26.

101 Article 2 of the African Charter.

(b) Everyone shall be equal before the law and entitled to equal protection of the law,[102] and all peoples shall be equal and enjoy the same respect and equal rights.[103]

(c) The state shall ensure the elimination of all discrimination against women and the protection of the rights of the woman and child as stipulated in international declarations and conventions.[104]

3.5.4.3 The South African Constitution

Justice and fairness are enshrined in the provisions in the Bill of Rights in the Constitution dealing with:

(a) equality and non-discrimination[105] (e.g. patients of different racial, social or economic classes should be treated equally);

(b) the right to dignity;[106]

(c) the right to lawful, reasonable and procedurally fair administrative action[107] (e.g. patients should be given written reasons for administrative decisions that deny them access to particular treatment).[108]

The Constitution lists the categories of persons who will be presumed to have been unfairly discriminated against once they can prove discrimination[109] In all other cases the persons being discriminated against will have to prove that the discrimination is unfair. The listed categories are persons discriminated against on the grounds of race, gender, sex, pregnancy, marital status, ethnic or social origin, colour, sexual orientation, age, disability, religion, conscience, belief, culture, language and birth.[110]

3.5.4.4 The South African Patients' Rights Charter

The Patients' Rights Charter[111] provisions regarding access to care include elements to prevent unfair discrimination.

---

102   Article 3.
103   Article 19.
104   Article 18.3. See also, Organization of African Unity African Charter on the Rights and Welfare of the Child (1990).
105   Constitution s 9.
106   Section 10.
107   Section 33(1).
108   Promotion of Administrative Justice Act 3 of 2000.
109   Constitution s 9(5).
110   Section 9(3) and (4).
111   https://www.safmh.org.za/documents/policies-and-legislations/Patient%20Rights%20Charter.pdf (accessed on 4 June 2020).

3.5.5 *Limitation of rights and patient responsibilities*

The rights of patients in the Bill of Rights in the South African Constitution are not absolute and may be limited under certain circumstances. In terms of section 36 of the Constitution, every right may be limited in terms of the law of general application to the extent that the limitation is reasonable and justifiable in an open and democratic society. There are a number of factors that will have to be taken into consideration when considering the limitation. These include:

(a) the nature of the right;

(b) how important it is to limit the right;

(c) the nature of the limitation and its extent;

(d) the relationship between the limitation and its purpose; and

(e) whether there are less restrictive means to achieve the purpose.

Similarly, although the Patients' Rights Charter[112] lists the rights of patients, it also imposes certain duties on patients, such as:

(a) to advise practitioners on their wishes regarding death;

(b) to comply with prescribed treatment or rehabilitation services;

(c) to enquire about related costs of treatment or rehabilitation and to make arrangements to pay for these;

(d) to look after health records in their possession;

(e) to take care of their health;

(f) to care for and protect the environment;

(g) to respect the rights of other patients and healthcare providers;

(h) to utilise the healthcare system properly and not to abuse it;

(i) to know their health services and what they offer; and

(j) to provide relevant and accurate information to healthcare providers for diagnostic, treatment, rehabilitation or counselling purposes.

---

112 https://www.safmh.org.za/documents/policies-and-legislations/Patient%20Rights%20Charter.pdf (accessed on 4 June 2020).

3.6   Compliance

If healthcare practitioners ensure that they comply with the four bioethical principles of patient autonomy, non-maleficence, beneficence and justice or fairness, they will be acting in accordance with the International Bill of Rights, the African Charter, the South African Constitution's Bill of Rights and the South African Patients' Rights Charter.

Some questions on which the rights of Steve Biko were violated

Steve Biko, the leader of the Black Consciousness Movement in South Africa, was arrested on 21 August 1977 under the Terrorism Act 83 of 1967. He was interrogated by police officers of the Port Elizabeth security police and suffered major head injuries while in police custody. On 11 September 1977, an injured and untreated Biko was loaded onto the back of a Land Rover and driven from Port Elizabeth to Pretoria to a prison with hospital facilities. He died shortly after arrival at the Pretoria prison on 12 September, having been left to die in his cell with an empty drip bottle attached to his arm. Biko was never charged with a crime or brought to trial.[113]

During his detention, Biko was kept naked in his cell, chained to a grille at night, and left lying on a urine-stained blanket on a rubber mat on the floor.

1.   Which rights of Biko in the Universal Declaration of Human Rights were violated?

2.   Which rights of Biko in the African Charter of Human and People's Rights would have been violated had it been applicable at the time that he died?

3.   Which rights of Biko in the South African Constitution would have been violated if the new Constitution had been applicable at the time that he died?

---

113   https://www.sahistory.org.za/people/stephen-bantu-biko (accessed on 4 June 2020).

CHAPTER 4

Health law – the basics

David McQuoid-Mason

By the end of this chapter readers will be able to:

1. List the different statutes relating to healthcare.
2. Explain how the common law of contract affects healthcare.
3. Explain how the common law of delict affects healthcare.
4. Explain how criminal law affects healthcare.
5. Explain what civil law is.
6. Explain the difference between civil and criminal law.

4.1   Introduction

In Chapter 3 there was a brief description of how the rights in the South African Constitution relate to the bioethical principles of autonomy, beneficence, non-maleficence and justice or fairness.

Apart from the Constitution, health law is affected by both statute law and common law. However, statute law and the common law have to comply with the Constitution and the constitutional issues will be considered in the relevant chapters dealing with particular aspects of health law.

There is a wide variety of statutes passed by parliament that affect health, but only the most important will be considered. Likewise, several aspects of common law affect health, but only those relating to contract, delict and criminal law will be considered.

4.2 Statute law affecting health

4.2.1 Introduction

There are a number of statutes affecting health including the National Health Act,[1] the Mental Health Care Act,[2] the Health Professions Act,[3] the Nursing Act,[4] the Pharmacy Amendment Act,[5] the Choice on Termination of Pregnancy Act,[6] the Sterilisation Act,[7] the Births and Deaths Registration Act,[8] the Children's Act,[9] the Older Persons Act[10] and the Medical Schemes Act.[11]

There are numerous other statutes that affect healthcare, such as the Boxing and Wrestling Control Act;[12] the Inquests Act;[13] the Medicines and Related Substances Act;[14] the Criminal Procedure Act;[15] the South African Medical Research Council Act;[16] the Prevention and Treatment of Substance Abuse Act;[17] the Compensation for Occupational Injuries and Diseases Act;[18] the Occupational Health and Safety Act;[19] the National Road Traffic Act;[20] the South African Institute for Drug-Free Sport Act;[21] the Correctional Services Act;[22] the Domestic Violence Act;[23] the Promotion of Access to Information Act;[24] the Promotion of Administrative Justice Act;[25] the Promotion of Equality and Prevention of Unfair Discrimination Act;[26] the Council for Medical Schemes

---

1   61 of 2003 (chapters 6 and 8 still have to be brought into effect).
2   17 of 2002 (Chapter 8 of the Mental Health Act 18 of 1973 still remains in effect).
3   56 of 1974.
4   33 of 2005.
5   88 of 1997.
6   92 of 1996.
7   44 of 1998.
8   51 of 1992.
9   38 of 2005.
10   13 of 2006.
11   131 of 1998.
12   39 of 1954.
13   58 of 1959.
14   101 of 1965.
15   51 of 1977.
16   58 of 1991.
17   20 of 1992.
18   130 of 1993.
19   85 of 1993.
20   93 of 1996.
21   14 of 1997.
22   111 of 1998.
23   116 of 1998.
24   2 of 2000.
25   3 of 2000.
26   4 of 2000.

Levies Act;[27] the Traditional Health Practitioners Act[28] and the Protection of Personal Information Act.[29]

In many cases the obligations imposed by the statutes are amplified by regulations issued by the appropriate minister.

It is intended to consider briefly the main provisions of the National Health Act and to tabulate a brief description of aspects of some of the other statutes relevant to health law.

4.2.2 National Health Act

The National Health Act[30] is fully in effect, except for Chapter 6 (dealing with health establishments) which is not as yet in full force. The Act provides a framework for a structured uniform health system in South Africa. It takes into consideration the Constitution and other laws on national, provincial and local governments regarding health services.

The National Health Act makes provision for the following:

(a) National health services across the country, including providers of public and private health services[31]

(b) The rights and duties of users and healthcare personnel[32]

(c) The establishment of national and provincial health councils[33]

(d) The establishment of a district health system and district health councils[34]

(e) The regulation of health establishments (not yet fully in force)[35]

(f) The establishment of academic health complexes[36]

(g) The control of use of blood, blood products, tissue and gametes in humans[37]

---

27   58 of 2000.
28   22 of 2007
29   4 of 2013.
30   61 of 2003.
31   Chapter 1.
32   Chapter 2.
33   Chapters 3 and 4.
34   Chapter 5.
35   Chapter 6.
36   Chapter 7.
37   Chapter 8.

(h) Health research and the establishment of a National Health Research Ethics Council and the National Health Research Committee[38]

(i)   The appointment of health officers and inspectors.[39]

The different sections and chapters of the National Health Act will be dealt with when discussing relevant aspects of health law.

4.2.3 Other statutes affecting health

Apart from the Constitution and the National Health Act, the following are some of the most important statutes that affect health:

(a) Children's Act[40] – provides for consent in the case of children and imposes reporting obligations on healthcare professionals when abuse or neglect is suspected.[41]

(b) Older Persons Act[42] – makes provision for the protection of the status, well-being, safety and security of older persons in institutions and imposes a duty on any person to report suspected abuse of older persons.

(c) Criminal Procedure Act[43] – makes provision for procedures and related matters in criminal proceedings including: (a) the collection of a blood sample from an accused at the request of any police officer; and (b) the collection of blood from a patient who is under the influence of alcohol at the request of a doctor, if the test may be needed for criminal proceedings at a later stage.

(d) Health Professions Act[44] – provides for the registration of certain healthcare professionals and prescribes the acts and omissions that may lead to disciplinary action by the Health Professions Council of South Africa.

(e) Mental Health Care Act[45] – provides for consent to medical treatment or operations on behalf of mental patients and imposes a duty on healthcare professionals to report dangerous patients to the authorities.

---

38   Chapter 9.
39   Chapter 10.
40   38 of 2005.
41   Amended by the Children's Amendment Act 41 of 2007 s 2.
42   13 of 2006.
43   51 of 1977.
44   56 of 1974.
45   7 of 2002.

(f) Occupational Health and Safety Act[46] – prescribes: (a) the general duties of employers to employees; (b) the general duties of employees at work; (c) the responsibilities of health and safety representatives; and (d) the responsibilities of health inspectors.

(g) National Health Laboratory Service Act[47] – provides for the management of all aspects of the National Health Laboratory Service.

(h) Choice on Termination of Pregnancy Act[48] – prescribes when termination of pregnancy may be lawfully conducted.

(i) Criminal Law (Sexual Offences and Related Matters) Amendment Act[49] – creates new definitions for the crime of rape; includes marital rape; creates new crimes of sexual assault and prohibits sexual acts with and sexual exploitation of children under prescribed ages; imposes a duty to report sexual offences against children and mentally disabled persons.

(j) Domestic Violence Act[50] – provides for the protection of victims of domestic abuse.

(k) National Road Traffic Act[51] – provides that blood alcohol levels may not exceed 0,05 g/100 ml for ordinary drivers.

(l) Promotion of Access to Information Act[52] – provides for the rights of patients to access information about themselves.

(m) Medical Schemes Act[53] – provides for the regulation of registered medical schemes.

(n) Protection of Personal Information Act[54] – provides for the protection of personal information and the regulation of personal information data banks.

4.3   The common law

The common law is the law brought to South Africa by the Dutch and English settlers and impacts on health law in the fields of contract, delict and criminal law.

---

46   85 of 1993.
47   37 of 2000.
48   92 of 1996.
49   32 of 2007.
50   116 of 1998.
51   93 of 1996.
52   2 of 2000.
53   131 of 1998.
54   4 of 2013.

4.3.1 Contract

A contract is an agreement between parties in which one person offers to do something and the other person accepts the offer. Contract is said to be the basis of most relationships between healthcare professionals and patients.[55]

A contract is an agreement between two or more parties to be bound by certain terms and conditions that come into effect by virtue of the will of the parties. A party to a contract that has been breached may sue in delict[56] or contract if all the essential elements of the delict have been satisfied – but may not sue twice. The same act or omission may be a delict or a breach of contract – especially in the medical sphere.[57] If one sues in contract, the damages claimed may only be for loss or damage that would have been within the contemplation of the parties. These are patrimonial loss or losses that can be measured in terms of money. One cannot claim for non-patrimonial loss such as pain and suffering, which can only be claimed in a delictual action (see below para 4.3.2).[58]

It has been held by the courts that where a defendant is protected from liability by an exclusion clause in a contract, a plaintiff may not sue in delict to get around the clause.[59] However, whether such protection will endure will depend on the exclusion clause complying with the provisions of the Consumer Protection Act.[60]

4.3.2 Delict

A delict is a breach of a general duty imposed by the law – it is not based on a contractual relationship between the parties.[61] Delictual duties are owed to people generally and not to a particular group of people, and are imposed by law independent of the will or acts of the parties involved. Like a breach of contract, a delict gives rise to a civil action at the suit of the injured party. Breaches of rights enshrined in the Constitution may result in delictual actions (e.g. a breach of the right to privacy).[62]

---

55   *Friedman v Glicksman* 1991 1 SA 1134 (W); cf *Afrox Healthcare Bpk v Strydom* 2002 6 SA 21 (SCA). See below para 6.2.
56   See delict below para 4.3.2.
57   *Van Wyk v Lewis* 1924 AD 438–443.
58   cf *ABC v Thomson Medical Pte Ltd and Others* [2017] SGCA (a Singapore case).
59   cf *Afrox Healthcare Bpk v Strydom* 2002 (6) SA 21 (SCA).
60   68 of 2008 s 52(3). See DJ McQuoid-Mason (2012) 'Hospital exclusion clauses limiting liability for medical malpractice resulting in death or physical or psychological injury: What is the effect of the Consumer Protection Act?' (2012) 5(2) *SAJBL* 65–68.
61   old ref 300 – ref missing *Van Wyk v Lewis* 1924 AD 438.
62   *C v Minister of Correctional Services* 1996 (4) SA 292 (T); *NM v Smith* 2007 3 SA 250 (CC).

4.3.2.1 Conditions of liability for a delict

Unlike in contract, the injured person can claim for patrimonial loss (i.e. loss that can be accurately measured in money, such as medical expenses, loss of wages, a dependant's action for loss of support, etc.) and pain and suffering, if the harm was caused through negligence (see below para 4.3.2.2). In claims for negligence, the plaintiff must prove that:[63]

(a) the defendant has committed an act or omitted to do something;

(b) the act or omission complained of is unlawful (i.e. it infringed a lawful right);

(c) he or she has suffered patrimonial loss (i.e. loss that can be measured in monetary terms);

(d) the act or omission of the defendant caused the harm to the plaintiff and is not too remote; and

(e) the defendant was at fault (i.e. acted negligently or intentionally).

In claims involving sentimental damages (i.e. damages for hurt feelings and infringements of bodily integrity, dignity, privacy or reputation that cannot be accurately measured in monetary terms), under the *actio injuriarum*:

(a) the plaintiff must prove that the defendant's act was wrongful;

(b) the plaintiff must prove that the defendant's act was an infringement of the plaintiff's personality rights (e.g. reputation, dignity, privacy or bodily integrity – common law or constitutional);

(c) the plaintiff must prove that the act complained of was done intentionally (i.e. *animus injuriandi*); and

(d) the plaintiff need not prove damages as these will be presumed – but an amount should be claimed (e.g. for defamation, infringement of dignity, invasion of privacy or assault).

Under the Aquilian action, the plaintiff has to prove that the defendant acted negligently or intentionally. Generally, under the *actio injuriarum* the plaintiff has to prove intention.

4.3.2.2 Negligence

Negligence means that a reasonable person in the position of the defendant would have foreseen the likelihood of harm and would have taken steps to guard against it. For example, where a person engages in a skilled profession, such as the medical profession, he or she is required to exercise the degree of skill and care

---

63   JC van der Walt and JR Midgley *Principles of Delict* 4 ed (2016) para 2.

of a reasonably competent person in that profession (i.e. a reasonably competent doctor). A breach of a statutory duty may lead to an inference of negligence, but a breach of such a duty is not negligence in itself – it may, however, be evidence of negligence.

4.3.2.3 Intention

Intention means that plaintiffs:

(a)   directed their minds to do the unlawful act; and

(b)   were conscious of the wrongfulness of their act.[64]

'Legal intention' means that plaintiffs:

(a)   subjectively foresaw the likelihood of harm to others; and

(b)   were reckless as to whether or not such harm resulted (referred to as eventual intention by lawyers).[65] This was applied in the notorious Oscar Pistorius case, where he intentionally fired bullets into a small toilet, knowing full well that he might kill someone – allegedly mistaking his girlfriend for a burglar.[66]

4.3.3 *Criminal cases*

A crime is a wrong against the state for which the wrongdoer (the criminal) is punished by the state. In a criminal case, the state brings a case against an accused person who is charged with a crime and the state has to prove that the accused person is guilty 'beyond a reasonable doubt'. The accused person does not have to prove that he or she is not guilty, but merely raise a doubt concerning his or her guilt in the state's case.[67]

Crimes may be created by both the common law and statutory law. Examples of common law crimes are murder, culpable homicide, assault and theft.[68] For instance, a gynaecologist was sentenced to imprisonment after being found guilty of culpable homicide in a case arising from medical negligence.[69] Examples of statutory crimes are rape, sexual assault, sexual exploitation of children and failure to report sexual offences under the Criminal Law (Sexual Offences and Related Matters) Amendment Act.[70]

---

64   *Moaki v Reckitt & Colman (Africa) Ltd* 1968 (3) SA 98 (AD) 103.

65   *S v De Bruyn* 1968 (4) SA 498 (A) 510.

66   *Director of Public Prosecutions, Gauteng v Pistorius* 2018 (1) SACR 115 (SCA).

67   See generally, J Burchell and J Milton *Principles of Criminal Law* 3 ed (2005).

68   Ibid.

69   *Van der Walt v Director of Public Prosecutions Mpumalanga* [2019] ZAMPMBHC 9.

70   32 of 2007.

The Constitution provides that arrested or detained persons are guaranteed the right to consult a lawyer and to have legal representation during the trial – at state expense, 'if a substantial injustice would result' because they cannot afford one.[71] Accused persons are entitled to be released on bail if they are not a threat to society, will not interfere with witnesses and will attend court during the trial. 'Bail' is a deposit paid to the court to make sure that the person attends the court hearing. If the accused person fails to appear, he or she will forfeit the bail to the state and may be arrested and detained.[72]

4.3.4 Civil cases

A civil wrong is a wrong against an individual for which the wrongdoer must pay compensation to the injured person. In a civil case, one person (the plaintiff) brings an action against another (the defendant) and the state is usually not involved – unless the state or its employees have injured a person or his or her property, or a person or his or her property has injured the state's interests or those of its employees.[73]

Plaintiffs have to prove their cases 'on a balance of probabilities'. This means that plaintiffs must prove that their version of the case is more likely than that of the defendants. If the plaintiffs succeed, the defendants will have to pay a certain amount in compensation to make up for the plaintiffs' losses. The aim of civil cases is to prevent or undo damage to the interests of plaintiffs without punishing defendants.[74]

4.3.5 Crimes and civil cases

Sometimes a person's act or omission may be both a crime and a civil wrong. For example, a person who assaults someone can be prosecuted by the state, convicted and punished (i.e. with a fine or imprisonment) for committing the crime of assault. The convicted person may also be sued for damages by the person injured in the assault and made to pay compensation for medical expenses, lost wages and pain and suffering.[75]

It is possible for a person who has been found not guilty of a crime – because the state could not prove its case beyond reasonable doubt – to be held liable for damages in a civil claim, because the plaintiff was able to prove his or her case on a balance of probabilities. This happened in the OJ Simpson civil case in which

---

71   Constitution of the Republic of South Africa, 1996 s 35.
72   Criminal Procedure Act 51 of 1977 s 35.
73   See below Chapter 8.
74   Ibid.
75   Ibid.

his wife's family recovered damages from him for killing his wife – even though he had been found not guilty of murdering her in the criminal case.[76]

Some questions on health law – the basics

Discuss the following scenarios and decide if the healthcare practitioner's conduct was a crime, a civil wrong or both:

1. A doctor terminates a pregnancy for a woman who is not legally entitled to have a termination of pregnancy.

2. A nurse tells her friends at a party that one of her patients is HIV positive and mentions the name of the patient who is known to the friends.

3. A surgeon negligently operates on a patient who is an architect and the patient dies. The architect is survived by a wife and four small children.

---

76 *Rufo v Simpson* [2001] Second District, Division 4, California (Court of Appeal); https://caselaw.findlaw.com/ca-court-of-appeal/1211279.html (accessed on 24 March 2020).

PART 2

Specific Topics

CHAPTER 5

Professionalism and the healthcare practitioner–patient relationship

David McQuoid-Mason and Ames Dhai

By the end of this chapter readers will be able to:

1. Explain the role of professionalism in healthcare practice.
2. Describe the challenges to professionalism in healthcare practice.
3. Explain the core foundational values in healthcare practice.
4. Explain why professionalism in healthcare practice should be regulated.
5. Describe the relationship between healthcare practitioners and patients.
6. Explain whether health practitioners are obliged to treat.
7. Describe the rights and duties of users of health services.
8. Describe the rights and duties of healthcare practitioners.
9. Describe the role of social media in healthcare.
10. Explain what is meant by telehealth.
11. Explain what is meant by dual loyalty.

5.1 What is professionalism in healthcare practice?

The healthcare practitioner–patient relationship can be viewed as the cornerstone of healthcare practice. In turn, healthcare practice can be considered as a moral and social contract between the profession and the public. Central to this lies professionalism and professional integrity. Professionalism sets the standard of what a patient should expect from his or her healthcare practitioner. Professionalism, which refers to the characteristics of a profession, can in the healthcare context be defined as:

> an occupation that is characterized by high moral standards, including a strong commitment to the well-being of others, mastery of a body of knowledge and skills, and a high level of autonomy.[1]

---

1   JR Williams 'The future of medical professionalism' (2009) 2 *The South African Journal of Bioethics and Law* 48–50. http://www.sajbl.org.za/index.php/sajbl/article/viewFile/55/50 (accessed on 27 July 2010).

The purpose of healthcare practice is always to care for the ailing and the sick, promote health interests and well-being, and strive towards healing environments.[2]

Healthcare practitioners are important agents through which scientific knowledge is applied to human health, thereby bridging the gap between science and society. However, healthcare practice goes beyond just clinical or technical excellence. It is more than just knowledge about disease. It is also about experiences, feelings and interpretations of human beings in often extraordinary moments of fear, anxiety and doubt. In this very vulnerable position, professionalism underpins the trust that the public has in healthcare practitioners,[3] and professional integrity and honesty should be a measure of the extent to which the professional's reputation and credibility remain untainted.

5.2   Challenges to professionalism in healthcare practice

Political, social and economic factors together with advances in science and technology have reshaped attitudes and expectations of the public and healthcare practitioners, whose roles and professional responsibilities up until now were clear and unequivocally well understood. In addition, several failures of professionalism, including financial pursuits, with concomitant adverse media coverage, have undermined public trust in health practice and have led to a questioning of traditional values and behaviour – challenging characteristics that were once seen as the hallmark of health practice.[4] Professional integrity can be easily tainted when the nature of the practitioner–patient relationship becomes somewhat transactional where patients are viewed as customers and healthcare as a commodity.

Moreover, we have progressed to an era where professional autonomy has had to give way to accountability. Perceptions of practitioners as healers have also been eroded by error and iatrogenic injury.[5] What is more, an emphasis on litigation as a tool in social justice has led to a greater level of public awareness of the harms of which practitioners can be guilty.[6] This has also had an adverse effect on public sector health budgets in South Africa,[7] and contributed to the sharp

---

2   RL Cruess, SR Cruess and SE Johnston 'Professionalism: An ideal to be sustained' (2000) 356 *Lancet* 156–169.

3   See generally, Royal College of Physicians *Doctors in Society: Medical Professionalism in a Changing World* (2005).

4   Royal College of Physicians *Doctors in Society: Medical Professionalism in a Changing World* (2005).

5   See generally, Institute of Medicine *Crossing the Quality Chasm: A New Health System for the Twenty First Century* (2001).

6   See generally, Association of American Medical Colleges *A Flag in the Wind: Educating for Professionalism in Medicine* (2003).

7   J Malherbe 'Counting the cost: The consequences of increased medical malpractice litigation in South Africa' (2013) 103(2) *SAMJ* 83–84.

increase in professional insurance premiums in high-risk medical specialities, such as obstetrics and gynaecology.[8]

Trust is critical to successful care and where patients cannot trust their practitioners, the quality of their care is seriously jeopardised. It is not because practitioners have special knowledge and technologies that they should be trusted. They are trusted only if this knowledge and technology is firmly attached to values that are explicit, understood and altruistic. The principal objective of practitioners is to treat their patients well. Unfortunately, survey data has revealed that the level of confidence and trust that was accorded the profession several decades ago has been substantially eroded.[9]

5.3   Core foundational values in healthcare practice

Compassion, competence and autonomy are judged to be core foundational values in the practice of healthcare. Understanding and concern for a person's distress are essential in this context. An extremely high degree of competence is expected and required of practitioners, measured in law by what a reasonably competent practitioner in that branch of their profession would be expected to do.[10] This is not limited to scientific knowledge and technical skills but also includes ethical knowledge, skills and attitudes, and an understanding of human rights and health law. As new ethical issues arise with changes in practice and its social and political environment, it is important that knowledge and skills are regularly updated through continuing professional development (CPD) and maintained in this arena. In South Africa, the HPCSA requires all practitioners to accumulate 30 continuing education units (CEUs) annually, of which five must be for ethics, law and human rights. Some categories, like dental assistants, are required to accumulated fewer points (15 general and 2 ethics).[11] Autonomy is the ethical principle that has changed the most over time with practitioner autonomy being moderated by governments and other authorities, and patient autonomy gaining widespread acceptance.[12] In South Africa, this has been influenced by

---

8   MS Pepper and MN Slabbert 'Is South Africa on the verge of a medical malpractice litigation storm?' (2011) 4(1) *SAJBL* 29–35.

9   M Schlesinger 'A loss of faith: The sources of reduced political legitimacy for the American medical profession' (2002) 80 *The Milbank Quart* 185–236.

10   *Van Wyk v Lewis* 1924 AD 438–444.

11   See HPCSA Continuing Professional Development Guidelines for the Health Professional Booklet 4 (2008): https://www.saphysio.co.za/media/83652/cpd-hpcsa-cpd-guidelines.pdf (accessed on 24 March 2020).

12   See generally, World Medical Association *Medical Ethics Manual* (2005).

the provisions of our democratic Constitution[13] which emphasises the right to equality,[14] dignity[15] and individual autonomy regarding health matters.[16]

The ethical and moral duties accorded to health practitioners impose an obligation of effacement of self-interest on the practitioner that distinguishes health practice from business and most other careers or forms of livelihood.[17]

Pellegrino states that there are at least three things specific to health practice that have led to this position:

(a) Firstly, it is the nature of illness itself with patients being in a uniquely dependent, anxious, vulnerable and exploitative state, being forced into a position of trusting the practitioner in a relationship of relative powerlessness. Furthermore, when practitioners offer to put knowledge at the service of the sick, they invite that trust. Hence, a health need, in itself, constitutes a moral claim on those equipped to help.

(b) Secondly, the knowledge gained by the practitioner is not proprietary as it is acquired through society sanctioning certain invasions of privacy, for example experimenting with humans and allowing for financial subsidisation of health education. The practitioner's knowledge is, therefore, not individually owned and should not be used primarily for personal gain, prestige or power.

(c) Thirdly, the oath that is taken at graduation is a public promise that the practitioner understands the gravity of his or her calling and undertakes to be competent and use that competence in the interests of the sick.[18]

5.4   Why professionalism in healthcare practice should be regulated

The three main purposes of regulating health practitioners are:

(a) to protect the public from unsafe practices;

(b) to set professional, ethical standards to ensure quality service; and

(c) to confer accountability, identity and professional status upon practitioners.

---

13   Constitution of the Republic of South Africa, 1996.
14   Section 9.
15   Section 10.
16   Section 12(2).
17   See generally, World Medical Association *Medical Ethics Manual* (2005).
18   ED Pellegrino 'Altruism, self-interest and medical ethics' (1987) 258 *JAMA* 1939–1940; see above para 2.1.

Thus, in South Africa, the HPCSA was established:

> In order to protect the public and guide the professions, council ensures that practitioners uphold and maintain professional and ethical standards within the health professions and ensure the investigation of complaints concerning practitioners and to ensure that disciplinary action is taken against persons who fail to act accordingly.[19]

Professionalism extends to relationships with patients, donors, colleagues and health practitioners themselves.[20]

The duties of healthcare practitioners towards patients, donors, colleagues, other professionals and themselves require them to act responsibly and to be accountable for their actions. There is a difference between responsibility and accountability:

> Responsibility denotes a duty to perform some function in a satisfactory manner. Accountability entails giving an account of one's acts or omissions.[21]

By accepting responsibility, a healthcare practitioner accepts the responsibilities that go with his or her work, whether this is in private practice as a self-employed person or in a salaried service situation. Accountability relates to how one exercises responsibility. One has to answer for one's actions. Responsibility is the basis for action that requires accountability.[22]

5.5   The relationship between healthcare practitioners and patients

A patient who consults a healthcare practitioner in private practice enters into a contractual relationship with the practitioner[23] but the practitioner also owes the patient a duty of care.[24] For example, where a pregnant woman was wrongly advised by a doctor that she was not at greater risk than normal of having an abnormal or disabled child, she could sue for damages in contract and in delict for the expenses of maintaining and rearing her disabled child and future medical and hospital expenses.[25] The court has gone further and suggested that an abnormal or disabled child whose mother was negligently not forewarned by the physicians when it could have been detected, may have an action for wrongful life.[26] However, a patient who goes to hospital for medical treatment by hospital

---

19   HPCSA 'Overview'; http://www.hpcsa.co.za (accessed on 24 March 2020).

20   HPCSA *General Ethical Guidelines for the Health Care Professions Booklet 1* (2016) paras 5–10.

21   See generally, MA Dada and DJ McQuoid-Mason *Phlebotomy Learnership Guide* (2007) 107–109.

22   Ibid.

23   *Friedman v Glicksman* 1996 (1) SA 1134 (W).

24   *Van Wyk v Lewis* 1924 AD 438–444.

25   *Friedman v Glicksman* 1996 (1) SA 1134 (W).

26   *H v Fetal Assessment Centre* 2015 (2) BCLR 127 (CC) para 80. cf TG Britz and M Slabbert (2015) 78 *THRHR* 577–588; J Neethling (2016) 79 *THRHR* 533–560.

staff enters into a contract with the hospital authority, and both the healthcare practitioners and the authority may be vicariously liable for any wrongful acts or omissions causing harm to patients.[27]

Individual employees who have committed wrongful acts or omissions for which their employers are responsible may not rely on the defence of 'superior orders' by claiming that they were ordered to carry out the procedure or treatment by their employers or their agents. If they knew or ought to have known that what they were doing was wrong, they will still be held liable.[28]

Legally, private practitioners can accept or refuse patients as they choose, provided they do not do so on unconstitutional grounds (e.g. unfair discrimination on racial or religious grounds).[29] However, the Constitution,[30] the National Health Act[31] and the ethical rules of the profession[32] require healthcare practitioners to provide emergency medical treatment by assisting people whose lives or health are seriously endangered unless they receive such help. Although the practitioner could have legitimate grounds for refusing to treat a patient (e.g. a full practice), there is potential for covert discrimination as practitioners do not have to account to anyone for refusing treatment in a non-emergency situation. Hence, the practitioner's conscience plays a role over and above ethical codes and the law regarding discriminatory practices on the ground.

Generally, the contract between healthcare practitioners and patients takes the form of an implied agreement that the practitioner will diagnose the patient's complaint and treat the person for it in the usual manner. In terms of the National Health Act,[33] health practitioners need to discuss the procedures and their consequences with their patients before treating them.[34] Consent by a patient to be treated by a particular practitioner means that only that practitioner may treat him or her, unless a medical emergency arises in which case other healthcare practitioners may assist without consent. In cases where health practitioners do not have the necessary skills, they are legally and ethically obliged to refer their patients to specialists, and a failure to do so may constitute negligence.[35]

---

27   cf *Esterhuizen v Administrator, Transvaal* 1957 3 SA 710 (T); *Dube v Administrator, Transvaal* 1963 4 SA 260 (W); *Buls v Tsatsarolakis* 1976 2 SA 891 (T); *Magware v Minister of Health* 1981 4 SA 472 (Z); *Mtetwa v Minister of Health* 1989 3 SA 600 (D). cf DJ McQuoid-Mason (2017) *SAJBL* 83–85.

28   DJ McQuoid-Mason 'Life Esidimeni deaths: Can the former ME11C for health and public officials escape liability for the deaths of the mental patients on the basis of obedience to "superior orders" or because the officials under them were negligent' (2018) *SAJBL* 5–7.

29   Constitution of the Republic of South Africa, 1996 ss 9 and 15.

30   Ibid s 27(3).

31   61 of 2003 s 5.

32   SA Strauss *Doctor, Patient and the Law* 3 ed (1993) 25.

33   38 of 2005 s 6.

34   See *Validity of consent* para 6.3 below.

35   *S v Mkwetshana* 1965 (2) SA 493 (N). See *Professional negligence* para 8.2 below.

Healthcare practitioners who fail to treat their patients in accordance with their agreement will be guilty of a breach of contract, may forfeit their fees and may be sued for damages.[36]

Healthcare practitioners do not guarantee that patients will be cured – unless they say so specifically (e.g. they guarantee that a pianist will recover 100% usage of her injured hand). Healthcare practitioners who guarantee the results of their treatment may face damages claims from patients if the desired outcome is not achieved. The courts do not expect healthcare practitioners to guarantee cures, but do expect them to treat patients with the amount of skill, competence and care that may reasonably be expected from practitioners in their branch of the profession.[37]

Inherent to the trust that is essential to the practitioner–patient relationship is the interpretation that once treatment commences, healthcare practitioners may not abandon their patients: the agreement only ends once the treatment has been completed or the patient no longer wishes to be treated or for some other justified reason. Patients are expected to make themselves available for treatment but if they do not, healthcare practitioners cannot force them to do so – unless they are a threat to public health and the court has ordered them to be treated (e.g. patients suffering from XDR TB).[38]

In law, patients who fail to keep appointments could be held liable by healthcare practitioners for any financial loss incurred (e.g. lost fees). The losses will be calculated by taking the fee which the practitioner would have earned from attending to the patient, less any sum the practitioner actually earned during the period set aside for the defaulting patient. The official tariff of fees for members of medical schemes includes rules for the cancellation of appointments. Timely steps must be taken to cancel an appointment: two hours for general practitioners and 24 hours for specialists – although each case will be treated on its merits.[39]

The Health Professions Council of South Africa (HPCSA), however, regards it as unethical for doctors to recover fees for services not rendered – including when patients do not honour appointments.[40]

---

36   *Edouard v Administrator of Natal* 1989 (2) SA 368 (D).

37   *Van Wyk v Lewis* 1924 AD 438–444. See *Medical malpractice* para 8.1 below.

38   *Minister of Health, Western Cape v Goliath* 2009 (2) SA 248 (C).

39   In terms of the Medical Schemes Rules under the Medical Schemes Act 131 of 1998 (rule D of the General Rules); cf MA Dada and DJ McQuoid-Mason *Introduction to Medico-Legal Practice* (2001) 6.

40   Booklet 11: *Guidelines on Over-servicing, Perverse Incentives and Related Matters* (2016) para 3.10.4; see Ethical Rules of Conduct for Practitioners registered under the Health Professions Act 56 of 1974, GN R717, 4 August 2006 rule 7.

5.6 Are health practitioners obliged to treat?

There is generally no liability for a mere omission in South African law – unless there is a legal duty to act (e.g. emergency medical treatment in terms of the Constitution),[41] or the circumstances are such that society would regard the failure to act as unlawful.[42] For example, a failure to prevent mentally ill patients from leaving hospital premises and harming members of the public may result in legal liability.[43] There may, however, be a contractual duty to treat people who present at a hospital (e.g. a casualty officer at a hospital must attend to patients brought in for treatment).[44]

As has been mentioned, in emergency cases healthcare practitioners are ethically and constitutionally obliged to treat persons who present at their clinics.[45] An emergency means 'a dramatic, sudden situation or event which is of a passing nature in terms of time' and not a chronic terminal illness such as a chronic kidney disease requiring dialysis.[46]

It has been said that although there is no obligation on healthcare practitioners to take on a case, once they do they must carry it through unless:

(a) the practitioner can leave it in the hands of another competent practitioner;
(b) the practitioner issues sufficient instructions for further treatment;
(c) the patient is cured or does not require further treatment;
(d) the patient refuses further treatment or discharges him- or herself from hospital (provided of course that the patient is mentally capable of doing so); and
(e) the practitioner gives the patient reasonable notice that he or she intends to discontinue his or her attendance, in which case the practitioner should ensure that other facilities are available (e.g. the practitioner should issue full instructions for further treatment and indicate his or her willingness to consult with the practitioner who takes over).[47]

In determining whether or not the failure to treat by healthcare practitioners is reasonable, the courts will probably take into account:

(a) the practitioner's actual knowledge of the patient's condition;
(b) the seriousness of the patient's condition;

---

41 See Constitution s 27(3).
42 *Magware v Minister of Health NO* 1981 (4) SA 472 (Z).
43 *Seema v Lid van die Uitvoerende Raad vir Gesondheid, Gauteng* 2002 (1) SA 771 (T).
44 cf *Magware v Minister of Health* 1981 (4) SA 472 (Z).
45 Constitution s 27(3).
46 *Soobramoney v Minister of Health, KwaZulu-Natal* 1998 (1) SA 765 (CC) 778.
47 DJ McQuoid-Mason 'The medical profession and medical practice' in WA Joubert and JA Faris (eds) *The Law of South Africa* vol 17(2) 2 ed (2008) para 206.

(c)   the professional ability of the practitioner to do what is asked;

(d)   the physical state of the practitioner (e.g. the practitioner was physically exhausted at the time);

(e)   the availability of other healthcare practitioners;

(f)   the interests of the other patients of the practitioner;

(g)   considerations of professional ethics;[48] and

(h)   the requirements of the Constitution (e.g. whether it was a medical emergency).[49]

Healthcare practitioners may treat patients only if they have consented to such treatment[50] as patients have a right to their bodily security.[51] Treating or operating on patients without consent may constitute a serious assault for which the practitioner can be criminally and civilly liable.[52] In some instances, however, the interests of society will override those of an individual and will justify medical action (e.g. quarantining people with XDR TB who are non-compliant[53] and those infected with the Covid-19 virus). In others, people may be treated without consent where, because of age or mental capacity, they are unable to consent. In such instances, the National Health Act requires somebody with the necessary legal capacity to consent on their behalf.[54] In emergency situations, people may be treated without consent if it is not against their previously expressed wishes.[55]

5.7   The rights and duties of users of health services

The National Health Act[56] states that healthcare users have the right to:

(a)   emergency medical treatment;[57]

(b)   participate in decision making;[58]

(c)   provide an informed consent themselves or by a legally competent person on their behalf;[59]

(d)   confidentiality;[60]

---

48   SA Strauss *Doctor, Patient and the Law* 3 ed (1993) 25.
49   Section 27(3).
50   *Stoffberg v Elliott* 1923 CPD 148.
51   Constitution s 12(1); see below para 6.5.
52   cf *Castell v De Greef* 1993 (3) SA 501 (C).
53   *Minister of Health, Western Cape v Goliath* 2009 (2) SA 248 (C).
54   National Health Act 38 of 2005 s 7(1)(*a*)–(*b*). See below paras 6.8 and 6.10.
55   See below para 6.4.
56   61 of 2003.
57   Section 5.
58   Section 8.
59   Section 7.
60   Section 14.

(e)   protection of their health records;[61]

(f)   access to information;[62]

(g)   complain;[63] and

(h)   to have complaints procedures displayed in all health establishments.[64]

The National Health Act also states that health users have the duty to:

(a)   adhere to the rules of health establishments when receiving treatment or health services;

(b)   provide accurate information to healthcare providers about their health;

(c)   cooperate with healthcare providers when using health services;

(d)   treat healthcare providers (i.e. professionally registered staff) and health workers with dignity and respect; and

(e)   to sign a discharge certificate or release of liability if they refuse to accept recommended treatment.[65]

5.8   Rights and duties of healthcare practitioners and personnel

All healthcare practitioners and personnel have the right:

(a)   not to be unfairly discriminated against on account of their health status – but may be subject to certain conditions;[66]

(b)   to measures to minimise injury or damage to their person or property at the health institution;[67]

(c)   to measures to minimise disease transmission at the health institution;[68] and

(d)   to refuse to treat a healthcare user who is physically or verbally abusive towards them or who sexually harasses them.[69]

All healthcare practitioners and personnel have the duty to:

(a)   provide emergency medical treatment;[70]

(b)   ensure that healthcare users participate in decision making;[71]

---

61   Section 17.
62   Sections 6 and 12.
63   Section 18.
64   Section 12(f).
65   Section 19.
66   Section 20(1) and (2).
67   Section 20(3)(*a*).
68   Section 20(3)(*b*).
69   Section 20(4).
70   Section 5.
71   Section 8.

(c) obtain an informed consent;[72]

(d) respect confidentiality;[73]

(e) protect health records;[74] and

(f) to provide access to information (including complaints procedures) – except where it will harm the user.[75]

5.9   Social media and healthcare

The popularity and use of social media have rapidly increased in the healthcare environment.

5.9.1   *Social media platforms*

Social media describes the online and mobile tools and electronic platforms that are used to share opinions and experiences, information, images, and video and audio clips, and includes websites and applications used for social networking. Popular media tools include the following:[76]

(a) Facebook – a networking site with over a billion users

(b) Twitter – a micro-blogging service where text-based posts of up to 140 characters known as 'tweets' are sent and read by its users

(c) LinkedIn – a platform offering features aimed at establishing professional networks

(d) YouTube – a video-sharing website

(e) Tumblr – a micro-blogging platform and social networking website allowing users to post multimedia and other content resulting in a short-form blog

(f) Flikr – an image and video hosting website where photographs are shared

(g) Blogs – regularly updated websites with commentaries or descriptions of events and maintained by individuals or organisations.

The term 'electronic messaging', which means the creating, storing, exchanging and managing of electronic data over a communications network, is also used in the social media setting.[77] Both practitioners and patients use these modalities in the

---

72   Sections 6 and 7.

73   Section 14.

74   Section 17.

75   Section 18.

76   C Grobler and A Dhai 'Social media in the healthcare context: Ethical challenges and recommendations' (2016) 9(1) *S Afr J BL* 22–25.

77   South African Medical Association Electronic Communications Guidelines (2020): https://www. samedical.org/file/1282 (accessed on 20 April 2020).

healthcare context. It is imperative that their benefits and risks are examined and high ethical and professional standards maintained by healthcare practitioners. While practitioners should be free to take advantage of the several personal and professional benefits of social media, concerns such as blurring of boundaries between an individual's public and professional life; maintaining privacy and confidentiality of patient information; the public image of the profession; and inter-professional relationships need to be taken into account[78]

5.9.1.1   Blurring of boundaries

Boundaries may be blurred between practitioners' private and professional lives. Practitioners may unknowingly expose themselves to risk by posting personal material intended for friends, especially where privacy settings have not been activated. This information may be accessible to a wider audience including patients who may attempt to strike up personal relationships with practitioners. This could lead to inappropriate boundary transgressions. Once content has been posted, even if it is deleted, this does not mean it has been removed. It could already have been copied or reproduced.

5.9.1.2   Confidentiality

Confidentiality is central to trust between practitioners and patients but may be difficult to maintain in the social media setting. Personal information could be uploaded during discussion of patients with fellow practitioners through blogs and other sites. Despite identifiers being removed, the patient could potentially be identifiable, resulting in unintentional ethical transgressions and possible legal recourse on the part of the patient. It would also be prudent to remember that many bits of information from multiple sources (e.g. postings from several different team members), when collated together, could identify a patient and result in a breach of patient confidentiality.

5.9.1.3   Public image of the profession

Media might routinely monitor online activity to research stories or look for potential stories. Information could be taken out of context and remain publicly available or permanently retrievable online. Online behaviour may harm the image of the profession. Documented public lapses include physicians taking digital photographs during surgery; posing with weapons and alcohol; making informal and derogatory comments about patients; making comments that could

---

78   C Grobler and A Dhai 'Social media in the healthcare context: Ethical challenges and recommendations' (2016) 9 *S Afr J BL* 22–25.

be perceived as racist, sexist or homophobic; and other unprofessional posts that ultimately could harm the practitioner and the profession.

5.9.1.4   Inter-professional relationships

While healthcare practitioners should be able to engage fully in online debates on healthcare matters, it is prudent to note that individual freedom to voice opinions is not absolute and can be restricted by the need to prevent harm to the rights and reputations of others. Unsubstantiated or negative comments about individuals or organisations must be avoided.

5.9.2   Regulation of social media in healthcare

5.9.2.1   The HPCSA

The HPCSA in its Ethical Guidelines for Social Media[79] reminds practitioners that their ethical obligations apply even in the social media context. It advises practitioners not to interact with patients via social media because of the possibility of a failure to maintain strictly professional relationships.[80] Where the patient, via social media, sends inappropriate messages, the practitioner needs politely to re-establish professional boundaries and explain the reasons for doing so.[81] If patients seek healthcare advice over social media, they should be advised by the practitioner to set up an appointment in person, except in an emergency, where appropriate assistance should be provided.[82] Where a patient persists in contacting the practitioner, a log of all contacts should be kept and the practitioner should contact the HPCSA for advice on how this should be managed.[83]

Opinions on the integrity, skills and professional reputation of colleagues should not be posted as these could result in the public losing faith in the profession.[84]

The HPCSA advises practitioners to include disclaimers in their profiles stating that the views therein are their own and not of the profession or health establishment. Nevertheless, this will not absolve them from their ethical obligations.[85]

Practitioners are cautioned by HPCSA to avoid conflicts of interest and not to engage in touting (e.g. advertising free coffee while waiting in the practice)

---

79   Booklet 16 (2019): https://www.hpcsa.co.za/Uploads/Professional_Practice/Conduct%20%26%20 Ethics/Ethical2%20Guidelines%20on%20Social%20Media.pdf (accessed on 20 April 2020).
80   Section 7.2.
81   Section 7.6.
82   Section 7.7.
83   Section 7.8.
84   Section 8.6.
85   Section 8.9.

or canvassing, or allowing others to do so on their behalf (e.g. declaring or posting patient reviews saying that he or she is the best practitioner in the field) in their social media activities.[86] Furthermore, they may not advertise, endorse or encourage the use of any medicine or health-related product in a manner which unfairly promotes the practitioner or organisation for financial or other gain.[87] Any financial interests should be declared.

5.9.2.2   Pertinent laws

Relevant laws include the Constitution (1996), National Health Act,[88] Children's Act,[89] Promotion of Access to Justice Act,[90] Protection of Personal Information Act[91] and the common law.

A person's right to an unimpaired reputation is protected by South Africa's law of defamation and is therefore available to vindicate damages suffered as a result of harmful or derogatory posts. Defamation is the act of making an unjustified statement about a person or organisation that could harm their reputation.[92] This could result in legal action against individuals and their organisations. An act is considered to be defamatory if it damages reputation or good name, lowers the esteem in which they are held in the minds of others or negatively affects what people think of them. Such content attacks a person's moral character, or exposes him or her to derision or ridicule.[93]

5.10 Telehealth

According to the World Health Organization (WHO), telehealth involves the use of telecommunications and virtual technology to deliver healthcare outside of traditional healthcare facilities. Video consultations or similar forms of technology allow for the replication of the interaction of traditional face-to-face consultations. Virtual home healthcare has now been made possible, where chronically ill or elderly patients may receive guidance in certain procedures while remaining at home. In addition, healthcare workers in remote field settings are now able to obtain guidance from professionals elsewhere in diagnosis, care and

---

86   Section 9.2.
87   Section 9.5.
88   61 of 2003.
89   38 of 2005.
90   3 of 2000.
91   4 of 2013.
92   British Medical Association 'The doctor–patient relationship' in *Medical Ethics Today: The BMA's Handbook of Ethics and Law* 3 ed (2012).
93   See generally E Sadleir and T de Beer *Don't Film Yourself Having Sex and Other Legal Advice for the Age of Social Media* (2014).

referral of patients. It is also possible to deliver training via telehealth schemes or with related technologies such as eHealth, which make use of small computers and the internet.[94]

5.10.1 Ethical considerations

There are both advantages and drawbacks to telehealth. Benefits are that telehealth schemes can improve healthcare access and outcomes, in particular for chronic disease treatment and for vulnerable groups. Costs and demands on crowded facilities are reduced. Patient referrals can be sped up. One practitioner can provide services to a number of different locations. At times of disasters, as experienced during the time of the Covid-19 pandemic and the lockdown, telehealth could be used as a platform for patient management and ongoing care.

Concerns include accuracy of images or text, security and confidentiality. In addition, telehealth consultations cannot convey the same information as a physical consultation.[95]

5.10.2 Regulation of telehealth

5.10.2.1 Relevant laws

Relevant laws include the following:

(a) National Health Act 61 of 2003

(b) Children's Act 38 of 2005

(c) Medical Schemes Act 131 of 1998 (as amended)

(d) Electronic Communications and Transactions Act 25 of 2002 (as amended)

(e) Protection of Personal Information Act 4 of 2013

(f) Consumer Protection Act 68 of 2008

(g) Promotion of Access to Information Act 2 of 2000.

---

94   WHO 'Telehealth' (2016): https://www.who.int/sustainable-development/health-sector/strategies/telehealth/en/ (accessed on 20 April 2020).

95   British Medical Association 'The doctor–patient relationship' in *Medical Ethics Today: The BMA's Handbook of Ethics and Law* 3 ed (2012).

5.10.2.2 The HPCSA

The HPCSA defines telemedicine as follows:[96]

> The practice of medicine using electronic communications, information technology or other electronic means between a healthcare practitioner in one location and a healthcare practitioner in another location for the purpose of facilitating, improving and enhancing clinical, educational and scientific healthcare and research, particularly to the under serviced areas in the Republic of South Africa.

The HPCSA stresses that core ethical values are also applicable in telemedicine practice, and the fact that a patient's information can be moved by electronic means does not alter the ethical duties of the healthcare practitioner.[97] Accountability of practitioners and their ethical duties remain the same. This includes obtaining informed consent and respecting confidentiality. It is the duty and responsibility of the consulting practitioner to obtain informed consent for telemedicine purposes.[98]

In terms of section 4.8.1(*a*) of the guidelines, patient-initiated or second opinion telemedicine is to be restricted to situations in which a previously existing healthcare–patient relationship exists. However, in the midst of the Covid-19 pandemic, the HPCSA acknowledged that new and increased demands for the treatment and care of South Africans infected and affected by the virus had arisen and on the 26 March 2020, it published the Guidance on the Use of Telemedicine Guidelines, replacing the term 'telemedicine' with 'telehealth', which included, inter alia, telemedicine, telepsychology, telepsychiatry, telerehabilitation and remote consultations with patients using telephonic or virtual platforms.[99]

A further guidance, published on 17 April 2020, stated that:

> Telehealth should preferably be practiced in circumstances where there is an already established practitioner–patient relationship, and where such a relationship does not exist, practitioners may still consult using Telehealth provided such consultations are done in the best clinical interest of patients.[100]

The HPCSA has allowed practitioners to charge fees for consultations undertaken through telehealth platforms, but strongly cautioned against practices that may amount to over-servicing and perverse incentives.

---

96   Booklet 10: *General Ethical Guidelines for Good Practice in Telemedicine* (2014): https://www.hpcsa.co.za/Uploads/Professional_Practice/Conduct%20%26%20Ethics/Booklet%2010%20Telemedicine%20September%20%202016.pdf (accessed on 20 April 2020).

97   Section 4.2.4.

98   Section 4.6.4.

99   https://www.hpcsa.co.za/Uploads/Events/Announcements/APPLICATION_OF_TELEMEDICINE_GUIDELINES.pdf (accessed on 21 April 2020).

100   Ibid.

The HPCSA stated that the guidance was only applicable during the Covid-19 pandemic, as it would assist practitioners to continue servicing patients while observing the regulations made in terms of section 27 of the Disaster Management Act, in particular regulation 11B(1)(*b*) which states as follows:

> During the lockdown, all businesses and other entities shall cease operations, except for any business or entity involved in the manufacturing, supply, or provision of essential goods or services, save where operations are provided from outside of the Republic or can be provided remotely by a person from their normal place of residence.

The HPCSA has undertaken to inform practitioners about the continued use, or otherwise, of this guidance soon after the end of the pandemic.[101]

5.11 Dual loyalty

Dual loyalty can be defined as simultaneous obligations, express or implied, to a patient or to a third party resulting in a clinical role conflict between professional duties to the patient and the interests of the third party.[102] This means that practitioners have responsibilities and are accountable both to their patients and to a third party, and these responsibilities and accountabilities are not compatible between parties.

Dual loyalty situations arise where healthcare practitioners may be employed by the state or private institutions to treat patients and a conflict of role arises between the interests of the employers and those of the patient. Other third parties that demand practitioner loyalty include family members, insurers, police, prison officials, military officials, managed-care organisations and sponsors of clinical research. The ethical challenge to the practitioner is how to optimise patient protection and act in the best interests of the patient in the face of external third party pressures. The dual loyalty conflict becomes especially problematic when the human rights of patients are violated.

Many societies hold healthcare professionals to an ethic of undivided loyalty to further the best interests of their patients. Clearly this was not the case with the Biko doctors (see the box on page 92). International ethical codes require complete loyalty to patients, and imply that such loyalty should extend above the interests of third parties even if the patients are alleged to be dangerous criminals or are prisoners, gangsters, terrorists, etc. The same applies to healthcare

---

101   https://www.hpcsa-blogs.co.za/hpcsa-covid-19-guidelines/ (accessed on 21 April 2020).
102   International Dual Loyalty Working Group *Dual Loyalty and Human Rights in Health Professional Practice: Proposed Guidelines and Institutional Mechanisms* (2002) 1–2: http://apha.confex.com/apha/132am/techprogram/paper_80265.htm (accessed on 20 May 2010).

practitioners employed in the private sector who may not put the interests (e.g. financial) of their employer above those of their patients.[103]

Health practitioners faced with a dual loyalty situation should reaffirm that their prime obligation is to their patients. They should inform their patients that they are acting on behalf of a third party but reassure them that they will put their interests first or refer them to someone else who can. In situations where practitioners feel that they should withdraw from the practitioner–patient relationship, they should do so by explaining the reasons to the patient after:

(a) identifying the role conflict and deciding that it cannot be resolved without compromising their ethical duty to the patient;

(b) finding that the pressures being exerted on them are real or perceived and legitimate;

(c) being satisfied that the third party has a legitimate claim on them; and

(d) appreciating that the conflict of interest will result in violation of the patient's human rights.[104]

Dual loyalty conflicts are particularly problematic when the health professional chooses to support the interests of the state instead of those of patients, which result in harms and wrongs to patients. While repressive governments can trigger some of the most insidious human rights violations as a result of dual loyalty conflicts, this situation can also be seen in open societies[105] as in the case of Gauteng and its Mental Health Marathon Project (also known as the Life Esidimeni tragedy).[106]

Violations of the right to access healthcare may also arise from policies imposed by governments compounding the problem when the health professional's conduct is constrained by the pressure to yield to these other powerful interests. Pressures include the culture of the institution where the professional practices, and fears or threats of professional harm. The fact that other parties may have interests that conflict with the medical interests of the person is irrelevant to the health professional's concern for the person as a patient.[107]

---

103   WMA 'Duties of Physicians in General' International code of medical ethics adopted by the 3rd General Assembly of the World Medical Association, London, England, October 1949; and amended by the 22nd World Medical Assembly, Sydney, Australia, August 1968; the 35th World Medical Assembly, Venice, Italy, October 1983; and the 57th WMA General Assembly, Pilanesberg, South Africa, October 2006 (accessed on 25 March 2019). See above para 2.3.

104   See DJ McQuoid-Mason and MA Dada *A to Z of Nursing Law* (2009); http://www.sahistory.org.za/pages/people/bios/biko-s.htm (accessed on 5 January 2010).

105   International Dual Loyalty Working Group *Dual Loyalty and Human Rights in Health Professional Practice: Physicians for Human Rights and School of Public Health and Primary Health Care* (2002) 1–3.

106   B Ferlito and A Dhai 'The Life Esidimeni tragedy: Some ethical transgressions' (2018) 108(3) *SAMJ* 157.

107   GR Mclean and T Jenkins 'The Steve Biko affair: A case study in medical ethics' (2003) 3(1) *Developing World Bioethics* 77–95.

5.11.1 The Life Esidimeni tragedy involving the deaths of mental healthcare patients

A clear understanding of the gravity of their calling as health professionals is necessary so they can have the courage to withstand the institutional pressures to which they are subjected. In the Gauteng Mental Health Project, 144 mental healthcare patients died after their move from Life Esidimeni facilities after October 2015 to unregistered NGO facilities, ostensibly to save the state money. An additional 1 418 were exposed to trauma and morbidity but fortunately survived. The Health Ombud was mandated to investigate this disaster in healthcare and according to his Report, three key players exerted tremendous power and created a culture of fear and disempowerment.[108] Two of them, the head of department and the director, were healthcare professionals and they clearly did not take their oaths seriously. Instead, they were responsible for putting practitioners to whom they issued directives into a situation of dual loyalty.[109] Justice Moseneke, who presided over the subsequent arbitration, aptly summarised the situation as follows:

> This is a harrowing account of the death, torture and disappearance of utterly vulnerable mental health care users in the care of an admittedly delinquent provincial government. It is also a story of the searing and public anguish of the families of the affected mental health care users and of the collective shock and pain of the many other caring people in our land and elsewhere in the world.[110]

Legally, the responsible political and public officials in the Esidimeni tragedy can be held criminally responsible for causing the deaths of many of the patients; however, it remains to be seen whether any of them will be prosecuted for homicide.[111]

---

108 *The Life Esidimeni disaster: The Makgoba report*: http://www.politicsweb.co.za/documents/the-life-esidimeni-disaster-the-makgoba-report (accessed on 1 April 2020).

109 A Dhai 'The Life Esidimeni tragedy: Moral pathology and an ethical crisis' (2018) 108(5) *SAMJ* 382–385.

110 DE Moseneke *The Life Esidimeni arbitration report*: http://www.saflii.org/images/LifeEsidimeni ArbitrationAward.pdf (accessed on 11 June 2018).

111 D McQuoid-Mason 'Life Esidimeni deaths: Can the former MEC for health and public health officials escape liability for the deaths of the mental health patients on the basis of obedience to "superior orders" or because the officials under them were negligent?' (2018) 11(1) *SAJBL* 5–7.

Some questions on professionalism and the healthcare practitioner–patient relationship

Steve Biko, the leader of the Black Consciousness Movement in South Africa, was arrested on 21 August 1977 under the Terrorism Act 83 of 1967. He was interrogated by police officers of the Port Elizabeth security police and suffered major head injuries while in police custody. On 11 September 1977, an injured and untreated Biko was loaded onto the back of a Land Rover and driven 750 km to Pretoria to a prison with hospital facilities. He died shortly after arrival at the Pretoria prison on 12 September, having been left to die in his cell with an empty drip bag attached to his arm. Biko was never charged with a crime or brought to trial.

During his detention, Biko was kept naked in his cell, chained to a grille at night, and left lying on a urine-stained blanket on a rubber mat on the floor.

The healthcare practitioners who attended to Biko while in custody did so at the request of the security police. It was subsequently found that the practitioners:

(a)   issued an incorrect medical certificate and a misleading medical record;

(b)   failed to examine Biko properly;

(c)   failed to enquire into and ascertain the possibilities of a head injury;

(d)   failed to obtain a proper medical history from Biko;

(e)   failed to conduct the necessary medical observations and keep appropriate notes;

(f)   failed to object to Biko being transported in the back of a police vehicle from Port Elizabeth to Pretoria;

(g)   failed to ensure transportation in an ambulance with competent medical attendants;

(h)   failed to do a proper medical examination before stating that Biko's central nervous system had shown no changes; and

(i)   examined Biko in the presence of the security police.

In their defence, the healthcare practitioners stated that they had no option but to agree to the demands of the security police.[112]

1. Discuss how the core foundational values in healthcare practice were breached by the healthcare practitioners who attended to Biko.

2. What should the practitioners have done in this situation?

3. What are some of the common law rights of Biko that were violated by the practitioners?

4. What are the lessons to be learnt in the Biko case in respect of dual loyalty in the context of healthcare?

---

112 http://www.sahistory.org.za/pages/people/bios/biko-s.htm (accessed on 5 January 2010).

CHAPTER 6

Consent

David McQuoid-Mason and Ames Dhai

By the end of this chapter readers will be able to:

1. Explain the ethical aspects of consent.

2. Explain what the law requires for a valid consent.

3. Explain when a healthcare practitioner may depart from the procedure consented to.

4. Explain how consent may be limited in terms of the Constitution.

5. Describe when children may consent to medical treatment and operations.

6. List who may provide consent on behalf of children unable to give a lawful consent.

7. List who may provide consent on behalf of mentally incompetent patients.

8. Describe the challenges concerning informed consent.

6.1 Ethical aspects of consent

The traditional Hippocratic belief that one could do almost anything on a patient as long as the principles of beneficence (best interests) and non-maleficence (no harm) were upheld was considerably revolutionised over the last century, with the recognition internationally of fundamental human rights. Paternalism, the belief that the healthcare practitioner should protect or advance the interests of the patient even if contrary to the patient's own immediate desires or freedom of choice, no longer has a place in the healthcare context. As a result of the Nuremburg Trials, and international instruments such as the International Bill of Rights adopted by member states of the United Nations,[1] as well as several other codes and guidelines emanating from international bodies such as the World Medical Association, the values of autonomy and self-determination have been recognised as paramount. Hence, two conditions are fundamentally

---

1   Consisting of the Universal Declaration of Human Rights (1948), the International Covenant on Civil and Political Rights (1966) and the International Covenant on Economic, Social and Cultural Rights (1966).

indispensable for autonomy: liberty (independence from controlling influences) and agency (capacity for intentional action).[2]

Autonomous actions are the outcome of deliberations and choices by rational agents as persons in the moral sense. Rational persons meet the criteria necessary to decide what is in their own best interests. Healthcare practitioners have a duty to recognise and respect this value in their patients. Not to do so would not only violate their patients' autonomy but would also be synonymous with treating them as less than persons.[3] An autonomous person is someone who has the ability to deliberate about personal goals and to act under the direction of such deliberation. Respecting autonomy denotes valuing autonomous persons' considered opinions and choices, and refraining from obstructing their actions unless they are clearly detrimental to others.[4]

While there has been widespread acceptance of patient autonomy, with patients being the ultimate decision makers in matters that affect themselves, the clinical autonomy and freedom in determining patient management that medical practitioners traditionally enjoyed has been significantly curbed by, inter alia, governments, medical insurers and the economic climate. For instance, in South Africa the National Health Act[5] deals specifically with issues of consent[6] and confidentiality.[7] Hence, autonomy or self-determination, one of the foundational principles in medical practice, has changed to a large extent over the years.[8]

Autonomy or the right to self-determination is a fundamental ethical principle underlying informed consent. However, other ethical principles are also key to informed consent. The information provided has to be useful and must assist the patient in making the best possible choice (beneficence). This is provided for in the National Health Act which specifically lists the information that must be provided.[9] Not providing information necessary to allow for an informed choice by the patient would constitute harm to the dignity of the patient. The practitioner would thereby fail to conform to the principle of not doing harm (non-maleficence). Therefore, the key ethical principles underlying informed consent include a combination of autonomy, beneficence and non-maleficence, with respect for patient autonomy being the overarching goal in the process.

---

2   TL Beauchamp and JF Childress 'Respect for autonomy' in TL Beauchamp and JF Childress (eds) *Principles of Biomedical Ethics* 7 ed (2013) 101–149.

3   R Munson *Intervention and Reflection* 7 ed (2004) 101–113.

4   National Commision for the Protection of Human Subjects of Biomedical and Behavioural Research *The Belmont Principles* (1979).

5   61 of 2003.

6   Sections 6 and 7.

7   Section 14.

8   World Medical Association *Medical Ethics Manual* (2005).

9   See below para 6.3.

6.1.1   *The meaning of informed consent in bioethics*

Founded on basic ethico-legal principles, the doctrine of informed consent entails a process of information sharing and decision making based on mutual respect and participation. It should be considered a process and procedure, and not merely an affirmation, ritual or signature on a piece of paper at a particular point in time. The idea behind informed consent is that it facilitates the performance of professional tasks in a morally defensible way by bringing the patient's informed preferences into the healthcare practitioner's plans. Being well informed on entering the decision-making process protects the patient's dignity in the healthcare environment.

The fundamental belief behind informed consent is that trust between the healthcare practitioner and the patient will be fostered and engendered.[10] An obvious requirement for ensuring that consent is truly informed is a healthcare practitioner with communication, listening and interpretative skills. In addition, it is an ethical imperative that the healthcare practitioner recognise and respect the patient's choice of decision, which may be that of informed refusal rather than consent. This is specifically provided for in the National Health Act.[11] The practitioner who provides information to a patient acknowledges an imbalance of information between them which, if not addressed, will compromise the patient's autonomy. It is this imbalance of information that is the root of patient vulnerability. Knowledge and information with regard to the patient's ailment will empower the patient to make the choice most suitable to his or her needs and desires.

6.2   Legal aspects of consent

In law, the healthcare practitioner–patient relationship is usually a contractual one[12] with the contract taking the form of an implied agreement that the healthcare practitioner will make a diagnosis and treat the patient in accordance with generally accepted standards.[13] A contract implies that the parties involved in the contract have full knowledge of the situation and that they have willingly contracted. All forms of management must be discussed with the patient first. A related legal concept is the idea of a fiduciary relationship, whereby the patient places a special trust or confidence in the healthcare practitioner. Hence

---

10   R Purtillo *Ethical Dimensions in the Health Professions* 3 ed (1999) 185–204.
11   Section 6.
12   cf *Friedman v Glicksman* 1996 (1) SA 1134 (W).
13   R Purtillo *Ethical Dimensions in the Health Professions* 3 ed (1999) 185–204.

the healthcare practitioner violates his or her legal duty if information that is necessary for a patient to make a rational decision regarding care is withheld.[14]

Whether or not there was consent in a particular case is a question of fact.[15] Consent to treatment can be expressed either orally or in writing (signed), or can be implied (tacit) by conduct. In law, there is no difference between written or oral consent, except that written consent is easier to prove should a dispute ensue.[16] It is the duty of the healthcare practitioner to ensure that consent has been obtained from the patient. The healthcare practitioner cannot rely on other healthcare professionals, including nursing staff, to ensure that consent has been obtained.[17]

6.3 Validity of consent

The ethical and legal elements of a valid consent process are:

    (a) disclosure;

    (b) understanding;

    (c) capacity; and

    (d) voluntariness.[18]

6.3.1 Ensuring that the consent it valid

Consent involves a patient agreeing to undergo a specific treatment or operation,[19] and is usually in writing in cases where patients enter hospitals or undergo surgery.[20] Healthcare practitioners who undertake the procedure consented to are required to ensure that a proper consent has been obtained, otherwise they may be guilty of assault. Sometimes a failure to obtain consent may amount to an invasion of privacy. For example, where a prison officer took a blood sample from a prisoner for HIV testing without following departmental procedures concerning informed consent, it was held that the conduct of the prison officer amounted to an invasion of privacy.[21]

Submission to treatment by a patient does not amount to consent – unless the patient submits after having full knowledge of the nature, consequences and

---

14   R Purtillo *Ethical Dimensions in the Health Professions* 3 ed (1999) 185–204; cf *Castell v De Greef* 1994 (4) SA 408 (C).

15   cf *Pandie v Isaacs* (A135/2013, 1221/2007) [2013] ZAWCHC 123 ; *Beukes v Smith* (211/2018) [2019] ZASCA.

16   MA Dada and DJ McQuoid-Mason *Introduction to Medico-Legal Practice* (2001) 5–32.

17   A Dhai 'Informed Consent' (2008) 1 *The South African Journal of Bioethics and Law* 27–30: http://www. sajbl.org.za/index.php/sajbl/article/viewFile/5/9 (accessed on 20 December 2009).

18   MA Dada and DJ McQuoid-Mason *Introduction to the Medico-Legal Practice* (2001) 5–32.

19   cf *Pandie v Isaacs* (A135/2013, 1221/2007) [2013] ZAWCHC 123; *Beukes v Smith* (211/2018) [2019] ZASCA.

20   cf *Stoffberg v Elliott* 1923 CPD 148.

21   *C v Minister of Correctional Services* 1996 (4) SA 292 (T).

risks involved in the proposed procedure. However, although submission may extend to premedication on admission and ordinary nursing care, it should not be extended to serious or irreversible treatment,[22] or cases involving young children or mentally disabled persons.[23]

The courts will not order a person to undergo a surgical procedure if it will violate his or her constitutional rights. For example, where the police applied for a court order to force an accused person to undergo a surgical operation to remove a bullet which could be used in evidence in a criminal trial, it was held that the granting of such an order would violate the accused's constitutional rights to a fair trial, bodily integrity and privacy.[24]

A concept that is closely related to informed consent is that of 'truth telling'. It is always assumed that telling the truth is the right thing to do. Truth telling is aligned to honesty, the moral value of which is unquestionable. Yet, the problem of telling the truth to patients is a topic of controversy, particularly when bad news must be conveyed.

6.3.2 The common law accepted standard of disclosure of the procedure and risks

In the past, the accepted standard of disclosure was that of the 'professional community standard'. The amount of information to be imparted was largely a matter of discretion by the healthcare practitioner concerned. This professional community standard has in most jurisdictions been replaced by the 'reasonable patient' standard, which entails a patient-centred approach to informed consent.[25] Consent will only be 'informed' if the patient has substantial knowledge about the nature, effect, consequences and risks involved in the treatment or procedure consented to.[26] This means that there is a duty on the healthcare practitioner to explain the procedures to be followed to the patient, what the alternatives are, the benefits of the treatment, how the patient would fare without treatment and to warn the patient about the 'material risks' involved in the proposed treatment.[27]

---

22 MA Dada and DJ McQuoid-Mason *Introduction to Medico-Legal Practice* (2001) 9.
23 DJ McQuoid-Mason 'The medical profession and medical practice' in WA Joubert and JA Faris (eds) *The Law of South Africa* 17(2) 2 ed (2008) para 33.
24 *Minister of Safety and Security v Xaba* 2003 (2) SA 703 (D); but *contra: Minister of Safety and Security v Gaqa* 2002 (2) SACR 654 (C), where the court held that such an order was reasonable and justifiable.
25 JD Lieberman and AR Derse 'HIV-positive health care workers and the obligation to disclose' (1992) 13 *Journal of Legal Medicine* 333–365; cf *Castell v De Greef* 1994 (4) SA 408 (C).
26 See National Health Act 61 of 2003 s 6; *Castell v De Greef* 1994 (4) SA 408 (C).
27 *Castell v De Greef* 1994 (4) SA 408 (C) 426.

A risk is 'material' if:

(a)   a reasonable person in the patient's position, if warned of the risk, would attach significance to it; and

(b)   the healthcare practitioner should reasonably be aware that the patient, if warned of the risk, would attach significance to it.[28]

However, a practitioner need not point out every possible complication that may arise,[29] but where a risk would be considered material by the patient, it would need to be explained to him or her, even though it might be remote.

The courts have held that doctors should at least inform the patient about the more serious risks involved in the operation or treatment (e.g. that disfigurement, cosmetic changes and necrosis resulting in the need to amputate limbs may flow from radiological treatment for cancer).[30] However, where the risk of a particular form of treatment is extremely uncommon, as is the case of partial paralysis from an injection known as a phenol block of the lower nerves, it would not be necessary to warn the patient.[31] However, where a 'high risk' procedure is proposed, a reasonable practitioner would give a patient a fair and balanced picture of the material risks involved.[32]

The defence of consent in medical matters applies where:

(a)   the patient has knowledge of the nature or extent of the harm or risk;

(b)   the patient appreciates and understands the nature of the harm or risk;

(c)   the patient has consented to the harm or assumed the risk;

(d)   the consent is comprehensive and extends to the entire transaction, inclusive of its consequences;[33]

(e)   the person giving the consent is legally capable of giving consent (e.g. not a mentally immature child or a mentally challenged person);[34] and

(f)   the patient has made the decision freely and voluntarily without being coerced into doing so.

Consent is a valid defence only if the act the patient consents to is in accordance with public policy – i.e. not contrary to good morals (e.g. consent to a statutorily prohibited termination of pregnancy would not render the doctor's conduct lawful).[35]

---

28   *Castell v De Greef* 1994 (4) SA 408 (C) 426.

29   *Castell v De Greef* 1993 (3) SA 501 (C).

30   *Esterhuizen v Administrator, Transvaal* 1957 (3) SA 710 (T). See generally, MA Dada and DJ McQuoid-Mason *Introduction to Medico-Legal Practice* (2001) 14.

31   *Richter v Estate Hamman* 1976 (3) SA 226 (C).

32   *Castell v De Greef* supra; cf DJ McQuoid-Mason 'The Medical Profession and Medical Practice' in WA Joubert and JA Faris (eds) *The Law of South Africa* 17(2) 2 ed (2008) para 40.

33   *Castell v De Greef* 1994 (4) SA 408 (C) 425.

34   MA Dada and DJ McQuoid-Mason *Introduction to Medico-Legal Practice* (2001) 8.

35   Ibid.

6.3.3 *Assessing the patient's ability to give an informed consent*

A requisite for the healthcare practitioner is the obligation to ascertain the level of a patient's ability to grasp the information given, i.e. the mental competence or capacity. One of the greatest challenges to the doctrine of informed consent is the difficulty in ascertaining whether or not the patient truly grasps the nature of his or her illness and the basis for consenting to or refusing the management proposed.

Of assistance are the four levels of competence that have been proposed by Appelbaum and Grisso.[36] Ideally, the patient should have all four levels for optimal competence:

(a) The ability to communicate choices
(b) The ability to understand relevant information upon which the choice is made
(c) The ability to appreciate the situation according to the patient's own values
(d) The ability to weigh various values to arrive at a decision.

A simple of method of determining whether patients have such competence is for practitioners to request their patients to paraphrase the information that has been conveyed to them.

Differences of language and culture are two major obstacles to good practitioner–patient communication, with differences in cultural understanding of the nature and cause of illness at times impeding the understanding of the diagnosis and treatment options provided by the practitioner.[37]

6.3.4 *The National Health Act requirements for an informed consent*

The National Health Act states that when obtaining an informed consent the healthcare provider must inform the user in a language that the user understands and in a manner that takes into account the user's level of literacy.[38] The Act provides that as part of informed consent, every healthcare provider must inform a user of:

(a) the user's health status – except where it would be contrary to the best interests of the user;
(b) the range of diagnostic procedures and treatment options available to the user;

---

36   PS Appelbaum and T Grisso 'Assessing patients' capacities to consent to treatment' (1988) 319 *N Engl J Med* 1635–1638.
37   World Medical Association *Medical Ethics Manual* 2015.
38   Section 6(2).

(c) the benefits, risks, costs and consequences generally associated with each option; and

(d) the user's right to refuse health services – including an explanation of the implications, risks and obligations of such refusal.[39]

The National Health Act requires health practitioners to inform patients of their diagnosis unless there is 'substantial evidence that the disclosure of the user's health status would be contrary to the best interests of the user'.[40] An example of such 'therapeutic privilege' would be where a cancer diagnosis may cause the patient to become so despondent that it undermines the treatment.[41] Where, however, the patient states that his or her consent is dependent upon being given a diagnosis of his or her condition, such diagnosis must be known to the patient – otherwise there is no proper consent.[42] An important consideration is that how the truth is conveyed is just as significant as what is conveyed.

6.3.4.1   The need to disclose the 'costs'

The reference to the 'costs' of each option in the National Health Act means that there is an obligation on healthcare practitioners to advise patients of their fees and other costs involved, including those likely to be incurred if the patient is referred to a specialist, laboratory or some other person or agency.[43]

Practitioners should also advise patients who are claiming against medical schemes that their account will reflect the International Code of Diseases (ICD) codes for the services that have been provided in terms of ICD-10.[44]

6.3.5   *Participation in decision making*

The National Health Act provides that healthcare users have the right to participate in any decision affecting their health and treatment.[45] If the informed consent is given by a person other than the user, such person must, if possible, consult the user before giving the required consent.[46] Healthcare users capable of understanding must be informed about their health and treatment even if they

---

39   Section 6(1).
40   Section 6(1)(*a*).
41   cf *Castell v De Greef* 1994 (4) SA 408 (C) 426.
42   MA Dada and DJ McQuoid-Mason *Introduction to Medico-Legal Practice* (2001) 14–15.
43   DJ McQuoid-Mason 'Is there an ethical duty and legal duty on doctors to disclose their fees before treatment?' (2015) 105(3) *SAMJ* 96–97.
44   See HPCSA Guidelines for Good Practice in the Health Care Professions Booklet 4 *Seeking Patients' Informed Consent: The Ethical Considerations* para 17: http://www.hpcsa.co.za (accessed on 26 March 2020); *Confidentiality: Protecting and Providing Information Booklet 5* para 8.2.2.1: http://www.hpcsa.co.za (accessed on 26 March 2020).
45   Section 8(1).
46   Section 8(2)(*a*).

lack legal capacity to give the informed consent required[47] (e.g. children under that age of 12 years). Health users unable to participate in decisions affecting their health and treatment must be informed about it after the provision of the health service in question unless the disclosure of such information would be contrary to the user's best interests[48] (e.g. where an emergency procedure is done on an unconscious patient).

6.4 Health practitioner departing from procedure consented to

Health practitioners may not depart materially from the treatment agreed upon – especially if the new treatment is far more radical than that originally consented to. For example, consent to superficial X-ray treatment with mild consequences does not extend to consent to radical radiological treatment with serious consequences.[49]

It has been suggested that in circumstances where a patient has consented to a specific type of operation, and while being operated upon under general anaesthetic, another serious condition is detected, the practitioner would be justified in trying to remedy such condition if:

(a) the extension of the operation is in accordance with good medicine;

(b) the extension takes place in good faith in order to alleviate the patient's complaint;

(c) the risk to the patient is not materially increased; and

(d) it would be against the patient's medical interests first to allow the person to recover from the anaesthetic in order to give consent to the operation being extended.[50]

The courts have held that in cases of emergency an extension of an operation without the patient's consent may be justified on the basis of necessity.[51]

6.4.1 Emergency medical treatment without consent

The National Health Act provides that emergency medical treatment may be provided where patients incapable of giving consent are faced with death or

---

47   Section 8(2)(*b*).

48   Section 8(3).

49   *Esterhuizen v Administrator, Transvaal* 1957 (3) SA 710 (T).

50   SA Strauss and MJ Strydom *Die Suid-Afrikaanse Geneeskundige Reg* (1967) 223–234; cf DJ McQuoid-Mason 'The Medical Profession and Medical Practice' in WA Joubert and JA Faris (eds) *The Law of South Africa* 17(2) (2008) para 41.

51   *Stoffberg v Elliott* 1923 CPD 148. For a full discussion of deviations from consent in medical interventions, see P Carstens and D Pearmain *Foundational Principles of South African Medical Law* (2007) 911–917.

irreversible damage to their health if such treatment is delayed and they have not refused consent.[52] The Constitution[53] and the National Health Act[54] provide that nobody may be refused emergency medical treatment. In cases of emergency, unqualified laypeople may render medical assistance if no healthcare practitioners are available.[55]

6.5   The South African Constitution and consent

The Constitution[56] states that everyone has the right to bodily and psychological integrity, which includes the right to security and control over their body.[57] Accordingly, all patients in South Africa have the right to free choice and informed consent and refusal in the healthcare context.

The Constitution, however, allows for the limitation of rights provided that the limitation is reasonable and justifiable in an open and democratic society.[58] Thus autonomy is not absolute. For example, where patients request illegal or non-therapeutic or other procedures that are against public policy, although their ability to make free choices is respected, the healthcare professionals may not accede to their requests.[59] In addition, recent involuntary admissions of patients with extensively drug-resistant tuberculosis in South Africa might be justified by invoking section 36.[60]

Every right has a corresponding responsibility. An important aspect of the informed consent process would be the need to highlight the importance of patients honouring their obligatory responsibilities as part of the healthcare practitioner–patient relationship. The rights and limitations to informed consent, informed refusal and the corresponding responsibilities are also detailed in the Patients' Rights Charter.[61]

---

52   Section 7(1)(*e*).
53   Section 27(3).
54   Section 5.
55   SA Strauss *Legal Handbook for Nurses and Health Personnel* 7 ed (1992) 11.
56   Constitution of the Republic of South Africa, 1996.
57   Section 12(2).
58   Section 36. See above para 3.4.
59   DJ McQuoid-Mason 'Michael Jackson and the limits of patient autonomy' (2012) 5(1) *SAJBL* 11–14.
60   *Minister of Health v Goliath, Western Cape* 2009 (2) SA 248 (C).
61   Department of Health National Patients Rights Charter: https://www.safmh.org.za/documents/policies-and-legislations/Patient%20Rights%20Charter.pdf (accessed on 4 June 2020). See above para 3.4.

6.6 Consent by spouses

Spouses may consent independently to medical treatment or operations, even if they are married in community of property, because the Constitution gives everyone the right to make decisions concerning their physical or psychological integrity.[62] For example, the consent of the father of a foetus in utero is not required for an abortion in terms of the Choice on Termination of Pregnancy Act,[63] nor may one spouse compel the other spouse to undergo an operation against his or her will, or even to submit to a medical examination. For example, where a husband and wife were living apart and in the process of divorce, the husband could not obtain a court order to force his wife to undergo a medical examination so that he could save money by getting her to join his medical aid scheme.[64]

6.7 Consent by children

Generally, in the case of a child under the age of 18 years, the consent of the parent or guardian is required.[65] However, there are certain exceptions to this rule in terms of the Children's Act[66] and the Choice on Termination of Pregnancy Act.[67]

6.7.1 Consent to medical treatment and surgical operations by children[68]

Consent by children to medical treatment and surgical operations is presently controlled by the Children's Act which has also lowered the age of majority from 21 to 18 years,[69] which means that people over the age of 18 years have full legal capacity.

The Children's Act provides that children may consent to their own medical treatment or to the medical treatment of their child if:

(a) they are over the age of 12 years; and
(b) they are of sufficient maturity and have the mental capacity to understand the benefits and risks, and social and other implications of the treatment.[70]

---

62 Constitution s 12(2).
63 Section 5.
64 *Palmer v Palmer* 1955 (3) SA 56 (O).
65 cf *Esterhuizen v Administrator, Transvaal* 1957 (3) SA 710 (T).
66 38 of 2005.
67 92 of 1996.
68 See generally, DJ McQuoid-Mason and MA Dada *A–Z of Nursing Law* (2009).
69 Section 17.
70 Section 129(2).

Children may consent to the performance of a surgical operation on themselves or their child if:

(a) they are over the age of 12 years;

(b) they are of sufficient maturity and have the mental capacity to understand the benefits and risks, and social and other implications of the surgical operation; and

(c) they are duly assisted by their parent/s or guardian.[71]

6.7.2 Consent by children to HIV testing[72]

The special provisions in the Children's Act regarding HIV testing of children state that consent for an HIV test on a child may be given by the child him- or herself if the following conditions are satisfied:

(a) Such test is in the best interests of the child; and

(b) The child is 12 years of age or older, or the child is under the age of 12 years and is of sufficient maturity to understand the benefits, risks and social implications of such a test.[73]

The Children's Act also provides that consent on behalf of children to HIV testing may be given by:

(a) the parent or caregiver;

(b) the provincial head of social development; and

(c) a designated child protection organisation arranging the placement of the child, where the child is under the age of 12 years and is not of sufficient maturity to understand the benefits, risks and social implications of such a test.

If the child has no parent or caregiver and there is no designated child protection organisation arranging the placement of the child, the superintendent or person in charge of the hospital may give consent. If the child or any of the above persons unreasonably withhold consent, or the child or the parent or caregiver of the child is incapable of giving consent, consent may be given by a children's court.[74] A 'caregiver' is any person, other than a parent or guardian, who factually cares for a child.[75]

71   Section 129(3).
72   See generally, MA Dada and DJ McQuoid-Mason *Introduction to Medico-Legal Practice* (2001).
73   Section 130(2)(*a*) read with s 130(1).
74   Section 132(*b*)–(*f*).
75   Children's Act 38 of 2005 s 1.

6.7.3　*Consent by children to contraception*[76]

The Children's Act provides that nobody may refuse to sell condoms to children over the age of 12 years or refuse to provide condoms to children over 12 years where such condoms are distributed free of charge.[77]

In the case of contraceptives other than condoms, they may be supplied to children without parental or caregiver consent if:

(a)　the child is at least 12 years old;

(b)　proper medical advice is given to the child; and

(c)　the child is medically examined to determine on medical grounds whether a specific contraceptive should not be supplied to the child.[78]

6.7.4　*Consent by children to termination of pregnancy*

The provisions allowing consent to a termination of pregnancy by girls of any age under the Choice on Termination of Pregnancy Act are not affected by the Children's Act.[79] In terms of the Choice on Termination of Pregnancy Act a minor girl of any age may consent to the termination of her pregnancy without her parent's or guardian's consent.[80] However, such a child must have sufficient understanding of the benefits, risks and social implications in order to give an informed consent.[81]

The definition of termination of pregnancy and purpose of the Choice on Termination of Pregnancy Act are wide enough to include terminations other than those for abortion purposes. Thus it has been suggested that the consent provisions relevant to a child of any age may include a child consenting to a live birth by caesarean section in emergency situations.[82]

76　DJ McQuoid-Mason 'The Medical Profession and Medical Practice' in WA Joubert and JA Faris (eds) *The Law of South Africa* 17(2) 2 ed (2008) para 36.

77　Section 134(1).

78　Section 134(2).

79　Section 129(1).

80　Section 5(2).

81　DJ McQuoid-Mason 'Termination of pregnancy and children: Consent and confidentiality issues' (2010) 100(2) *SAMJ* 213–214; 'Termination of pregnancy and children: Professor McQuoid-Mason replies' (2011) 101(2) *SAMJ* 212.

82　DJ McQuoid-Mason 'Can the consent provisions in the Choice on Termination of Pregnancy Act, which do not require children to be assisted by a parent or guardian, be used for live births caesarean section in emergency situations?' (2018) 11(1) *SAJBL* 43–45.

6.8 Consent on behalf of children with no legal capacity to consent[83]

Consent to medical treatment on behalf of children who do not have legal capacity in terms of the Children's Act has to be provided by the parent, guardian, caregiver of the child or some other person with legal capacity to do so.[84]

Consent to surgical treatment on behalf of children who do not have legal capacity in terms of the Children's Act has to be provided by the parent, guardian or some other person with legal capacity to do so.[85]

In terms of the provisions of the Children's Act, the parent/s, guardian or caregiver of a child may consent to the medical treatment of a child if the child is:

(a) under the age of 12 years; or

(b) over the age of 12 years but is of insufficient maturity or is unable to understand the benefits, risks and social implications of the treatment or operation.[86]

The same would apply to surgical treatment – except that the consent must be given by a parent or guardian[87] or someone appointed by the court, not a caregiver.

Furthermore, the superintendent of a hospital, or the person in charge of the hospital in the absence of the superintendent, may consent to the medical treatment of or a surgical operation on a child if:

(a) the treatment or operation is necessary to preserve the life of the child or to save the child from serious or lasting physical injury or disability; and

(b) the need for the treatment or operation is so urgent that it cannot be deferred for the purpose of obtaining consent that would otherwise have been required.[88]

The Minister of Social Development may consent to the medical treatment of or surgical operation on a child if the parent/s or guardian of the child:

(a) unreasonably refuses to give consent or to assist the child in giving consent;

(b) is incapable of giving consent or of assisting the child in giving consent;

(c) cannot readily be traced; or

(d) is deceased.[89]

---

83   See generally, DJ McQuoid-Mason and MA Dada *Introduction to Medico-Legal Practice* (2001).
84   Section 129(4).
85   Section 129(5).
86   Section 129(4) and (5).
87   Section 129(5).
88   Section 129(6).
89   Section 129(7).

The minister may consent to the medical treatment of or surgical operation on a child if the child unreasonably refuses to give consent.[90] A high court or children's court may consent to the medical treatment of or a surgical operation on a child in all instances where another person that may give consent refuses or is unable to give such consent.[91] A parent, guardian or caregiver of a child may not refuse to assist a child in terms of the Act or withhold consent on the sole grounds of religious or other beliefs, unless such parent or guardian can show that there is a medically accepted alternative choice to the medical treatment or surgical operation concerned.[92]

As previously mentioned, in terms of the National Health Act,[93] if children are too young to consent legally but capable of understanding, they must be given sufficient information to enable them to participate in the decision-making process.[94]

Legal age of consent by children for medical treatment and surgical operations	
Procedure	Age at which children can legally consent
Medical treatment	12 years and are 'of sufficient maturity'
Surgical operation	12 years and are 'of sufficient maturity' and assisted by a parent or guardian
HIV testing	12 years if 'of sufficient maturity'
Contraception	12 years
Termination of pregnancy	Any age
Male circumcision	16 years

Notes:

1. *'Of sufficient maturity':* The term 'of sufficient maturity' is linked to the child also having 'the mental capacity to understand the benefits and risks, and social and other implications' of the medical treatment or surgical operation.[95]
2. *Informed consent:* In all the above instances the child must be able to give an informed consent, which means that (a) the child knows the nature and extent of the harm or risk; (b) the child appreciates and understands the nature of the harm or risk; (c) the child consents to the harm or assumed risk; and (d) the child's consent is comprehensive and extends to the entire transaction, including its consequences.[96]

---

90 Section 129(8).
91 Section 129(9).
92 Section 129(10).
93 61 of 2003.
94 Section 8(2)(*a*); see paras 6.3 and 6.7.
95 Act 32 of 2007 s 1(1)(*b*).
96 Act 32 of 2007 s 57.

6.9   Sexual intercourse and consent

The age at which a child is considered by law to be mature enough and capable of consenting to sexual intercourse is 16 years of age.[97] In terms of the Criminal Law (Sexual Offences and Related Matters) Amendment Act, an adult or child having sex (penetrative or non-penetrative) with a child under the age of 12 years will be guilty of committing the crime of rape or sexual violation, and consent by the child is no defence because such a child has no legal capacity to consent.[98] Where the accused is a child below the age of 10 years (the age of criminal capacity), the child cannot be prosecuted. If the accused is a child between 10 and 14 years of age, the child can be prosecuted, but the prosecution will have to prove that the child has criminal capacity.

Children under 12 years of age are not legally capable of giving consent to sexual penetration or a sexual violation. Therefore, any sexual act with a girl or boy under 12 years of age constitutes rape or sexual assault. It is an offence for an adult to have sexual intercourse with, or to sexually violate, a child who is between 12 and 16 years of age, even with the consent of the child.[99] Where accused persons are deceived into believing that the child is older than 16 years of age, they may use this in their defence.[100] The Director of Public Prosecutions has a discretion whether or not to criminally charge children who engage in consensual sexual activities if both are between 12 and 16 years old. However, it is not criminal offence for children under 16 years of age to engage in sexual activities with a partner who is less than two years younger than them.[101]

It is also an offence to have sexual intercourse with mentally incompetent persons as this would amount to rape. Other sexual activities with them also amount to a crime.[102] There is a duty on anyone who is aware of sexual offences against children or mentally incompetent persons to make a report to a police official.[103]

6.10   Consent on behalf of mentally incompetent persons[104]

Generally, a person with mental capacity is a person who understands the nature and effect of what he or she is doing. A patient without mental capacity is a mentally

---

97   Act 32 of 2007 s 1(1)(*b*).
98   Act 32 of 2007 s 57.
99   Section 15.
100   Act 32 of 2007 ss 15 and 16.
101   Section 16.
102   Sections 23–26.
103   Section 54.
104   See DJ McQuoid-Mason 'The medical profession and medical practice' in WA Joubert and JA Faris (eds) *The Law of South Africa* 17(2) 2 ed (2008) para 39.

incompetent patient. Such a patient is unable to understand the nature, effects and consequences of the proposed healthcare services. The Mental Health Care Act[105] provides that a healthcare practitioner or establishment may provide care, treatment and rehabilitation services or admit a mental healthcare user only if:

(a) the user consented to the care, treatment, rehabilitation services or admission;

(b) the practitioner or institution is authorised by a court order or review board; or

(c) due to mental illness, any delay in providing care, treatment, rehabilitation services or admission may result in:

    (i) death or irreversible harm to the health of the user;

    (ii) the user inflicting serious harm to him- or herself or others; or

    (iii) the user causing serious damage to or loss of property belonging to him or her, or others.[106]

A mental healthcare user includes:

(a) the person him- or herself;

(b) the person's next-of-kin;

(c) a person authorised by any other law or court order to act on that person's behalf; or

(d) an administrator appointed in terms of the Act.[107]

The National Health Act[108] also deals with situations where patients are unable to give informed consent. In such cases, consent may be given by:

(a) a person mandated by the user in writing to give consent on his or her behalf; or

(b) a person authorised to give consent by any law or court order;

(c) the spouse or partner of the user, a parent, grandparent, an adult child or a brother or sister in the specific order as listed where no person has been mandated or authorised to give consent on the patient's behalf.[109]

Hence, where patients are not competent to make decisions, these are made on their behalf by substitute decision makers. Problems may arise when appropriate substitute decision makers are not in agreement, or when a decision is made, it conflicts with the best interests of the patient as perceived by the practitioner.

---

105   17 of 2002.
106   Section 9(1).
107   Section 1.
108   61 of 2003.
109   Section 7(1)(*b*).

It is recommended that the practitioner, when faced with this challenge, counsels the family and uses the appropriate sections of the law as discussed above towards resolution of any conflicts.

6.11 Challenges in respect of informed consent

Informed consent poses numerous challenges. These are due, for the most part, to resource constraints, understaffing of healthcare facilities, and language and cultural barriers. Often South African healthcare workers find themselves faced with patient loads and responsibilities which are all but unmanageable. This means that although these health professionals wish to provide the best possible treatment to their patients, it is not always possible. Consultation time is limited by the sheer volume of patients awaiting treatment. These time restraints mean that healthcare workers often cannot devote the large amount of time needed for informed consent to each patient.

Furthermore, continuity of care, when a patient is treated by the same doctor over a long period of time, is difficult to establish in these circumstances. This poses problems when it comes to assessing capacity, as the healthcare professional has limited or no previous experiences with the patient upon which to gauge his or her present capacity.

The South African population is also culturally diverse. Healthcare practitioners in this country recognise that different cultural norms and beliefs should be respected but it is often difficult to establish what these are. Where the doctor cannot speak the patient's language and where many medical conditions (like HIV/AIDS) are clouded in superstition, it will require ongoing dialogue between healthcare providers and patients to ensure that the patient's beliefs are recognised.

HIV is another issue which poses a challenge to informed consent. Because of the stigma surrounding the disease, patients are either unwilling to disclose their HIV status to healthcare professionals or they are unwilling to consent to HIV testing.

6.11.1 Patient noncompliance and working with difficult patients

The noncompliant patient is the patient who, for whatever reason, does not cooperate with the practitioner's management programme. Often, this is not in the patient's best interests and is counterproductive to the pursuit of good health. Patients who are noncompliant may hold back on necessary information, may not at all be inclined to change their unhealthy behaviours or may default prescribed treatment.[110] In some instances, when it is necessary to protect the health of the public, a court order may be required to ensure that such noncompliant patients are quarantined (e.g. as in the case of XDR TB patients).[111]

On 17 March 2020, just as South Africa had found itself in the grips of the Covid-19 pandemic, an urgent application was heard in the High Court of South Africa, Gauteng Local Division, Johannesburg involving a case where a mother and daughter who had tested positive for the Covid-19 virus refused to be quarantined and the father refused to be tested for the virus. The application had been filed by the Gauteng Department of Health. The court ordered that the South African Police Service trace and test the father for the infection and that the mother and daughter be quarantined at the Charlotte Maxeke Johannesburg Academic Hospital until such time as the department was satisfied that they (mother and daughter) did not pose a risk of transmission to the public.[112]

6.11.1.1   Impact on the practitioner

Working with difficult patients can be emotionally stressful to the practitioner, who at times may have to develop defence mechanisms to cope with these tensions. Feeling useful and being useful are integral to the practitioner achieving satisfaction with the work that he or she does. The noncompliant, uncooperative patient will deny those that provide care the chance to feel that usefulness and satisfaction.[113] It is understandable that practitioners who work really hard to improve the patient's condition and whose efforts are met with noncompliance will feel frustrated and dissatisfied. Emotional reactions and responses that are adverse towards the patient could follow and trigger a rift from the practitioner's ethical and moral ideals. Moreover, a core value of professionalism (the obligation to transcend the personal and serve the needs of others) could be eroded. The practitioner may find him- or herself in a very disconcerting position where he or she is challenged to maintain the duty of compassionate and concerned care for all patients while faced with situations that undermine this responsibility.[114]

---

110   R Martinez 'Losing empathy – commentary' in TK Kushner and DC Thomasma (eds) *Ward Ethics: Dilemmas for Medical Students and Doctors in Training* (2001) 104–108.

111   *Minister of Health v Goliath, Western Cape* 2009 (2) SA 238 (C).

112   A Mthethwa 'Court orders quarantine after mother and daughter test positive for Covid-19 but refuse isolation' *Daily Maverick* 18 March 2020: https://www.dailymaverick.co.za/article/2020-03-18-court-orders-quarantine-after-mother-and-daughter-test-positive-for-covid-19-but-refuse-isolation/ (accessed on 1 April 2020).

113   R Martinez 'Losing empathy – commentary' in TK Kushner and DC Thomasma (eds) *Ward Ethics: Dilemmas for Medical Students and Doctors in Training* (2001) 104–108.

114   Ibid.

6.11.1.2 Responding to the noncompliant patient

How should a practitioner respond to the noncompliant patient? The empathic and compassionate practitioner will listen to the rejection of management. Empathy and compassion are not only the ability to feel a patient's pain and suffering but also to have an awareness of the whole person, the person's ideas, feelings, attributes and prejudices. It is also important to remember that we can learn from our patients. Practitioners should learn to adjust to specific patients and their behaviour, and guard against allowing their own reactions to interfere with the general ethical rule in medicine that all patients should be treated alike.[115]

The practitioner could begin by asking him- or herself what the patient understood about the proposed management. Successful relationships between healthcare practitioners and patients depend upon mutual trust.[116] The Health Professions Council of South Africa (HPCSA) stresses that effective communication is key to enabling patients to make informed decisions. It advises practitioners to take appropriate steps to find out what patients want to know and ought to know about their condition and its treatment. Such dialogue with patients would lead to clarity of objectives and understanding, and strengthen the quality of the relationship between practitioners and patients. It would also provide an agreed framework within which practitioners could respond effectively to the individual needs of patients.

Patients are more likely to cooperate fully with the agreed management of their conditions if they make properly informed decisions about their healthcare.[117] Patients may need more information to make informed choices about procedures which are associated with a high risk of failure or adverse side effects, or about investigations for conditions which, if present, could have serious implications for their employment, social or personal life. In addition, information should be presented to patients in a language that they understand and they should be asked whether they have understood the information and whether they would like more information before making a choice.

It is important to bear in mind that patient retention in a management programme will depend to a large extent on how much the patient really understands about the proposed processes. If a patient has not truly understood, would it be fair of the practitioner to label him or her as noncompliant?[118]

---

115 Ibid.

116 See generally, Health Professions Council of South Africa Guidelines for Good Practice In the Health Care Professions Booklet 4: *Seeking Patients' Informed Consent: The Ethical Considerations*: http://www.hpcsa.co.za (accessed 26 March 2020).

117 Ibid.

118 Ibid.

6.11.1.3 Using a patient-centred approach

Practitioners have an obligation to enquire about patients' individual needs and priorities when providing information to them. In the context of South Africa's multicultural diversity, patients' beliefs, culture, occupation or other factors may have a bearing on the information they need in order to reach a decision and this should not be ignored. Assumptions should not be made about patients' views. During discussion, patients should be asked about concerns they may have about the treatment or the risks that the treatment may involve. Patients may attach particular significance to certain risks, and practitioners need to be aware of this.[119] Practitioners need to respond honestly and as comprehensively as possible to any questions the patient raises.[120]

It is imperative that patients are given sufficient time to reflect before and after making a decision, especially where the information is complex or the severity of the risks is great. According to the HPCSA, where patients have difficulty understanding information, or the information to absorb is in excess, it may be appropriate to provide this in manageable amounts. Supplementing the information with appropriate written or other back-up material, over a period of time, or repeating the information as often as is reasonably necessary is also recommended. In addition, involving nursing or other members of the healthcare team in discussions with the patient, where appropriate, may prove to be useful as they could have valuable knowledge of the patient's background or particular concerns.[121]

6.11.1.4 Obtaining advice and assistance in dealing with difficult patients

Despite a strict adherence to the core ethical values in healthcare practice by the empathic, altruistic and compassionate practitioner, the angry, abusive, self-destructive, noncompliant and perhaps even vindictive patient is sometimes a reality. The unfortunate situation of an inquiry at the level of the HPCSA and/or legal sanction as a result of interacting with such patients may arise. Generally, good note-keeping as part of management guidelines is recommended to practitioners. This usually assists with patient management during follow-up and could be used in the practitioner's defence should a legal challenge arise. The value of accurate record keeping cannot be sufficiently emphasised.

---

119 See generally, Health Professions Council of South Africa Guidelines for Good Practice in the Health Care Professions Booklet 4: *Seeking Patients' Informed Consent: The Ethical Considerations*: http://www.hpcsa.co.za (accessed 26 March 2020).

120 Ibid.

121 Ibid.

Being aware of the challenges imposed by the difficult patient, and discussing these with peers and other colleagues, as well as seeking advice from medical insurers, could assist in finding ways to deal with these patients. Discussing thoughts and feelings about the difficult patient could help the practitioner understand the issues associated with dealing with such patients and how to overcome them. The practice of empathy and compassion could be understood by discussing why one loses empathy and how the situation could be adjusted to allow for fair and just treatment of the patient. Talking about these dilemmas could go a long way towards assisting practitioners in coping with such patients.

Some questions on consent

Read the following scenarios and decide whether the persons concerned may consent or refuse to consent to the following healthcare procedures:

1. An HIV-positive 12-year-old mother of a baby asks a doctor to test her baby for HIV.

2. A 15-year-old boy refuses to consent to a blood transfusion for religious reasons.

3. A wife consents to a termination of pregnancy without consulting her husband.

4. The parents of a baby refuse to consent to their child receiving a blood transfusion on religious grounds.

5. An 11-year-old girl asks a family planning clinic to provide her with condoms.

CHAPTER 7

Confidentiality

David McQuoid-Mason and Ames Dhai

By the end of chapter readers will be able to:

1. Explain the ethical aspects of confidentiality.
2. Explain the legal aspects of confidentiality.
3. Describe how the courts deal with confidentiality.
4. Explain what the law is regarding access to medical records.

7.1   Ethical aspects of confidentiality[1]

Confidentiality is one of the longest standing dictums in healthcare codes of ethics and has been a cornerstone of healthcare ethics since the time of Hippocrates. According to the Hippocratic Oath, written in the 4th century BC:

> What I may see or hear in the course of the treatment or even outside of the treatment in regard to the life of men, which in no account one must spread abroad, I will keep to myself holding such things shameful to be spoken about.[2]

The updated, modern version of the Hippocratic Oath that was originally introduced in the Declaration of Geneva by the WMA in 1948, and subsequently amended, in the clause on confidentiality it simply states: 'I will respect the secrets that are confided in me, even after the patient has died'.[3]

Throughout the ages, confidential information has been perceived as sensitive information, as judged by the patient. This sensitive information could be shameful, harmful and embarrassing to the patient. Confidentiality can be perceived as the need to keep such personal information within proper bounds. The patient, therefore, must have a reasonable expectation that this sensitive information will not be disclosed to others. When healthcare practitioners obtain

---

1   See generally, Health Professions Council of South Africa Guidelines for Good Clinical Practice in the Health Care Professions Booklet 5 *Confidentiality: Protecting and Providing Information* (2016).

2   O Temkin and CL Temkin (eds) *Ancient Medicine: Selected Papers of Ludwig Edelstein* (1967) 6.

3   WMA 'The Physician's Pledge' *Declaration of Geneva* (1948), as amended (2017): https://www.wma.net/policies-post/wma-declaration-of-geneva/.

confidential information from patients, the latter have a right to expect that the practitioner will honour his or her professional promise of confidentiality.

7.1.1 Privacy and confidentiality

The notion of confidentiality is often discussed within the framework of privacy. While these concepts are closely linked, there are some differences between the two. Privacy relates to aspects of a person's being into which no one else should intrude. When patients share private information with their practitioners, they choose to relinquish some aspects of their privacy. Patients have a reasonable expectation that such information will only be shared with specific people to further their (the patients') welfare and with no one else. Confidentiality therefore involves a relationship, whereas privacy does not.[4]

7.1.2 Confidentiality and patient autonomy

It is clear that confidential information must be treated with utmost care. The reasons for this are:

(a) to exclude unauthorised people from being privy to this information; and

(b) to facilitate the sharing of sensitive information with the goal of helping the patient.[5]

Confidential information may be shared with other healthcare practitioners involved in managing the patient on condition that this information pertains to that aspect of management and has relevance to the case.

There are three sources from which confidentiality draws such a high value. These are autonomy, respect for persons and trust.[6] The principle of autonomy prescribes that personal information belongs to an individual and should not be made known to others without their consent, except where there is a legitimate requirement to breach confidentiality.[7] Individuals have a right to privacy and this right allows them autonomy over their personal information. Because people deserve respect, it is essential that the confidences they impart to the healthcare practitioner are upheld and respected. In this manner, their privacy will be preserved.

---

4   R Purtilo *Ethical Dimensions in the Health Professions* 3 ed (1999) 147–162.

5   Ibid.

6   World Medical Association *Medical Ethics Manual* (2015) 34–63.

7   See para 7.1.4 below.

7.1.3 Confidentiality and trust

The practitioner–patient relationship is one built on trust. Keeping confidences assists in building that trust thereby maintaining patient dignity. Eroding that trust will most certainly harm the relationship. Often practitioners are total strangers to patients who end up revealing their most intimate and personal information to them. Frequently this is information that they would not want anyone else to know. If there was no understanding by patients that practitioners have ethical and legal duties to keep their disclosures secret, they would withhold information which would hinder practitioners in their efforts to provide effective interventions.

7.1.4 Breaching patient confidentiality

Generally, confidential information cannot be shared with others unless authorised by the patient personally or by the law. In most cases, patients are unaware of the limits to patient confidentiality. Good clinical practice entails that they are advised before rather than after their information has been divulged. Where a breach of confidentiality is necessary and justifiable, this should be kept to a minimum and those who gain access to this information should be made aware of the need for them to uphold it as confidential. In healthcare institutions, breaches may also occur when others (e.g. laboratory technicians, students and interpreters) require access to the patient's information.[8]

It should be remembered that breaching confidentiality always involves a harm – that of creating distrust in the practitioner–patient relationship. When faced with such a dilemma, it is important that the following questions are asked:[9]

(a) Does the benefit of breaching confidentiality outweigh the harm of threatening the trust in the practitioner–patient relationship?

(b) How can the amount of harm be kept to a minimum when it is ethically appropriate to breach confidentiality?

While questions surrounding the practice of keeping patient confidences are not easily resolved, it is always the duty of the practitioner to ensure that the harms as a result of making disclosures are minimised and patient benefits optimised.

8   World Medical Association *Medical Ethics Manual* (2015) 34-63.
9   R Purtilo *Ethical Dimensions in the Health Professions* 3 ed (1999) 147–162.

7.2 Health Professions Council of South Africa ethical rules on confidentiality

The Minister of Health, in consultation with the HPCSA, has promulgated rules on confidentiality[10] and the HPCSA has published guidelines to assist healthcare practitioners in interpreting them.[11] Ethically medical practitioners may divulge verbally or in writing information regarding a patient which they ought to divulge only (a) in terms of a statutory provision; (b) at the instruction of a court of law; or (c) where justified in the public interest.[12]

Any other information may be divulged by a practitioner only (a) with the express consent of the patient; (b) in the case of a minor under the age of 12 years, with the written consent of his or her parent or guardian; or (c) in the case of a deceased patient, with the written consent of his or her next-of-kin or the executor of such deceased patient's estate.[13]

The ethical rule regarding disclosures of the patient's condition after death is stricter than the common law, as usually a deceased person's rights die with them except if the pleadings in the court case had been joined beforehand.[14] It is submitted, however, that the health status of deceased persons may be ethically disclosed if their health condition endangers third parties.

7.3 Legal aspects of confidentiality

7.3.1 Introduction

According to the law, confidentiality is the duty of healthcare professionals to ensure that all information concerning a patient is not disclosed without the consent of the patient or under the conditions prescribed by law. The Constitution

---

10   HPCSA Ethical Rules of Conduct for Practitioners Registered Under the Health Professions Act, 1974: GN R717 of 4 August 2006; see HPCSA Ethical and Professional Rules of the Health Professions Council of South Africa Booklet 2 *Ethical and professional rules of the Health Professions Council of South Africa as promulgated in* Government Gazette *R717/2006* (2016): http://www.hpcsa.co.za (accessed 26 March 2020).

11   See generally, Health Professions Council of South Africa Guidelines for Good Clinical Practice in the Health Care Professions Booklet 5 *Confidentiality: Protecting and Providing Information* (2016) (accessed on 26 March 2020).

12   HPCSA Ethical Rules of Conduct for Practitioners Registered Under the Health Professions Act, 1974: GN R717 of 4 August 2006, rule 13(1); cf *Tshabalala-Msimang and Another v Makhanya and Others* 2008 (6) SA 102 (W).

13   Rule 13(2). See also Health Professions Council of South Africa Guidelines for Good Clinical Practice in the Health Care Profession Booklet 5 *Confidentiality: Protecting and Providing Information* (2016) para 9.5 (accessed on 26 March 2020); cf DJ McQuoid-Mason 'Disclosing details about the medical treatment of a deceased public figure in a book: Who should have consented to the disclosures?' (2017) 107(12) *SAMJ* 1072–1074.

14   cf *Spendiff v East London Despatch Ltd* 1929 EDL 113.

states that everyone has the right to privacy, which includes the right not to have the privacy of their communications infringed.[15] The National Health Act provides that all information concerning healthcare users, including information regarding their health status, treatment or stay in a healthcare establishment should be kept confidential.[16] Subject to the provisions of the Promotion of Access to Information Act,[17] no person may disclose any information about a patient unless:

(a) the patient consents to that disclosure in writing;

(b) a court order or any law requires that disclosure; or

(c) non-disclosure of the information represents a serious threat to public health.[18]

A breach of such confidence may result in an action for invasion of privacy in terms of the Constitution[19] and the common law.[20]

The common law right to privacy requires healthcare practitioners to maintain the confidentiality of their patients unless:

(a) a court of law orders them to make a disclosure;[21]

(b) an Act of parliament requires the disclosure to be made;[22]

(c) there is a threat to an endangered third party;[23]

(d) there is a moral, social or legal obligation to make a disclosure to a person or agency that has a reciprocal moral, social or legal obligation to receive the information;[24]

(e) where patients make complaints against practitioners to their regulatory bodies regarding their treatment and the practitioners are obliged to make certain disclosures as part of their defence; or

(f) the patient consents to the disclosure being made.

---

15   Section 14.
16   Section 14(1).
17   Act 2 of 2000.
18   National Health Act s 14(2).
19   Section 14. *C v Minister of Correctional Services* 1996 (4) SA 292 (T).
20   *Jansen van Vuuren v Kruger* 1993 (4) SA 842 (A).
21   *Parkes v Parkes* 1916 CPD 702; *Botha v Botha* 1972 (2) SA 559 (N).
22   For example, the duty to report (a) child abuse under the Children's Amendment Act 41 of 2007 s 110; (b) sexual offences against children of mentally disabled persons under the Criminal Law (Sexual Offences and Related Matters) Amendment Act 32 of 2007 s 54; and (c) abuse of older persons under the Older Persons Act 13 of 2006 s 26.
23   For example, in the American case of *Tarasoff v Regents of the University of California* (1976) Cal SCt 17 Cal Rep 3rd series 425, a student told a university psychologist that he was going to kill his ex-girlfriend because she had left him. The psychologist warned the campus security but not the girl or her family. The girl was killed and her family sued the university. The court held that there was a legal duty on the psychologist to warn the girl or her family because she was an endangered third party and 'the protective privilege ends where the public peril begins'.
24   *Jansen van Vuuren v Kruger* 1993 (4) SA 842 (A).

These exceptions may be raised as defences to actions for invasion of privacy, defamation or breach of contract arising from a breach of confidentiality.[25] An additional exception is where a person is a public figure and it is in the public interest to make a public disclosure about his or her conduct when it is in conflict with his or her duties as a public official.[26]

7.3.2 Confidentiality and children

Under the Children's Act,[27] there is a legal duty on healthcare practitioners not to divulge information about their child patients without the latters' consent if they are over 12 years of age or with the written consent of their parents or guardians if they are minors under 12 years of age.[28] Information about children old enough to obtain condoms[29] or consent to HIV tests[30] may not be communicated to third parties (including their parents or guardians) without their consent.

A girl of any age may consent to disclosures about her termination of pregnancy without the consent of a parent or guardian.[31]

7.3.3 Confidentiality and court proceedings

The courts treat the relationship between healthcare practitioners and patients as a qualified privilege irrespective of whether the relationship involves physical or psychological injuries or illnesses.

The courts have decided against an absolute privilege for the psychiatrist–patient relationship and have exercised discretion regarding whether they will permit psychiatrists to refuse to give evidence. For example, during a custody dispute one of the spouses wished to lead evidence from a psychiatrist who had treated the other spouse. The court held it could exercise its discretion if it was in the best interests of the child and justice that the evidence should be led.[32] In custody disputes, psychiatric evidence concerning one or other spouse may be crucial for the well-being of the children. The court is the upper guardian of all minors and the best interests of the child (not the parents) is paramount. The courts, however, are conscious of the fact that psychiatric treatment may be inhibited if patients fear disclosures.

---

25   MA Dada and DJ McQuoid-Mason *Introduction to Medico-Legal Practice* (2001) 20–22.
26   cf *Tshabalala-Msimang and Another v Makhanya and Others* 2008 (6) SA 102 (W).
27   38 of 2005.
28   Children's Act s 129.
29   Ibid. s 134(3).
30   Ibid. s 133.
31   Choice on Termination of Pregnancy Act 1996 s 5(2).
32   *Botha v Botha* 1972 (2) SA 559 (N).

Likewise, in a criminal case an accused person was sent for psychiatric observation. During the interview with the psychiatrist he made certain statements which conflicted with statements made previously to a magistrate. The prosecutor wished to lead evidence of what the accused had said about the crime to the psychiatrist. The court refused the prosecutor's request because he was trying to admit evidence in order to establish certain facts concerning the offence, rather than the accused's state of mind at the time the offence was committed. This was not the purpose of psychiatric observation. Furthermore, justice might suffer if persons sent for observation began to fear that what was told to a psychiatrist may be used against them in court.[33] However, the courts have held that statements made to a psychiatrist that do indicate the accused's state of mind at the time of the alleged offence can be admitted as evidence.[34]

In cases involving physical injuries or illnesses – even if they are embarrassing (e.g. evidence of sexually transmitted infections) – the courts will order disclosure if it is necessary in the interests of the administration of justice. For example, in a divorce case a medical practitioner was asked whether he had examined the defendant husband for venereal disease and the practitioner claimed privilege. The plaintiff wife had sued for divorce on the basis of the husband's adultery and wanted evidence from the husband's doctor concerning the sexually transmissible infection which her husband had not contracted from her. The court had to decide whether the husband had committed adultery and ordered the medical practitioner to answer the question.[35]

In civil matters, refusal by a healthcare practitioner to comply with a court order to breach the confidentiality of their patient will result in prosecution for contempt of court. In criminal matters, such refusal is also contempt and the practitioner could be sentenced to imprisonment in terms of the Criminal Procedure Act.[36]

7.3.4 Access to medical records

Technically doctors, healthcare centres, community health clinics and hospitals own the patients' records held by them. However, this is really custodial ownership, because their right to use the records is subject to the confidentiality rule.

---

33 *S v Forbes* 1970 (2) SA 594 (C).
34 *S v Webb* 1971 (2) SA 340 (T).
35 *Parkes v Parkes* 1916 CPD 702; cf *Botha v Botha* 1972 (2) SA 559 (N).
36 51 of 1977 s 189.

7.3.4.1   Access in terms of the Constitution

The Constitution provides that everyone has the right of access to information held by the state as of right and to information held by private bodies (e.g. private hospitals) where he or she requires such information to exercise or protect a right.[37] The courts have held that the Health Professions Council is not an organ of the state and that a patient may have access as of right only to those parts of medical records held by the council on behalf of the public hospital that handed them over for inquiry purposes – the balance of the records would have to be obtained directly from the public hospital.[38]

7.2.4.2   Access under the Promotion of Access to Information Act

In terms of the Promotion of Access to Information Act,[39] an information officer must be appointed by public and private bodies to provide access to information at reasonable cost.[40] Access to medical records must be provided to patients in terms of the Act but may be refused where such access would cause serious harm to the patient's physical or mental well-being.[41]

7.2.4.3   Access under the Protection of Personal Information Act

Personal information is also protected by the Protection of Personal Information Act,[42] most of which is now in effect. The Act provides that it is prohibited to process personal information about a person's religion or philosophy of life, race, political persuasion, health or sexual life, trade union membership, criminal behaviour, or unlawful or objectionable conduct connected with a ban on such behaviour, except if the data subject has given his or her explicit consent to the processing of the information or the Act provides otherwise.[43] An exception to the consent requirement is in the case of medical professionals, healthcare institutions or facilities, or social services, where such information is necessary for the proper treatment and care of the data subject, or for the administration of the institution or professional practice concerned.[44] The Act requires data subjects (a) to be notified that data about them is being held,[45] (b) to be allowed to have access to their data[46] and (c) to be allowed to correct their data.[47]

---

37   Section 31(1).
38   *Korf v Health Professions Council of SA* 2000 (1) SA 1171 (T) 1178–1179.
39   2 of 2000.
40   Section 30.
41   MA Dada and DJ McQuoid-Mason *Introduction to Medico-Legal Practice* (2001) 17–22.
42   4 of 2013.
43   Section 26.
44   Section 32(1).
45   Section 18.
46   Section 23.
47   Section 24.

7.2.4.4   Access under the National Health Act

The National Health Act provides that a health worker or any healthcare provider that has access to the health records of a user may disclose such personal information to any other person, healthcare provider or health establishment as is necessary for any legitimate purpose within the ordinary course and scope of his or her duties where such access or disclosure is in the interests of the user.[48]

The Act also provides that a healthcare provider may examine a user's health records for the purposes of:

(a)   treatment with the authorisation of the user; and

(b)   study, teaching or research with the authorisation of the user, head of the health establishment concerned and the relevant health research ethics committee.[49]

If the study, teaching or research reflects or obtains no information as to the identity of the user concerned, it is not necessary to obtain the above authorisations.[50] The person in charge of a health establishment in possession of a user's health records must set up control measures to prevent unauthorised access to those records and the storage facility in which or system by which records are kept.[51]

Some questions on confidentiality

Consider the following scenarios and decide whether the healthcare practitioners can be held legally liable:

1.   A doctor tells a patient's wife that her husband has tested positive for HIV after the husband said that he would not tell his wife because she would think that he was having an affair.

2.   A nurse tells a patient's family with whom he is living that the patient suffers from TB.

3.   A doctor reports to the police that a 12-year-old girl is having sex with a 43-year-old man.

4.   A nurse at a clinic notifies the health authorities that there has been a cholera outbreak and mentions the names of some of the patients to them.

5.   A clerk at a hospital informs an insurance company that a patient had died from an AIDS-related illness.

---

48   Section 15(1).
49   Section 16(1).
50   Section 16(2).
51   Section 17(1).

CHAPTER 8

Medical malpractice and professional negligence

David McQuoid-Mason and Ames Dhai

By the end of this chapter readers will be able to:

1. Explain the meaning of medical practice.
2. Explain the meaning of professional negligence.
3. Explain how professional negligence is proved.
4. Define what is meant by vicarious liability.
5. Explain how exclusion or exemption clauses work.
6. Explain the Impact of medical negligence claims.
7. Describe the role of mediation as an alternative dispute resolution process.

8.1 Medical malpractice

Medical malpractice refers to negligent or intentional unlawful conduct on the part of healthcare practitioners that causes injury or damage to their patient or their patient's property. At common law, malpractice occurs where professional persons, intentionally or negligently, unlawfully cause harm to another person – usually their client or his or her family. Malpractice goes further than professional negligence because it includes negligent or intentional acts.[1] An example of malpractice would be where a healthcare practitioner intentionally breaches the confidence of his or her patient.

8.2 Professional negligence

Professional negligence occurs when health practitioners negligently fail to exercise the degree of skill and care of a reasonably skilled practitioner in their field of practice.[2] Healthcare practitioners may give evidence as to procedures that should be followed, but the courts will decide whether such procedures

---

1   DJ McQuoid-Mason and MA Dada 'Malpractice' in *A–Z of Nursing Law* 3 ed (2017) 184.
2   *Mitchell v Dixon* 1914 AD 519; *Castell v De Greef* 1993 (3) SA 501 (C); cf *S v Mahlela* 1966 (1) SA 226 (A).

are reasonable.[3] Specialists are expected to exercise a greater degree of skill and care than general practitioners.[4] Greater skill and care is also required where more complicated medical procedures are used.[5] Therefore general practitioners would be negligent if they undertook work for which they did not have the required specialist skills – unless it were an emergency situation and no specialist was available.[6] Practitioners may be negligent if they fail to warn patients about the meaning of certain symptoms.[7]

8.2.1   Types of medical negligence cases

An attempt has been made to classify professional negligence cases into actions arising from (a) illegal operations; (b) defective medical instruments or equipment; (c) wrongful diagnoses; (d) wrongful blood transfusions; (e) incompetent anaesthesia; (f) incompetent procedures; (g) carelessness of patients; (h) careless treatment; (i) overdoses of medicines or drugs; (j) excessive radiotherapy; (k) the leaving of instruments or equipment inside patients; (l) incompetent follow-up treatments; (m) premature discharges from hospital; (n) transfusing patients with HIV-infected blood; (o) 'baby-swaps' in maternity wards; (p) a failure to move patients to hospitals; (q) a failure by general practitioners to refer patients to specialists; (r) failed sterilisations; (s) failed abortions; (t) a failure to warn a pregnant woman about the risk of delivering a defective baby so she could terminate the pregnancy; and (u) a failure to properly inform patients.[8]

Other examples may be (a) allowing patients to succumb to a hospital-acquired infection;[9] (b) giving nurses telephonic instructions about patients without seeing the patient or following up properly on their condition;[10] or (c) communicating electronically with patients who have been diagnosed with a life-threatening illness – without checking they have actually received the information.[11] A failure to cure, however, may not necessarily give rise to a claim based on negligence.[12]

---

3   *Michael v Linksfield Park Clinic (Pty) Ltd* 2001 (3) SA 1188 (SCA).

4   *Van Wyk v Lewis* 1924 AD 438–457.

5   cf *Collins v Administrator, Cape* 1995 (4) SA 73 (C) 82.

6   cf *S v Mkwetshana* 1965 (2) SA 493 (N) 497.

7   *Dube v Administrator, Transvaal* 1963 (4) SA 260 (T).

8   Carstens and Pearmain 646–647; see also DJ McQuoid-Mason 'The medical profession and medical practice' in WA Joubert and JA Faris (eds) *The Law of South Africa* 17(2) 2 ed (2008) para 45.

9   DJ McQuoid-Mason 'Hospital-acquired infections – when are hospitals legally liable?' (2012) 102(6) *SAMJ* 353–354.

10 DJ McQuoid-Mason 'When may doctors give nurses telephonic instructions? (2016) 106(8) *SAMJ* 787–788.

11 DJ McQuoid-Mason 'Sending patients electronic reminders of the need for urgent treatment to prevent life-threatening illnesses – some lessons to be learned and a cautionary reminder that self-representation can be dangerous (2019) 109(11) *SAMJ* 845–847.

12 cf *Coppen v Impey* 1916 CPD 309 321; *Richter v Estate Hamman* 1976 (3) SA 226 (C).

8.2.2 Standard of care

The test for the standard of care required of healthcare practitioners is whether a reasonably competent practitioner in that branch of the profession would have foreseen the likelihood of harm and would have taken steps to guard against its occurrence.[13]

Healthcare practitioners have been successfully sued by patients:[14] (a) where a plaster cast was applied too lightly around a fractured arm and the practitioner failed to detect the resultant ischaemia, with sepsis and necrosis causing the arm to be amputated;[15] (b) where a plaster cast was applied too tightly causing a fractured arm to be reduced to a 'shrunken, clawlike appendage of extremely limited functional value';[16] (c) where careless administration of excessive radiotherapy resulted in the loss of limbs;[17] (d) where excessive radiation resulted in burns;[18] and (e) where a patient suffered brain damage from cerebral hypoxia arising from a negligently attached tracheotomy tube.[19]

Healthcare practitioners have not been held liable:[20] (a) where a doctor failed to pay a follow-up visit to a patient who had been treated for a broken leg and it could not be proven that, if he had visited the patient, he could have done anything to the leg;[21] (b) where a platinum needle used in a syringe to explore a patient's chest cavity broke and remained in his body and the patient failed to prove negligence by the practitioner;[22] (c) where a swab was left in a patient after an appendectomy and gall bladder operation, and the court found that it was the duty of the theatre sister, not the surgeon, to count the swabs;[23] and (d) where a casualty officer failed to detect on an X-ray plate a patient's fracture and the court found that the doctor was not experienced in the matter but had acted reasonably in the circumstances.[24]

Negligence is determined by the criteria of reasonableness and foreseeability. Therefore, there may be no liability when unforeseeable complications arise during treatment (e.g. due to idiosyncrasy or hypersensitivity).[25] However, this does not apply if such idiosyncrasy or hypersensitivity were foreseeable and could

---

13   *Buls v Tsatsarolakis* 1976 (2) SA 891 (T).
14   See generally, MA Dada & DJ McQuoid-Mason *Introduction to Medico-Legal Practice* (2001) 23.
15   *Dube v Administrator, Transvaal* 1963 (4) SA 260 (W).
16   *Blythe v Van den Heever* 1980 (1) SA 191 (A).
17   *Esterhuizen v Administrator, Transvaal* 1957 (3) SA 710 (T).
18   *Dale v Hamilton* 1924 WLD 184.
19   *Collins v Administrator, Cape* 1995 (4) SA 73 (C).
20   See generally, MA Dada & DJ McQuoid-Mason *Introduction to Medico-Legal Practice* (2001) 23–24.
21   *Webb v Isaac* 1915 EDL 273.
22   *Mitchell v Dixon* 1914 AD 519.
23   *Van Wyk v Lewis* 1924 AD 438–444.
24   *Buls v Tsatsarolakis* 1976 (2) SA 891 (T).
25   cf *Coppen v Impey* 1916 CPD 309 321; *Richter v Estate Hamman* 1976 (3) SA 226 (C).

have been tested for beforehand.[26] The greater the likelihood of harm arising from the procedure (e.g. where a practitioner works with dangerous substances) the greater will be the degree of care required.[27] The same applies where the practitioner has special knowledge of circumstances that increased the risk.[28] A different level of skill and care may be justifiable in cases of 'sudden emergency' – depending on the circumstances.

8.2.3   Evidence of negligence

The degree of skill and care that can be expected of a reasonably competent healthcare practitioner who is facing legal action is largely a question of evidence.[29] The court, however, will not rely on the medical evidence alone in deciding which risks are the result of a particular treatment. Where expert opinion is not supported by logic, it will be ignored by the court,[30] and the same applies if the body of professional opinion overlooks an obvious risk which could have been guarded against.[31] The court will decide for itself whether the healthcare practitioner's conduct conforms to the standard of reasonable care demanded by the law – and will not delegate its task to any body of professional opinion.[32] If a defendant knowingly raises false defences that waste the court's time, the court may make a special order of costs against the defendant.[33]

The courts in some countries allow patients to use the maxim 'the facts speak for themselves' (*res ipsa loquitur*) to assist them in proving their cases in situations where an inference could be drawn that the healthcare practitioner concerned had acted negligently. This does not apply in South Africa and the *res ipsa loquitur* maxim is not used in our courts for medical negligence cases.[34] This approach has, however, been criticised.[35]

---

26   Ibid.
27   cf *R v Van Schoor* 1948 (4) SA 349 (C).
28   DJ McQuoid-Mason 'The medical profession and medical practice' in WA Joubert and JA Faris (eds) *The Law of South Africa* 17(2) 2 ed (2008) para 219.
29   *Blythe v van den Heever* 1980 (1) SA 191 (A); *Castell v De Greef* 1994 (4) SA 408 (C) 426.
30   *Michael v Linksfield Park Clinic (Pty) Ltd* 2001 (3) SA 1188 (SCA) para 36.
31   Ibid. para 38.
32   *Castell v De Greef* 1994 (4) SA 408 (C) 426.
33   *Michael v Linksfield Park Clinic (Pty) Ltd* 2001 (3) SA 1188 (SCA) para 36.
34   *Van Wyk v Lewis* 1924 AD 438–444.
35   Carstens and Pearmain 857–860; see generally, P Carstens and P Van den Heever *Res Ipsa Loquitur and Medical Negligence: A Comparative Survey* (2011).

8.3   Vicarious liability

8.3.1   Meaning of vicarious liability

Vicarious liability refers to a situation where one person is liable for another person's unlawful conduct even if the first person is not at fault. Vicarious liability is mainly covered by the common law, especially in respect of the employer–employee relationship. In order for employers to be vicariously liable for the wrongful conduct of their employees, plaintiffs must show that:

(a) there was an employer–employee relationship (i.e. the employers can tell their employees what to do and how to do it);

(b) the employees had committed an unlawful act or omission; and

(c) the employees were involved in the performance of their work (i.e. were acting in the course and scope of their employment).[36]

While employers may be sued because they have more money than their employees, the latter may also be sued. However, double damages may not be claimed. If employers pay the full amount, employees may not be sued for the same amount – although employers may recover from employees the amount paid to the plaintiff.[37]

Where a medical practitioner and a hospital are jointly responsible for a loss suffered by a patient, the court will apportion the damages between them in terms of the Apportionment of Damages Act.[38]

8.3.2   Vicarious liability and healthcare institutions

Healthcare institutions such as hospitals and nursing homes are vicariously liable for the unlawful acts of their employees where the latter commit wrongful acts or omissions during the course and scope of their employment.[39] Hospitals and nursing homes will be liable even though they have warned their employees against using certain procedures, or the employees' acts or omissions amount to intentional wrongdoing[40] – provided such acts or omissions fall within the course and scope of the employees' employment.

Although hospitals and nursing homes are liable for the acts and omissions of healthcare practitioners employed by them, the courts have held that where there

---

36   *Minister of Police v Rabie* 1986 (1) SA 117 (A).

37   DJ McQuoid-Mason and MA Dada *A–Z of Nursing Law* (2009).

38   58 of 1971; *Wright v Medi-Clinic Ltd* 2007 (4) SA 327 (C).

39   cf *Esterhuizen v Administrator, Transvaal* 1957 (3) SA 710 (T); *Dube v Administrator, Transvaal* 1963 (4) SA 260 (W).

40   *Zungu v Administrator, Natal* 1971 (1) SA 284 (D).

is a shortage of resources, a standard of excellence cannot be expected which is beyond the financial resources of the hospital authority.[41]

8.3.3 Vicarious liability of healthcare practitioners

The vicarious liability of healthcare practitioners for the acts and omissions of their employees will depend on whether they have the right of control over their employees (i.e. they can tell them what to do and how to do it).[42] Healthcare practitioners are clearly liable for the wrongful acts and omissions of assistants directly employed by them. However, where hospitals or nursing homes provide healthcare practitioners with assistants, this will depend upon whether they are under the practitioner's control (i.e. the practitioner can tell them what to do and how to do it).[43] Thus the courts have held that a doctor is not vicariously liable for the wrongful acts of a qualified theatre sister because she has 'independent duties to discharge',[44] and a surgeon is not liable for the wrongful omissions of an anaesthetist working with him in theatre.[45]

It is submitted that generally nurses can be regarded as under the control of the healthcare practitioners concerned. It could be argued, however, that whenever the assistant performs an independent task at her own discretion, she is not acting as the servant of the practitioner.[46] However, even if the assistant is exercising an independent task, if the practitioner was in a position to intervene in order to prevent harm and failed to do so, he or she may also be liable for negligence.[47] Even though a principal (e.g. a hospital) is vicariously liable for the wrong of a healthcare practitioner, the latter will also be liable for any harm caused (i.e. both are responsible).

8.4 Exclusion or exemption clauses

Exclusion or exemption clauses are conditions in contracts in terms of which people who supply goods or services restrict their liability should the goods or services prove to be defective. The courts will only exclude liability for harm resulting from a defective product or service where the particular condition that was excluded has occurred. Where the wording in a clause is ambiguous, or

---

41   *Collins v Administrator, Cape* 1995 (4) SA 73 (C) 82.
42   *Jones v Manchester Corp* [1952] 2 All ER 126.
43   MA Dada and DJ McQuoid-Mason *Introduction to Medico-Legal Practice* (2001) 25.
44   *Van Wyk v Lewis* 1924 AD 438–444.
45   *S v Kramer* 1987 (1) SA 887 (W).
46   MA Dada and DJ McQuoid-Mason *Introduction to Medico-Legal Practice* (2001) 25.
47   DJ McQuoid-Mason 'The medical profession and medical practice' in WA Joubert and JA Faris (eds) *The Law of South Africa* 17(2) 2 ed (2008) para 51.

the condition is not clearly excluded, the courts will read the exemption clause against the person who is relying on it to exclude liability and in favour of the person who has been harmed.

As previously mentioned, in the past the courts have held that once people sign contracts that exclude liability for harm should they or their property be injured or damaged, they are bound by such clauses – even if the terms are unfair. Thus where hospitals have contracted out of harm to patients caused by negligence on the part of their employees, the courts have held that such a condition is not contrary to public policy or against the Constitution.[48] However, this has now changed because the Consumer Protection Act[49] provides that people will not be able to sign away their rights in contracts or consent to terms in contracts that are unfair or unconscionable.[50]

8.5 Defences to actions for professional negligence

Practitioners may raise the following defences to a claim for professional negligence: (a) consent; (b) contributory negligence (a partial defence);[51] (c) necessity;[52] (d) statutory authority;[53] and (e) order of court.[54]

8.6 Impact of medical negligence claims

The past few decades have witnessed a spiraling of medical negligence claims, both in terms of frequency and quantum. While medical malpractice systems in the country are exorbitantly costly, they are also inefficient.[55] This impacts directly on access to healthcare, a basic human right in the country, as enshrined in the Bill of Rights of the Constitution of South Africa.[56] Practising defensive medicine, irrespective of the sector in which healthcare is delivered, has now become the norm with the focus being not just patient health and best interests,

---

48   *Afrox Healthcare Bpk v Strydom* 2002 (6) SA 21 (SCA).
49   68 of 2008.
50   Section 49.
51   *Wright v Medi-Clinic Ltd* 2007 4 SA 327 (C).
52   *Stofberg v Elliott* 1923 CPD 148 150.
53   Criminal Procedure Act 51 of 1977 ss 37(2) and 225(2); cf *S v Human* 1996 (1) SA 232 (W); *Minister of Safety and Security v Gaqa* 2002 (1) SACR 654 (C); *S v Orrie* 2004 (3) SA 584 (C); contra *Minister of Safety and Security v Xaba* 2003 2 SA 703 (D).
54   See Carstens and Pearmain (2007) 871–941.
55   See generally, South African Law Reform Commission *Medico-Legal Claims* Issue Paper 33 Project 141 (2017): https://www.justice.gov.za/salrc/ipapers/ip33_prj141_Medico-legal.pdf (accessed 3 April 2020).
56   Constitution 1996 s 27.

but also that of safeguarding against possible medical malpractice liability, thereby increasing unnecessary clinical and diagnostic procedures.[57]

The unequivocal situation is that currently the fear of lawsuits holds hostage practitioners' options and preferences for delivery of ethically exercised care to their patients, leading to frustration and dissatisfaction to both practitioners and patients.[58] In 2009–2010, the Gauteng Provincial Health Department was facing medical negligence claims of R573 million.[59] In 2016, the total quantum of claims was in the region of R3.5 billion,[60] and by July 2019 it had spiraled to R29 billion.[61] The 2017 contingent liabilities claim for medical negligence for the South African National Department of Health was an amount in excess of R55 billion.[62]

8.6.1 Reasons for litigation

There are several reasons why patients institute court claims against healthcare professionals. These include the following:[63]

(a) The desire for monetary compensation

(b) Touting and advertising by lawyers, despite touting in the legal fraternity being illegal. Advertising, however, is legal.

(c) Claims being instituted on a contingency fee basis. This means that there is no risk for the claimant because the attorney is not paid should the claim fail, but the attorney will receive 25% of any amount if the claim is successfully recovered.

(d) Poor communication between the healthcare practitioner and the patient, including not obtaining valid informed consent

(e) Adverse outcomes because of deterioration of services as a result of overburdened and understaffed medical personnel and faulty equipment

---

57 A Dhai 'Medical negligence: Alternative claims resolution an answer to the epidemic?' (2016) 9(1) *SAJBL* 2–3.

58 WHO *Rapid Scoping Review of Medical Malpractice Policies in Obstetrics* (2015): http://www.who-report_malpracticemodels_-12aug2015_final.pdf (accessed on 1 April 2020).

59 J Malherbe 'Counting the cost: The consequences of increased medical malpractice litigation in South Africa' (2013) 103(1) *SAMJ* 83–84.

60 N Claassen 'Mediation as an alternative solution to medical malpractice court claims' (2016) 9(1) *SAJBL* 7–10.

61 Times Live: https://www.timeslive.co.za/news/south-africa/2019-07-11-da-slams-r29bn-medical-negligence-claims-against-gauteng-health/ (accessed on 15 August 2019).

62 South African Law Reform Commission *Medico-Legal Claims* Project 141 (2017): http://salawreform.justice.gov.za/ipapers/ip33_prj141_Medico-legal.pdf (accessed on 3 April 2020).

63 N Claasen 'Mediation as an alternative solution to medical malpractice court claims' (2016).

(f) Criminal conduct, where healthcare staff unlawfully sell the hospital records to attorneys

(g) A greater awareness of the protection of rights of patients in the Constitution:[64] (i) section 10 (right to human dignity); (ii) section 11 (right to life); (iii) section 12(2) (right to bodily and psychological integrity); (iv) section 27 (right to healthcare services, ability to support dependants, right not to be refused emergency medical treatment); (v) section 28 (children's rights to basic healthcare services, protection from maltreatment, neglect, abuse or degradation, entitlement to legal representation in civil proceedings); and (vi) section 34 (the right to go to court or other tribunal or forum).

(h) The Consumer Protection Act[65] has limited the protective effect of exclusion clauses that seek to limit the liability of persons or organisations that cause harm to consumers: (i) section 22 (right to information in plain language); (ii) section 48 (right to fair, reasonable and just contract terms); (iii) section 49 (right to proper notice of certain terms and conditions); (iv) section 51 (prohibited terms and conditions); (v) section 54 (right to quality service); (vi) section 58 (warning concerning nature of risks); and (vii) section 61 (faultless liability for damage caused by goods and services).

8.6.2 Disadvantages of litigation

There are several disadvantages to litigation. These include the following:[66]

(a) The costs have become prohibitive. While contingency fee-based cases mean that the litigants will not pay their attorney's fees should they lose the case, they will, however, be required to pay the costs of the winning party.

(b) It is extremely time consuming, with some cases taking several years before coming to trial. Interim procedures, postponements and/or further appeal processes could further extend the final conclusion of the matter.

(c) Opposing parties are prevented by their lawyers from communicating with one another, thereby precluding any early amicable settlement.

(d) Professional careers could be destroyed by adverse publicity and cross-examination even where there is no merit in the case.

(e) The patient's dignity could be undermined by adverse publicity and cross-examination even in successful claims.

---

64   Constitution, 1996.
65   68 of 2008.
66   N Claasen 'Mediation as an alternative solution to medical malpractice court claims' (2016).

(f) All adverse outcomes or errors do not necessarily constitute negligence justifying the institution of a claim.[67]

(g) The entire experience could be very traumatic, in particular to the healthcare professional.

(h) The judges and magistrates who preside over the cases usually do not have an understanding of complex medical procedures and complications, and this could lead to their arriving at unjust decisions.

(i) Litigation does not usually result in the opposing parties reconciling.

(j) Court decisions could be based on legal technicalities (e.g. exceptions, prescription and lack of compliance with notice periods). These decisions are usually not based on the parties' needs. Both parties could end up being dissatisfied.

8.7   Alternative dispute resolution

The problems with litigation as described above, coupled with the adversarial nature of the process, has resulted in parties being encouraged to use alternative dispute resolution processes (ADR). These include negotiation, mediation and arbitration. Negotiation is the primary form of consensus seeking and is the simplest and most effective way of resolving disputes. It is flexible, informal, party-directed, closest to the parties' own circumstances and control, and geared to each party's concerns. Mediation (which is essentially negotiation between the parties with the assistance of a third party), while not a soft option, offers a crucial opportunity for the early and effective resolution of disputes. Arbitration is often slow and costly. Proponents of arbitration argue that it is quicker and less expensive than litigation. This is, however, not the case in practice.[68]

8.7.1   Mediation as an alternative to medical litigation.

Mediation is recognised by the civil justice system, with court-annexed mediation being inaugurated in certain magistrates courts in Gauteng and North West province in 2014 when magistrates court rules on mediation were promulgated.[69] Mediation in the rules is defined as the:

> process by which a mediator assists the parties in actual or potential litigation to resolve the dispute between them by facilitating discussions between the parties, assisting them

---

67   In *Buthelezi v Ndaba* 2013 SA 437 (SCA), the Supreme Court of Appeal in Bloemfontein determined that the mere admission that 'something went wrong' does not amount to negligence.

68   J Brand, F Steadman and C Todd (eds) 'Mediation among the range of processes for resolving disputes' *Commercial Mediation: A User's Guide* 2 ed (2016) 12–23.

69   GN 855 of 31 October 2014.

in identifying issues, clarifying priorities, exploring areas of compromise and generating options in an attempt to resolve the dispute.[70]

On 7 February 2020, the Rules Board for Courts of Law Act[71] were amended and Rule 41A was inserted.[72] Mediation, in terms of Rule 41A, is:

> a voluntary process entered into by agreement between the parties to a dispute, in which an impartial and independent person, the mediator, assists the parties to either resolve the dispute between them, or identify issues upon which agreement can be reached, or explore areas of compromise, or generate options to resolve the dispute, or clarify priorities, by facilitating discussions between the parties and assisting them in their negotiations to resolve the dispute.

As can be seen from the above, the courts are placing more reliance on mediation as a means to resolve disputes. In terms of 41A3(*b*), a judge, or a case management judge or the court may at any stage before judgment direct the parties to consider referral of a dispute to mediation.

The main purpose of mediation is to promote restorative justice,[73] preserve relationships between litigants or potential litigants which may become strained or destroyed by the adversarial nature of litigation,[74] facilitate an expeditious and cost-effective resolution of a dispute,[75] ... [and] provide litigants ... with solutions ... which are beyond the scope and powers of judicial officers.[76]

Several countries require mediation as a necessary step prior to instituting litigation in their judicial systems. Success rates are estimated to be between 80 and 90%.[77] This is because mediation is less costly and less time consuming. Mediation is a flexible, voluntary and confidential process facilitated by a neutral third party. It is consensus based and parties remain in ultimate control of the decision. Joint and private meetings are utilised. Discussions are confidential, without prejudice, off the record and cannot be used as evidence in court proceedings should a settlement not be arrived at. It is less formal than arbitration and court litigation. The mediator does not sit in judgment but is involved with assisting the parties through negotiation to come to their own solutions. There are no witnesses or public observers.[78]

---

70   Rule 73.
71   107 of 1985.
72   *Government Gazette*, 7 February 2020, No 43000: http://www.gpwonline.co.za (accessed on 20 April 2020).
73   Rule 71(*b*).
74   Rule 71(*c*).
75   Rule 71(*d*).
76   Rule 71(*f*).
77   N Claasen 'Mediation as an alternative solution to medical malpractice court claims' (2016).
78   J Brand, F Steadman and C Todd (eds) 'Mediation among the range of processes for resolving disputes' (2016).

There are certain key considerations to take into account when making a decision to mediate:[79]

(a) Would settlement be appropriate under the circumstances?

(b) Are relationships important?

(c) Do the parties want to retain control of the outcome?

(d) Do both sides believe they have a good case?

(e) Is there great disparity in power between the parties?

(f) Is speed important?

(g) Are bad communication and misunderstanding largely to blame for the dispute?

(h) Are highly complex technical issues involved?

(i) Would an adverse precedent be a nuisance for both sides?

(j) Is confidentiality important?

(k) Would the case probably settle out of court?

(l) Do both sides need, above all else, the opportunity to let off steam?

(m) Do the parties really want to litigate?

Some questions on medical malpractice

Read the following scenarios and decide whether the healthcare practitioner's conduct amounted to medical malpractice or professional negligence, and where appropriate, whether his or her employer can be held vicariously liable:

1. A surgeon operates on a patient without obtaining an informed consent.

2. A nurse at a rape crisis clinic shouts out to a patient that they 'do not do abortions on schoolgirls'.

3. Nurses and doctors in a labour ward pinch the thighs of patients during delivery.

4. A doctor prescribes the wrong drug for a patient and the patient becomes severely ill.

5. A psychiatrist does not warn the wife of a patient that her husband has threatened to kill her.

---

79   Ibid.

CHAPTER 9

Reproductive health

David McQuoid-Mason and Ames Dhai

By the end of this chapter readers will be able to:

1. Explain the ethical aspects of reproductive healthcare.
2. Explain the meaning of artificial fertilisation.
3. List the objections to artificial fertilisation.
4. Explain the meaning of surrogate motherhood.
5. Explain the ethical issues involving termination of pregnancy.
6. Explain when terminations of pregnancy may be legally procured.
7. Explain the consent procedures regarding terminations of pregnancy.
8. Appreciate when health practitioners may and may not exercise their freedom of conscience, religion or belief in respect of terminations of pregnancy.
9. Explain the law regarding sterilisation with and without consent.
10. Explain the law regarding contraception.

9.1 Ethical aspects of reproductive healthcare

Many dilemmas, some amounting to crises, often arise in the context of reproductive health. Problems arising in reproductive health do not occur in a vacuum. They are often influenced by values, culture, traditions, social practices and laws which, in the main, have not been unbiased towards issues of human reproduction. In addition, rapid advances in science and technology, especially from the second half of the 20th century, have led to the provision of certain aspects of reproductive healthcare which, in previous years, was not possible. Several ethical, legal and human rights challenges have emerged as a result.

Reproductive health extends beyond just being that of a health issue. It is also a development and human rights issue. While reproductive health is an important component of health both for men and women, it can be viewed as more critical an issue for women who have complex and vulnerable reproductive systems. In addition, a major burden of disease in women is related to their reproductive potential and function, and societal treatment of women. Women are subject to social dysfunctions that impact on their physical, mental and social health. Often women's human rights are infringed, compromising their reproductive health. Women should not be viewed as a means in the process of reproduction and as targets in the process of fertility control.[1]

9.1.1   Meaning of reproductive health

The meaning of reproductive health developed by the United Nations, based on the International Conference on Population and Development in Cairo in 1994 and the International Conference on Women in Beijing in 1995, is as follows:[2]

> Reproductive health is a state of complete physical, mental and social well-being and not merely the absence of disease and infirmity in all matters relating to the reproductive system and its functions and processes. Reproductive health therefore implies that people are able to have a satisfying and safe sex life and that they have the capability to reproduce and the freedom to decide if, when and how often to do so. Implicit in this last condition are the right of men and women to be informed and to have access to safe, effective, affordable and acceptable methods of family planning of their choice, as well as other methods of their choice for regulation of fertility which are not against the law, and the right of access to appropriate health-care services that will enable women to go safely through pregnancy and child birth and provide couples with the best chance of having a healthy infant.

The above definition offers a comprehensive and integrated approach to health needs related to reproduction. By putting women at the centre of the process, it recognises, respects and responds to the needs of women and not only those of mothers. In addition, it is broad enough to include sexual health which includes the ability to enjoy mutually fulfilling sexual relationships, freedom from sexual abuse, coercion or harassment, safety from sexually transmitted diseases and success in achieving or preventing pregnancy.[3] It is clear that sex and sexuality are important psychosocial components of the well-being of both women and men.

9.2   Artificial fertilisation

Louise Browne was the first baby born from the process of in vitro fertilisation (IVF) in 1978.[4] Since then, there has been rapid progress and advancement in artificial fertilisation technologies, also known as assisted reproduction.[5] Techniques other than sexual intercourse between a woman and a man are used

---

1   RJ Cook, BM Dickens and MF Fathalla (eds) *Reproductive Health and Human Rights* (2003) 8–33.
2   United Nations Department of Public Information *Platform for Action and Beijing Declaration: Fourth World Conference on Women, Beijing, China, 4–15 September 1995* (1995) para 94.
3   RJ Cook, BM Dickens and MF Fathalla (eds) *Reproductive Health and Human Rights* (2003) 8–33.
4   S Soini 'The interface between assisted reproductive technologies and genetics: technical, social, ethical and legal issues' (2006) 14 *European Journal of Human Genetics* 588–645.
5   Ibid.

for creating babies. Despite criticism and objections to these technologies and processes, the demand for artificial fertilisation continues.[6]

Some objections to artificial fertilisation are as follows:[7]

(a) It separates sex and reproduction, and alters traditional relationships.

(b) It reinforces and promotes sexism.

(c) Artificial insemination of donor sperm could lead to men being detached from children to whom they are not genetically related.

(d) Whether children born as a result of gamete donation should have information on their genetic donor parent is the subject of much speculation and debate, which is far from reaching resolution.

(e) Ovum donations are risky and involve hormonal stimulation, multiple egg production, frequent blood tests and sonograms, and uncomfortable retrieval processes.

(f) Risks associated with IVF include ectopic pregnancy, early pregnancy loss and multiple births, including higher order multiple gestations with complications of prematurity that could be prevented by foeticide.

(g) In most cases, more embryos are created than necessary. Extra embryos are usually discarded leading to debates on the moral status of the embryo.

(h) The costs of the procedures and the low success take-home baby rates have also raised concerns.

(i) Practitioners ought to advise their patients to adopt the many children needing parents rather that utilise scarce resources to create more children.

(j) It is immoral to spend scarce resources on these procedures when most people lack basic care.

(k) Cryopreservation is still very much in its infancy. Long-term risks to children are as yet not fully known.

(l) Storing embryos has a potential for mix-ups. Couples may disagree with regard to the future of the stored embryo and problems may arise when embryos are 'orphaned'.

---

6   LM Purdy 'Assisted reproduction, prenatal testing, and sex selection' in H Kuhse and P Singer (eds) *A Companion to Bioethics* (2009) 178–192.

7   S Soini 'The interface between assisted reproductive technologies and genetics: Technical, social, ethical and legal issues' (2006) 14 *European Journal of Human Genetics* 588–645.

Despite all these objections, artificial fertilisation is not prohibited and continues being used as management in women who request the procedures and can afford to pay for them. What is given moral and legal weighting is that people have reproductive rights and women are competent to make informed choices after being given all the necessary information, including the risks associated with the procedures.

9.2.1   Definition of artificial fertilisation

The Children's Act[8] defines artificial fertilisation as the introduction, by other than natural means, of a male gamete into the internal reproductive organs of a female person for the purpose of human reproduction, including:

(a)   the bringing together of a male and female gamete outside the human body with a view to placing the product of a union of such gametes in the womb of a female person; or

(b)   the placing of the product of a union of male and female gametes, which have been brought together outside the human body, in the womb of a female person.[9]

9.2.2   Status of children artificially conceived

The Children's Act provides that whenever the gamete or gametes of any person other than a married person or his or her spouse have been used with the consent of both such spouses for the artificial fertilisation of one spouse, any child born of that spouse as a result of such artificial fertilisation must for all purposes be regarded to be the child of those spouses as if the gamete or gametes of those spouses had been used for such artificial fertilisation.[10] In such cases it is presumed, until the contrary is proved, that both spouses have granted the relevant consent.[11] Despite this presumption, before undertaking an artificial fertilisation procedure, it would be advisable for a practitioner to ensure that there is a proper informed consent from the woman, and her husband if the latter is going to be held responsible for the expenses of the procedure and the maintenance of the child.[12]

---

8   38 of 2005.
9   Section 1.
10   Section 40(1)(*a*).
11   Section 40(1)(*b*).
12   DJ McQuoid-Mason 'The medical profession and medical practice' in WA Joubert and JA Faris (eds) *The Law of South Africa* 17(2) 2 ed (2008) para 63.

The Children's Act states that subject to any surrogacy agreement entered into in terms of the Act,[13] whenever the gamete or gametes of any person have been used for the artificial fertilisation of a woman, any child born of that woman as a result of such artificial fertilisation must for all purposes be regarded to be the child of that woman.[14] Furthermore, subject to any such surrogacy agreement, no right, responsibility, duty or obligation arises between a child born of a woman as a result of artificial fertilisation and any person whose gamete has or gametes have been used for such artificial fertilisation or the blood relations of that person, except when:

(a) that person is the woman who gave birth to that child; or

(b) that person was the husband of such woman at the time of such artificial fertilisation.[15]

In a case where a same sex couple adopted a child as a result of artificial insemination of the gametes of one of the partners and an anonymous father as donor, the Department of Home Affairs was ordered to construct an appropriate form to reflect who the parents are rather than stating that they cannot register the birth because there was no father.[16]

9.2.3 Access to information regarding their genetic parents by children born of artificial fertilisation or surrogacy

The Children's Act provides that children born of artificial fertilisation or surrogacy may have access to biographical and medical information concerning their genetic parents. A child born as a result of artificial fertilisation or surrogacy or the guardian of such a child is entitled to have access to: (a) any medical information concerning that child's genetic parents; and (b) any other information concerning the child's genetic parents but not before the child reaches the age of 18 years.[17] However, the information disclosed may not reveal the identity of the person whose gamete was or gametes were used for such artificial fertilisation or the identity of a surrogate mother.[18] The director-general of health or any other person specified by regulation may require a person to receive counselling before any information is disclosed about the genetic parents concerned.[19]

---

13   In terms of s 296.
14   Section 40(2).
15   Section 40(3).
16   *J and Another v Director-General, Department of Home Affairs* 2003 (5) SA 605 (D).
17   Section 41(1).
18   Section 41(2).
19   Section 41(3).

9.2.4   *Legal liability for wrongful acts or omissions*

If a doctor is negligent in the selection of semen (e.g. by obtaining semen from a donor suffering from venereal disease or too closely related to the recipient) so that a defective child is born, the doctor may face an action for 'wrongful life'.[20] In terms of the National Health Act,[21] unless authorised by the minister,[22] the following tissue, blood, blood products or gametes may not be removed or withdrawn from a living person for any prescribed medical or dental purposes:

(a)   Tissue, blood, a blood product or a gamete from a person who is mentally ill within the meaning of the Mental Health Care Act[23]

(b)   Tissue which is not replaceable by natural processes from a person younger than 18 years

(c)   A gamete from a person younger than 18 years

(d)   Placenta, embryonic or foetal tissue, stem cells and umbilical cord, excluding progenitor cord umbilical cells.[24]

As in all medical procedures, the physician must ensure that a proper informed consent has been obtained before engaging in artificial insemination. Failure to obtain such a consent may result in the practitioner being charged with sexual assault under the Criminal Law (Sexual Offences and Related Matters) Amendment Act.[25] It will also be a violation of the person's constitutional and common law personality rights which could give rise to a claim for damages.

9.2.5   *Surrogate motherhood*

Surrogacy involves a contractual agreement allowing for one woman to gestate a baby to be raised by another. The ovum could be derived from the gestational mother, the commissioning mother or a donor. Surrogate motherhood gives rise to several ethical concerns, some of which are as follows:

(a)   The term 'surrogate mother' should be reconsidered because the pregnancy involves a contractual agreement and perhaps should be called 'contract' pregnancy.

---

20   cf *H v Fetal Assessment Centre* 2015 (2) BCLR 127 (CC). See also the Singapore case of *ABC v Thomson Medical Pte Ltd and Others* [2017] SGCA.
21   61 of 2003.
22   Section 56(2)(*b*).
23   17 of 2002.
24   National Health Act 61 of 2003 s 56(2)(*a*).
25   Act 32 of 2007 s 5.

(b) Problems arise when gestational mothers change their minds and refuse to give up the child.[26]

(c) Problems arise when the commissioning parents and the gestational mother refuse to take custody of the child as may occur with the birth of a deformed baby.[27]

(d) There is a danger that surrogate transactions may be reduced to commercial arrangements.

(e) Human life may be commodified and reduced to baby selling. At issue is the rental of gestational services and the sale of a right to parental relationship to a child.[28]

Some of these concerns have been addressed in the surrogacy provisions in the Children's Act.[29]

Chapter 19 of the Children's Act has detailed provisions regarding surrogate motherhood:

(a) Such agreements must be in writing and confirmed by the High Court[30]

(b) The need for consent by the husband or partner of the commissioning parent[31]

(c) The need for the gametes of at least one of the commissioning parents to be used[32]

(d) The conditions under which surrogate agreements will be confirmed by the court[33]

(e) The conditions under which artificial fertilisation of the surrogate mother may take place[34]

(f) The effect of surrogate motherhood agreements on the child[35]

(g) When surrogate motherhood agreements terminate[36]

---

26 See generally, DL Spar *The Baby Business: How Money, Science and Politics Drive the Commerce of Conception* (2006).
27 Ibid.
28 LM Purdy 'Assisted reproduction, prenatal testing, and sex selection' in H Kuhse and P Singer (eds) *A Companion to Bioethics* (2009) 178–192.
29 Act 38 of 2005.
30 Section 292.
31 Section 293.
32 Section 294.
33 Section 295.
34 Section 296.
35 Section 297.
36 Section 298.

(h) The effect of terminating surrogate motherhood agreements[37]

(i) The termination of pregnancies during surrogacy[38]

(j) The prohibition against payments for surrogate motherhood[39]

(k) The protection of the identity of parties to a surrogacy agreement[40]

(l) The prohibition against certain other acts (e.g. fertilising a surrogate mother otherwise than in terms of the Act or paying compensation to induce a person to enter into a surrogacy agreement).[41]

Any unfair clauses in a surrogacy agreement may fall foul of the Consumer Protection Act.[42]

9.3 Termination of pregnancy

9.3.1 Ethical issues involving termination of pregnancy

To terminate a pregnancy or have an abortion is not an easy decision to make. Both women and their practitioners grapple with such a decision. Central to the dilemma is that of the moral status of the embryo or foetus. This is a century-old debate with century-old arguments, most hinging around the question: 'When does life begin?' Proponents of life beginning at conception accord the embryo or foetus full moral status. On the other hand, the proponents of life beginning at birth accord the embryo or foetus no moral status whatsoever. In the spectrum between these two extremes are the proponents of limited moral status at various gestational ages. Others argue that abortions are wrong, not because the embryo or foetus has any moral status but because the embryo or foetus is a potential human being. If the lives of human beings are of value, then the lives of potential human beings should be of value too. Permitting abortions will devalue human life.[43]

Reproductive health implies that people are able to have a satisfying and safe sex life and that they have the capability to reproduce and the freedom to decide if, when and how often to do so. Implicit in this is the requirement that women's reproductive choices, including whether or not to terminate a pregnancy, are respected.

---

37   Section 299.
38   Section 300.
39   Section 301.
40   Section 302.
41   Section 303.
42   68 of 2008 s 49.
43   For a discussion of the different arguments, see generally RJ Cook, BM Dickens and MF Fathalla (eds) *Reproductive Health and Human Rights* (2003) 8–33.

9.3.2   Legal aspects of termination of pregnancy

The Choice on Termination of Pregnancy Act[44] defines a termination of pregnancy as 'the separation and expulsion, by medical or surgical means, of the contents of the uterus of a pregnant woman'. The Act also defines the 'gestation period' as 'the period of pregnancy of a woman calculated from the first day of the menstrual period which in relation to the pregnancy is the last' and states that it applies to females of any age.[45]

9.3.2.1   Conditions for termination of pregnancy

The Act provides that a pregnancy may be terminated:

(a) in terms of s 2(1)(*a*), upon the request of a woman during the first 12 weeks of the gestation period of her pregnancy;

(b) in terms of s 2(1)(*b*), from the 13th up to and including the 20th week of the gestation period if a medical practitioner, after consultation with the pregnant woman, is of the opinion that:

    (i)   the continued pregnancy would pose a risk of injury to the woman's physical or mental health; or

    (ii) there exists a substantial risk that the foetus would suffer from a severe physical or mental abnormality; or

    (iii) the pregnancy resulted from rape or incest; or

    (iv) the continued pregnancy would significantly affect the social or economic circumstances of the woman;

(c) in terms of s 2(1)(*c*), after the 20th week of the gestation period if a medical practitioner, after consultation with another medical practitioner or a registered midwife, is of the opinion that the continued pregnancy:

    (i)   would endanger the woman's life;

    (ii) would result in a severe malformation of the foetus; or

    (iii) would pose a risk of injury to the foetus.

The termination of a pregnancy may be carried out only by a medical practitioner, except for a pregnancy terminated during the first 12 weeks, which may also be carried out by a registered midwife who has completed the prescribed training course.[46] The surgical termination of pregnancy may take place only at a facility designated by the Minister of Health by notice in the *Government Gazette*.[47]

---

44   92 of 1996.
45   Section 1.
46   Section 2(2).
47   Section 3(1).

The minister may designate any facility for the purpose contemplated subject to such conditions and requirements as he or she may consider necessary. The minister may withdraw any designation after giving 14 days' prior notice of such withdrawal in the *Gazette*.[48]

The state shall promote the provision of non-mandatory and non-directive counselling, before and after the termination of a pregnancy.[49] A woman who requests the termination of pregnancy from a medical practitioner or a registered midwife, as the case may be, shall be informed of her rights under the Act by the person concerned.[50]

9.3.2.2 Consent to termination of pregnancy

Subject to certain exceptions, the termination of a pregnancy may only take place with the informed consent of the pregnant woman.[51] Notwithstanding any other law or the common law, but subject to the exceptions, no consent other than that of the pregnant woman shall be required for the termination of a pregnancy.[52]

In the case of a pregnant child, a medical practitioner or a registered midwife, as the case may be, shall advise such child to consult with her parents, guardian, family members or friends before the pregnancy is terminated, provided that the termination of the pregnancy shall not be denied because such child chooses not to consult them.[53]

Consent on behalf of severely mentally disabled or unconscious women

Where a woman is:

(a) severely mentally disabled to such an extent that she is completely incapable of understanding and appreciating the nature or consequences of a termination or her pregnancy; or

(b) in a state of continuous unconsciousness and there is no reasonable prospect that she will regain consciousness in time to request and to consent to the termination of her pregnancy

her pregnancy may be terminated during the first 12 weeks of the gestation period, or from the 13th up to and including the 20th week of the gestation period, on the grounds set out above for the same period in respect of mentally competent patients in terms of s 2(1)(*b*) of the Choice Act:

---

48 Section 3(2) and (3).
49 Section 4.
50 Section 6.
51 Section 5(1).
52 Section 5(2).
53 Section 5(3).

(a) upon the request of and with the consent of her natural guardian, spouse or legal guardian; or

(b) if such persons cannot be found, upon the request and with the consent of her *curator personae*.

However, such pregnancy may not be terminated unless two medical practitioners or a medical practitioner and a registered midwife who has completed the prescribed training course, consent thereto.[54]

Where two medical practitioners or a medical practitioner and a registered midwife who has completed the prescribed training course, are of the opinion that:

(a) during the period up to and including the 20th week of the gestation period, in respect of such a pregnant mentally incompetent or continuously unconscious woman as referred to above:

    (i) the continued pregnancy would pose a risk of injury to the woman's physically or mental health;

    (ii) there exists a substantial risk that the foetus would suffer from a severe physical or mental abnormality;

(b) after the 20th week of the gestation period, in respect of such a pregnant mentally incompetent or continuously unconscious woman as referred to above, the continued pregnancy:

    (i) would endanger the woman's life;

    (ii) would result in a severe malformation of the foetus; or

    (iii) would pose a risk of injury to the foetus,

they may consent to the termination of the pregnancy of such woman after consulting her natural guardian, spouse, legal guardian or *curator personae*, as the case may be.

However, the termination of the pregnancy shall not be denied if the natural guardian, spouse, legal guardian or *curator personae*, as the case may be, refuses to consent thereto.[55]

9.3.2.3 Keeping of records

Any medical practitioner or a registered midwife who has completed the prescribed training course, who terminates pregnancy during the first two trimesters of the pregnancy in terms of the Act,[56] shall record the prescribed information in the

---

54   Section 5(4).

55   Section 5(5).

56   Section 2(1)(*a*) or (*b*).

prescribed manner and give notice to the person in charge of the facility where the abortion is carried out.[57]

The person in charge of a facility shall within one month of the termination of pregnancy at such facility, collate the prescribed information and forward it by registered post confidentially to the Director-General of Health. However, the name and address of a woman who has requested or obtained a termination of pregnancy shall not be included in the prescribed information.[58] The director-general shall keep a record of the prescribed information he or she receives in terms of the Act.[59] The identity of a woman who has requested or obtained a termination of pregnancy shall remain confidential at all times unless she herself chooses to disclose that information.[60]

9.3.2.4 Offences and penalties

Any person who:

(a) is not a medical practitioner or a registered midwife who has completed the prescribed training course and who performs a termination of a pregnancy referred to in s 2(1)(*a*) of the Act;

(b) is not a medical practitioner and who performs the termination of a pregnancy referred to in s 2(1)(*b*) or (*c*) of the Act; or prevents the lawful termination of a pregnancy or obstructs access to a facility for the termination of a pregnancy,

shall be guilty of an offence and liable on conviction to a fine or to imprisonment for a period not exceeding 10 years.[61]

Any person who contravenes or fails to carry out the notification and keeping of records requirements of s 7 of the Act shall be guilty of an offence and liable on conviction to a fine or to imprisonment for a period not exceeding six months.[62]

The minister may delegate his or her powers to the director-general or any other officer in the service of the state except the power to make regulations.[63] The minister may make regulations relating to any matter he or she may consider necessary or expedient to prescribe for achieving the objects of the Act.[64]

---

57   Section 7(1) and (2).
58   Section 7(3).
59   Section 7(4).
60   Section 7(5).
61   Section 10(1).
62   Section 10(2).
63   Section 8.
64   Section 9.

9.3.2.5 Freedom of conscience

Unlike the previous Abortion and Sterilization Act,[65] the Choice on Termination of Pregnancy Act does not contain a conscience clause, but doctors and health professionals are protected by the freedom of conscience, religion and belief provisions of the 1996 Constitution.[66] However, in cases of emergency or where there are no other available facilities, it is submitted that doctors and health professionals employed by the state may have to assist with terminations of pregnancy against their conscience, religion or belief.[67]

9.4 Sterilisation

According to the Constitution, everyone has the right to make decisions concerning reproduction and therefore it is not necessary for a spouse or partner to obtain consent from the other party before undergoing a sterilisation operation.[68] However, where the other party is required to pay for the cost of such sterilisation, his or her consent to the cost of the procedure should be obtained unless it is an emergency situation.

The Sterilisation Act[69] defines sterilisation as 'a surgical procedure performed for the purpose of making the person on whom it is performed incapable of procreation, but does not include the removal of any gonad'.[70]

9.4.1 Sterilisation with consent

The Sterilisation Act provides that persons may not be prohibited from being sterilised if they are:

(a) capable of consenting; and
(b) aged 18 years or above.[71]

The Act stipulates that such persons may not be sterilised without their consent.[72]

---

65 2 of 1975.
66 Constitution s 15(1).
67 DJ McQuoid-Mason 'State doctors, freedom of conscience and termination of pregnancy' (1997) 1 no 6 *Human Rights and Constitutional Law Journal of SA* 15–17.
68 Constitution s 12(2).
69 44 of 1998.
70 Section 1.
71 Section 2(1). cf *Pandie v Isaacs* (A135/2013, 1221/2007) [2013] ZAWCHC 123, where a successful claim for sterilisation without consent after a caesarean section was overturned on appeal.
72 Section 2(2).

The Act also provides that persons under the age of 18 years may not be sterilised unless a failure to do so would threaten their life or seriously injure their physical health. In such cases consent must be given by:

(a) a person who is lawfully entitled to give consent; and

(b) an independent medical practitioner who, before a panel is convened,[73] has consulted with the person to be sterilised and has provided a written opinion to the effect that the sterilisation is in the best interests of that person.[74]

For purposes of the Act, 'consent' means consent given freely and voluntarily without any inducement and may only be given if the person giving it has:

(a) been given a clear explanation and adequate description of the:

    (i) proposed plan of the procedure; and

    (ii) consequences, risks and the reversible or irreversible nature of the sterilisation procedure;

(b) been given advice that the consent may be withdrawn any time before the treatment; and

(c) understood and signed the prescribed consent form.[75]

9.4.2 Sterilisation without consent

The Sterilisation Act[76] provides that sterilisation may be performed on any person who is incapable of consenting or incompetent to consent provided all the following conditions are satisfied:

(a) A request has been made to the person in charge of a hospital.

(b) The parent, spouse, guardian or curator of the incompetent person has consented.

(c) A panel convened by the person in charge of the hospital agrees that sterilisation may be performed after considering all relevant information, including the fact that:

    (i) the incompetent person is 18 years of age, unless the physical health of the person is threatened; and

    (ii) there is no other safe and effective method of contraception except sterilisation.

---

73   The panel established in terms of s 3(2) of the Act.

74   Section 2(3).

75   Section 4.

76   44 of 1998.

(d) The person is mentally disabled to such an extent that he or she is incapable of:

    (i) making his or her own decision about contraception or sterilisation;

    (ii) developing mentally to a sufficient degree to make an informed judgement about contraception or sterilisation; and

    (iii) fulfilling the parental responsibility associated with giving birth.[77]

For the purposes of the above section, a person may only be sterilised if he or she suffers from a 'severe mental disability',[78] which, in terms of the Act, means:

> a range of functioning extending from partial self-maintenance under close supervision, together with limited self-protection skills in a controlled environment through limited self-care and requiring constant aid and supervision, to severely restrained sensory and motor functioning and requiring nursing care.[79]

The person in charge of the hospital who is required to convene a panel to consider the request for sterilisation must convene a panel consisting of:

(a) a psychiatrist, or medical practitioner, if no psychiatrist is available;

(b) a psychologist or social worker; and

(c) a nurse.[80]

Where the person to be sterilised is in custodial care, no member of the panel may be an employee of the custodial institution.[81] If the sterilisation is to be performed in a private healthcare facility, the members of the panel may not be employees of, or have a financial interest in, that facility.[82] The person performing the sterilisation must ensure that the method of sterilisation used holds the least health risk to the person on whom sterilisation is performed.[83]

    Sterilisation may be performed only at facilities designated by the member of the executive council responsible for health in the province concerned, or by the head of a provincial department of health to whom the member of the executive council has delegated his or her powers.[84] Persons in charge of designated facilities or persons delegated by them must be notified of every sterilisation performed in the facility and must keep a record of every such sterilisation.[85]

---

77   Section 3(1).
78   Section 3(6).
79   Section 3(7).
80   Section 3(2).
81   Section 3(3).
82   Section 3(4).
83   Section 3(5).
84   Sections 5(1) and 7(1).
85   Section 6.

9.4.3   Freedom of conscience and sterilisation

Healthcare practitioners have a constitutional right to refuse to participate in sterilisation operations on religious grounds or grounds of conscience,[86] except in cases of medical emergency treatment.[87]

9.4.4   Failed sterilisation

Where a healthcare practitioner negligently carries out a sterilisation operation which results in an unwanted child being born, the practitioner may be held liable for the maintenance of the child. For example, in a case in where a sterilisation operation was not done due to negligence by the hospital staff and the wife fell pregnant and gave birth to a normal child the family could not afford, the hospital was liable for damages to cover maintenance of the child.[88]

9.5   Contraception

In terms of the Constitution, everyone has the right to bodily integrity, including the right to make decisions about reproduction, which clearly includes contraception.[89] As has been mentioned, special provisions apply to children in terms of the Children's Act. In terms of the Act, children of 12 years or older may not be refused condoms[90] and may be provided with other forms of contraception if they have been given proper advice and medically examined to ensure that the contraceptive will not harm them.[91] The provision of contraception is governed by the general ethical and legal rules regarding healthcare practice such as consent, confidentiality, etc.[92]

In terms of the Children's Act, a person who refuses to sell or distribute condoms to a child over 12 years of age commits a criminal offence.[93] However, in terms of the Act, a healthcare practitioner who prescribes contraceptives for children under the age of 12 years in contravention of the Act does not commit a punishable offence (this is not listed as an offence in the Act). Nonetheless it is submitted that in such circumstances, the health practitioner may be sued civilly by the child's parents for interfering with their parental authority.[94]

---

86   Constitution s 15(1).
87   Constitution s 17.
88   *Edouard v Administrator of Natal* 1989 (2) SA 368 (D).
89   Section 12(2)(*a*).
90   Section 134(1).
91   Section 134(2).
92   SA Strauss *Doctor, Patient and the Law* 3 ed (1993) 169.
93   Section 305(1)(*c*).
94   cf SA Strauss *Doctor, Patient and the Law* 3 ed (1993) 172; cf *Gillick v W Norfolk & Wisbeck Health Authority* (1985) 2 All ER 402 (HL).

It is also submitted that if a health practitioner provides contraception to a child below the age of 12 years, he or she cannot be held criminally liable for aiding and abetting a contravention of the Sexual Offences Act,[95] unless it can be shown that the practitioner had expressly or impliedly encouraged the commission of the offence.[96]

Some questions on reproductive health

Read the following scenarios and decide whether the reproductive rights of the patients were respected:

1. A rural mission hospital refuses on religious grounds to carry out terminations of pregnancies and turns away pregnant women seeking terminations without referring them to institutions that provide termination of pregnancy services.

2. A nurse refuses on religious grounds to assist in an elective sterilisation procedure.

3. A pharmacist refuses to sell condoms to a 13-year-old girl.

---

95   23 of 1957.
96   SA Strauss *Doctor, Patient and the Law* 3 ed (1993) 172.

CHAPTER 10

Human genomics and genetics

Ames Dhai and David McQuoid-Mason

By the end of this chapter readers will be able to:

1. Describe some of the relevant terms used in the fields of genomics and genetics.
2. Discuss the ethical issues that arise in the context of genomics and genetics.
3. List the pertinent legislation applicable to genomics and genetics.
4. Discuss the ethico-regulatory complexities in these fields.
5. Explain the problems associated with gene editing.

10.1 Introduction

Heritable traits are determined at conception and are transmitted through DNA from parent to child. 'Genomics' refers to all the inherited information contained in the DNA of an individual. 'Genetics' is the field where this information is applied so as to understand how characteristics of living organisms are transmitted from one generation to the next through DNA. In other words, genetics is the study of heredity.

In human genetics, heritable factors in individuals, families and populations are studied. Epigenetics is the study of how environmental factors influence gene expression and is usually included under the term 'genetics'. Precision medicine refers to the use of genetic and genomic tests in the clinical setting towards making the correct diagnosis and identifying the therapy with the best chance of improving the health of the patient with the fewest side effects. Therefore, precision medicine is more than looking at heritable components.[1]

---

1   Academy of Science of South Africa *Human Genetics and Genomics in South Africa: Ethical, Legal and Social Implications: A Consensus Study* (2018) para 2.3: http://research.assaf.org.za/bitstream/handle/20.500.11911/106/2018_assaf_ethical_genetics_genomics_consensus.pdf?sequence=1&isAllowed=y (accessed on 25 March 2020).

DNA information is particularly helpful in the clinical setting in the management of heath. It is also useful in individual identification as applied in forensics and for the establishment of kinship. In healthcare, DNA is typically extracted from blood samples, dried blood spots, buccal swabs, saliva, tissue, and urine and stool samples. In forensic science, other sources have also been used, for example bone, tooth pulp and dandruff. Isolated DNA can survive in storage intact for decades. However, the quality of the DNA is affected by the method of storage. Temperature, chemicals, contaminants, enzymes or other adverse environmental conditions can result in the degradation of DNA.[2]

Terms like 'race' and 'ethnicity' are currently still in use. This is because appropriate terms which are still regarded as socially relevant for expression of externally visible differences are currently lacking. Genomic and genetic work is important to challenge such unscientific notions, particularly in South Africa's constitutional context with regard to respect and equality.[3]

Rapid advances in science and technology have resulted in rapid developments in genetics and genomics with new ethical, legal and social questions emerging. Speedy and responsible responses are needed.[4] Some examples of these developments are next-generation sequencing, genetic cohort studies and biobanks.

10.2 Ethical issues

10.2.1 The shared nature of DNA

A unique overall genome is possessed by each individual, but DNA is shared among biological family members. It is only in identical twins that genomes are identical. By definition, genomics and genetics will involve families, communities and population groups. A genetic diagnosis in an individual could have implications for other biological family members. Some communities may have a higher incidence of certain genetic diseases. This could also apply to larger population groups. Therefore, responsibilities and obligations to family members, communities and population groups may be as important as responsibilities and obligations to individuals. In addition, genetic information may predict the future health of the individual and family members. Choices in response to genetic information obtained may also affect future generations.[5] It is therefore

---

2   Ibid.
3   Academy of Science of South Africa *Human Genetics and Genomics in South Africa: Ethical, Legal and Social Implications: A Consensus Study* (2018) para 2.
4   MS Pepper 'Launch of the South African Human Genome Programme' (2011) 101(5) *SAMJ* 287–288.
5   Academy of Science of South Africa *Human Genetics and Genomics in South Africa: Ethical, Legal and Social Implications: A Consensus Study* (2018) para 2.

not surprising that unique ethical and legal issues arise in the context of genomic and genetic work.

The common-good approach is rapidly gaining popularity in genomics and genetics, and a set of norms have emerged as a result. These include mutuality, solidarity, citizenry, universality and reciprocity:[6]

(a) Mutuality is an important concept and has to do with the sharing of genetic information with family members.

(b) Solidarity has to do with the right to know or not to know and the duty to make responsible decisions when it comes to reproductive choices and predictive testing.

(c) Citizenry is a notion that encourages public understanding of science and in that way, promotes universality. For success in genomics and genetics work, it is vital that there is an informed public.

(d) Universality has to do with the idea that all people need to contribute to science and health improvement.

(e) Reciprocity is the notion that there should be a bi-directional relationship between research participants and researchers. Participant choice as to whether to bank DNA for future research is an example of reciprocity.

10.2.2 Challenges to informed consent

Owing to the shared nature of DNA, genetic information is individual, familial and communal, giving rise to challenges to the superiority of individual autonomy and consent.[7] In clinical genetics services, there are several role players in the informed consent process, including the patient, the family, a clinician and often a genetic counsellor. Pre- and post-test counselling are necessary. The patient's consent for the genetic testing is obtained after pre-test counselling. This allows for adequate understanding of the implications of the test.[8]

(a) Sharing findings with family members coupled with implications for privacy and confidentiality need to be discussed during the informed consent process.

---

6   BM Knoppers and R Chadwick 'Human genetic research: Emerging trends in ethics' (2005) 6 *Nature Reviews Genetics* 75.

7   PC Kuszler 'Biotechnology entrepreneurship and ethics: Principles, paradigms, and products' (2006) 25 *Medicine & Law* 491.

8   AL McGuire and LM Beskow 'Informed consent in genomics and genetic research' (2010) 11 *Annual Review of Genomics and Human Genetics* 361–381.

(b) Methods of genomic characterisation are now able to read every part of the genome. Therefore, genetic variants that are known to be associated with genetic disorders will need to be included in the informed consent process as they could arise as incidental findings of the testing both in clinical testing and research.[9]

(c) It is important to inform patients and research participants that there is ongoing decoding of genomic and genetic information. Hence it is difficult to predict everything in advance as new information is emerging all the time. Moreover, some information may only become known several years after obtaining consent.[10]

(d) A particular ethical challenge in genomics care and research is that of feeding back of results of incidental findings to patients or research participants. Results that should be fed back include where there is an indication of susceptibility to conditions that are life-threatening, manageable and unlikely to have been diagnosed without the genetic test.[11]

10.2.3 Exploitation and vulnerability

Africa is rich in diversity. Historically and even today, there is unfair exploitation of Africa's vulnerability by funders from abroad:[12]

(a) Data and samples are often mined without regard to the interests of data and sample providers or even the local researchers or practitioners.

(b) This is being seen more frequently with biobanks (biorepositories) which are established in Africa with foreign funding and where preferential data and sample access are allowed to foreign researchers. Ethically appropriate collaborations and capacity building are often disregarded.

(c) The situation is further complicated by asymmetrical power relationships between funders and local researchers and practitioners, and also by asymmetrical power relationships between local practitioners or scientists, and patients or research participants, respectively.

---

9   Academy of Science of South Africa *Human Genetics and Genomics in South Africa: Ethical, Legal and Social Implications: A Consensus Study* (2018) para 4.1 http://research.assaf.org.za/bitstream/handle/20.500.11911/106/2018_assaf_ethical_genetics_genomics_consensus.pdf?sequence=1&isAllowed=y (accessed on 25 March 2020).

10 AJ Clarke 'Managing the ethical challenges of next-generation sequencing in genomic medicine' (2014) 111(1) *British Medical Bulletin* 17–30.

11 L Eckstein, JR Garrett, BE Berkman 'A framework for analysing the ethics of disclosing genetic research findings' (2014) 42(2) *The Journal of Law, Medicine & Ethics* 190–207.

12 Academy of Science of South Africa *Human Genetics and Genomics in South Africa. Ethical, Legal and Social Implications. A Consensus Study* (2018) para 2.

(d) Commercialisation of products with little to no benefit sharing with the local researchers, institutions, and data and sample donors is often seen in these unequal relationships.

The rights to share in scientific advancement and its benefits, protection of authorship, and protection of moral and material interests resulting from scientific production in the Universal Declaration of Human Rights[13] offer some protection to sample donors and researchers involved in the research.

10.2.4 Stigmatisation and discrimination

Respecting privacy and confidentiality are essential in order to avoid social harms like stigmatisation and discrimination.[14] Genetic discrimination results when people are treated differently because of having a genetic condition that causes or may increase the risk of an inherited disorder. These harms could extend beyond individuals and affect groups and communities with wide-ranging implications including in the area of finance, education and employment.[15]

In the context of population groups being involved in genomics research, there is the risk that research results could worsen the existing stigma for those groups. This is of particular importance where genomics research involves stigmatised conditions or where there is pre-existing political, social or economic marginalisation.[16]

10.2.5 Increasing disparities

Transactional costs of genomic and genetic work could result in the technologies not being available to those who are at a disadvantage because of poverty. Hence, a danger could be that of increasing the disparities between the rich and the poor. For example, in precision medicine, there are ethical implications with

---

13   Universal Declaration of Human Rights, UN General Assembly, 1948:http://www.ohchr.org/EN/UDHR/Documents/UDHR_Translations/eng.pdf (accessed on 20 March 2020).

14   See generally JD Watson *A passion for DNA: Genes, genomes and society* (2000); MN Slabbert and MS Pepper 'A room of our own? Legal *lacunae* regarding genomic sovereignty in South Africa' (2007) 70 *THRHR* 622–637.; MN Slabbert 'Genetic privacy in South Africa and Europe: A comparative perspective' (Part II) (2008) 71 *THRHR* 81–100.

15   MA Rothstein 'Genetic screening in employment: Some legal, ethical, and societal issues' (1990)1 *International Journal of Bioethics* 239–244; MA Rothstein *Genetic secrets: Protecting privacy and confidentiality in the genetic era* (1997); J Kupfer 'The ethics of genetic screening in the workplace' (1993) 3(1) *Business Ethics Quarterly* 17–25.

16   J De Vries , M Jallow, TN Williams, D Kwiatkowski, M Parker and R Fitzpatrick 'Investigating the potential for ethnic group harm in collaborative genomics research in Africa: Is ethnic stigmatisation likely?' (2012) 75 *Social Science & Medicine* 1400–1407; J De Vries, M Slabbert and MS Pepper 'Ethical, legal and social issues in the context of the planning stages of the Southern African Human Genome Programme' (2012) 31 *Medicine & Law* 119.

regard to health and wealth disparities and also sufficient knowledge generation for implementation in understudied populations.[17]

10.2.6 Direct-to-consumer testing

The marketing of genomic and genetic tests directly to consumers has increased in prevalence and comes with its own set of challenges which include the following:[18]

(a) Recipients receive results directly without healthcare professionals assisting them to understand what the results actually mean. This could result in severe anxiety.

(b) Most of these tests are based on studies of populations in the West and have not been validated locally.

(c) The data could be used irresponsibly by risk assessment businesses such as insurers to implement discriminatory practices.

(d) There is no regulatory framework to control direct-to-consumer testing in South Africa.

10.2.7 Data dissemination in the forensics sector

Similar to clinical genetics, data dissemination in the forensic science sector is complex and challenging, and requires relevant education of the public in this context. Globally, forensic science is viewed as a field that needs to be practised with transparency and accountability so that trust can be built between the government, the justice system and society. Citizens need to trust that they will receive effective social protection.[19]

10.3 Legal issues

10.3.1 Pertinent legislation

Legislation dealing with genomics and genetics in South Africa is limited. The pertinent legislation is as follows:

---

17 Academy of Science of South Africa *Human Genetics and Genomics in South Africa: Ethical, Legal and Social Implications: A Consensus Study* (2018) para 2.3.1: http://research.assaf.org. za/bitstream/handle/20.500.11911/106/2018_assaf_ethical_genetics_genomics_consensus. pdf?sequence=1&isAllowed=y (accessed on 25 March 2020).

18 Ibid para 3.4.

19 Academy of Science of South Africa *Human Genetics and Genomics in South Africa: Ethical, Legal and Social Implications: A Consensus Study* (2018) 3.4.1: http://research.assaf.org.za/ bitstream/handle/20.500.11911/106/2018_assaf_ethical_genetics_genomics_consensus.pdf? sequence=1&isAllowed=y (accessed on 25 March 2020).

10.3.1.1 Constitution of the Republic of South Africa, 1996

The Constitution protects the right not to have the privacy of a person's communications infringed,[20] unless it can be shown that it was reasonable and justifiable to do so. Thus, this protects the privacy of any communication between a person undergoing genetic testing and his or her health practitioner. Not obtaining consent prior to taking a genetic sample, doing the genetic testing itself, and disclosing or publishing the results constitutes an infringement of the right to privacy.

For instance, in the case of *S v Orrie*,[21] a DNA blood test was taken for a criminal investigation without informed consent and was held to be an invasion of the person's constitutional right to 'personal autonomy privacy' (not to have intrusions into his or her private life) and his or her right to 'informational privacy' (not to have disclosures made about his or her DNA made to third parties – without his or her consent or where it threatened the health and safety of others). Such an invasion may however be allowed if it was a 'reasonable and justifiable' limitation of the right.[22] Therefore, in *S v Orrie*, the court allowed the test and disclosure because 'the taking of blood samples for DNA testing for the purposes of a criminal investigation is a reasonable and necessary step to ensure that justice is done and is reasonable and necessary in balancing the interests of justice against those of individual dignity'.[23]

10.3.1.2 National Health Act (NHA)[24]

The Constitution recognises the right to privacy,[25] and the National Health Act ensures that this is applied to health matters.[26] The National Health Act protects the confidentiality of health information held by hospitals and other health establishments, and provides that no person may disclose such information unless that person has given consent for the disclosure; or if required by court order; or if non-disclosure constitutes a serious threat to public health.[27] In the context of genomics and genetics, the privacy of personal information could be threatened when a person's genetic results are stored, processed or kept in a databank by institutions or persons in the insurance or financial, health or employment sectors.

---

20   Section 14(*d*).
21   *S v Orrie* 2004 3 SA 584 (C).
22   Constitution s 36.
23   *S v Orrie* 2004 (3) SA 584 (C) 589.
24   Act 61 of 2003.
25   Section 14.
26   Ibid.
27   Ibid.

Chapter 3 mandates the Director-General of Health to provide for genetic services and 'must issue and promote adherence to, norms and standards on health matters, including genetic services'.[28] Chapter 8 deals with blood and blood products, assisted reproductive technology, cell-based therapy, transplantation, tissue banks, forensic medicine/pathology, and reproductive and therapeutic cloning. With regard to the latter, the Act prohibits the manipulation of human genetic material from gametes, zygotes and embryos for purposes of reproductive cloning.[29] The Minister of Health may, under such conditions as may be prescribed, permit therapeutic cloning utilising adult or umbilical cord stem cells.[30] Therapeutic cloning is defined as 'the manipulation of genetic material from either adult, zygotic or embryonic cells in order to alter, for therapeutic purposes, the function of cells or tissues'.[31] No person may import or export human zygotes or embryos without the prior written approval of the minister.[32] The minister may permit research on stem cells and zygotes which are not more than 14 days old on written application and if (a) the applicant undertakes to document the research for record purposes; and (b) prior consent is obtained from the donor of such stem cells or zygotes.[33] Any person who contravenes or fails to comply with these provisions is guilty of an offence and is liable on conviction to a fine or to imprisonment for a period not exceeding five years or to both a fine and such imprisonment.[34]

Written informed consent is required prior to the removal of biological material from a living donor.[35] Where the person is deceased, consent to remove and use biological materials may be found in the person's will, in a written statement or in a witnessed oral statement[36] or may be provided by 'the spouse, partner, major child, parent, guardian, major brother or major sister of that person in the specific order mentioned'.[37]

The Minister of Health has made regulations in terms of the Act dealing with the use of human biological material;[38] the general control of human bodies, tissue blood, blood products and gametes;[39] the registration of microbiological laboratories; and the acquisition, importation, handling, maintenance and supply

---

28   Section 21(*b*)(vii).
29   Sections 57(1)(*a*) and (6)(*a*) & (*b*).
30   Section 57(2).
31   Section 57(6)(*b*).
32   Section 57(3).
33   Section 57(4).
34   Section 57(5).
35   National Health Act ss 56 and 62.
36   National Health Act s 62(1)(*a*).
37   National Health Act s 62(2).
38   GN R177 of 2 March 2012.
39   GN R180 of 2 March 2012; GN 392 of 26 April 2017.

of human pathogens;[40] the import and export of human tissue, blood, blood products, cultured cells, stem cells, embryos, foetal tissue, zygotes and gametes;[41] and the regulations relating to tissue banks.[42]

10.3.1.3 The Protection of Personal Information Act (the POPI Act)[43]

The Protection of Personal Information Act places emphasis on the privacy of health and other information about individuals, and the definition of personal information in the Act includes 'the biometric information of the person'.[44] Most of the Act is now in effect. The Act defines biometrics as 'a technique of personal identification that is based on physical, physiological or behavioural characterisation including blood typing, fingerprinting, DNA analysis, retinal scanning and voice recognition'.[45]

The POPI Act gives effect to the constitutional right to privacy.[46] This is achieved by safeguarding personal information when it is processed by a 'responsible party' and by regulating the manner in which personal information may be lawfully processed in line with international standards.[47] A general prohibition against the processing of 'special' personal information is provided for, but is subject to specific exceptions. For example, the Act provides that personal information concerning inherited characteristics may not be processed in respect of a data subject from whom the information concerned has been obtained, unless (a) a serious medical interest prevails; or (b) the processing is necessary for historical, statistical or research activity.[48] Furthermore, access to health information must be done in accordance with the provisions of the Promotion of Access to Information Act.[49]

10.3.1.4 Promotion of Access to Information Act[50]

The Promotion of Access to Information Act states that before an information officer releases personal health information to a patient or authorised requester, the information officer may consult with the health practitioner treating the patient if he or she 'is of the opinion that the disclosure of the record to the relevant person might cause serious harm to his or her physical or mental health, or well-being'.[51]

---

40 GN R178 of 2 March 2012.
41 Ibid.
42 Ibid.
43 Protection of Personal Information Act 4 of 2013.
44 Section 1.
45 Ibid.
46 Constitution s 14.
47 Protection of Personal Information Act s 2.
48 Section 32(5).
49 2 of 2000.
50 Ibid.
51 Section 30.

10.3.1.5 The Criminal Law (Forensic Procedures) Amendment Act[52]

The Criminal Law (Forensic Procedures) Amendment Act and its Forensic DNA Regulations of 2015[53] address the collection, use, storage and destruction of DNA samples in forensics. Genetic testing performed in the field of forensics includes applications of individual identity in criminal cases, family relationships in immigration disputes, parentage testing and identification in mass disasters. The Forensic DNA Regulations of 2015 allow for the right of the arrested person to request the removal of his or her DNA profile from the National Forensic DNA Database after acquittal or exclusion from a criminal case. The removal must be executed within 30 days of application.[54] The regulations specify that buccal samples as well as DNA samples need to be destroyed within 30 days of obtaining a forensic DNA profile or after the sample has been processed by the Forensic Science Laboratory.[55] This may not be a realistic timeframe with regard to the requirements of the justice system.[56]

10.3.1.6 The Medicines and Related Substances Amendment Act[57]

The Medicines and Related Substances Amendment Act[58] establishes the South African Health Products Regulatory Authority (SAHPRA) under the Medicines Control Council. The Act's mandate includes medical devices. Medical devices include diagnostic tests and would therefore also cover genetic tests. The Medicines Control Council Guidelines for the Registration of Medicines[59] in the section on 'biological medicines' refer to genetically modified material, including recombinant DNA technology. Under the Guidelines, applications for the registration of 'biological medicine', which includes medicine prepared for 'human gene therapy' have to be made to the biological sub-unit of SAHPRA.[60]

---

52 Criminal Law (Forensic Procedures) Amendment Act 37 of 2013.
53 Forensic DNA Regulations GN R 207 of 13 March 2015.
54 Regulation 12.
55 Regulation(10)(1).
56 Academy of Science of South Africa *Human Genetics and Genomics in South Africa: Ethical, Legal and Social Implications: A Consensus Study* (2018) para 5.2.2: http://research.assaf.org.za/bitstream/handle/20.500.11911/106/2018_assaf_ethical_genetics_genomics_consensus.pdf?sequence=1&isAllowed=y (accessed on 25 March 2020).
57 72 of 2008.
58 Ibid.
59 Medicines Control Council *Guidelines for the Registration of Medicines: General Information* (2012) Guideline 8.
60 Guideline 8.2.6.

10.3.2 The common law

The right to privacy has been recognised by the common law for many years.[61] For instance, in the case of an application to court – predating the Constitution – to allow a blood sample to be taken from a child to establish paternity, the court held that it was not in the 'best interests of the child' and was an infringement of the child's right to privacy, and refused to grant the application.[62]

10.3.3 Protection against discrimination

Section 9 of the Constitution provides that everyone is equal before the law and that everyone has the right to equal protection. Unfair discrimination is prohibited on one or more grounds including disability. This Constitutional provision of equality is given effect by the Promotion of Equality and Prevention of Unfair Discrimination Act.[63] A person who suffers from a genetic disease resulting in a disability severely impacting his or her life cannot be unfairly discriminated against.

Several key international human rights instruments provide for protection against genetic discrimination and include provisions requiring states to protect citizens against such discrimination. The United Nations Educational, Scientific and Cultural Organisation's (UNESCO) Universal Declaration on the Human Genome and Human Rights (1997)[64] provides that 'no one should be subjected to discrimination based on genetic characteristics that is intended to infringe or has the effect of infringing human rights, fundamental freedoms and human dignity'.[65] UNESCO's International Declaration on Human Data[66] (2003) provides that 'every effort should be made to ensure that human genetic data are not used for purposes that are discriminatory or in any way that would lead to the stigmatisation of an individual, a family or a group'.[67] At the supranational level, the Council of Europe's European Convention on Human Rights and

---

61 *Jansen van Vuuren v Kruger* 1993 (4) SA 842 (A).
62 *Seetal v Pravitha NO* 1983 (3) SA 827 (D).
63 Promotion of Equality and Prevention of Unfair Discrimination Act 4 of 2000.
64 United Nations Educational, Scientific and Cultural Organisation *Universal Declaration on the Human Genome and Human Rights* (1997): http://portal.unesco.org/en/ev.phpURL_ID=13177&URL_DO=DO_TOPIC&URL_SECTION=201.html (accessed on 27 March 2020).
65 Article 6.
66 United Nations Educational, Scientific and Cultural Organisation International Declaration on Human Data: http://portal.unesco.org/en/ev.php-URL_ID=17720&URL_DO=DO_TOPIC&URL_SECTION=201.html (accessed on 27 March 2020).
67 Article 7.

Biomedicine (1997)[68] prohibits any form of discrimination based on a person's genetic heritage.[69] Article 21 of the European Union's Charter of Fundamental rights (2000)[70] prohibits discrimination relating to genetic characteristics.

10.4 Gene editing

Gene editing involves precise additions, deletions and alterations to the genome. Clinical applications involving somatic (non-reproductive) cells are in the early stages. There is great potential for the use of this technology in germline cells.[71] Gene therapy where genetic changes are made to somatic cells is already established as a therapeutic modality. Genome editing for somatic applications is a form of gene therapy. Somatic genome editing could pose technical challenges in that the gene-editing tools may not find their target genes efficiently, resulting in off-target effects, or may inadvertently affect germline cells; however, clinical trials using this technology for some diseases are already under way in some countries.[72]

While somatic cell gene editing does evoke ethical concerns, it is germline gene editing that is fraught with ethical complexities.[73] Currently, South Africa does not have an ethico-legal framework in place for the governance of gene editing and while we contemplate catching up in this regard, the first CRISPR-edited babies have already arrived.[74]

10.4.1 Benefits of germline genome editing

Already in use for some decades are prenatal and pre-implantation genetic diagnosis for the purpose of avoiding disease transmission. However, these technologies do not work in some cases and where they do work could result in discarding affected embryos or in selective abortion, resulting in debates over the moral status of the embryo. Germline genome editing could provide some

---

68 Council of Europe *Convention for the Protection of Human Rights and Dignity of the Human Being with Regard to the Application of Biology and Medicine* (1997): https://rm.coe.int/168007cf98 (accessed on 27 March 2020).

69 Article 11.

70 European Union *Charter of Fundamental Rights* (2009): https://www.europarl.europa.eu/charter/pdf/text_en.pdf (accessed on 27 March 2020).

71 A Dhai 'Advances in biotechnology: Human genome editing, artificial intelligence and the Fourth Industrial Revolution: The law and ethics should not lag behind' (2018) 11(2) *SAJBL* 58–59.

72 The National Academies of Sciences Engineering Medicine *Human Genome Editing: Science, Ethics and Governance* (2017): http://nap.edu/24623 doi 10.17226/24623 (accessed on 28 March 2020).

73 A Dhai 'Genetics, genomics, biobanks and health databases in research ethics' in A Dhai (ed) *Health Research Ethics: Safeguarding the Interests of Research Participants* (2019) 166–211.

74 A Opar 'CRISPR-edited babies arrived, and regulators are still racing to catch up' (2019) 25 *Nature Medicine* 1634–1636: https://www.nature.com/articles/s41591-019-0641-x (accessed on 25 November 2019).

families with the most appropriate option for preventing disease transmission. The resulting genetic changes would then be passed down the generations. This shift from individual level effects is viewed as contentious by some.[75] Social and ethical concerns including those involving the acceptance of children with disabilities, the risk of inheriting off-target genome effects, equitable access, and slippery slope cautions in the contexts of enhancement and eugenics are issues that require consideration.[76] Both somatic and germline processes could be used for enhancement purposes. Enriching traits and capacities beyond levels considered adequate for health are realistic possibilities.

10.4.2 International guidelines on genome editing

Considerations of fairness, social norms and need require public debate and regulations on somatic and germline processes.[77] The Nuffield Council, on the ethical acceptability of genome editing in the context of reproduction, has proposed two principles that need to be satisfied. Firstly, the intention of the intervention must be to secure the welfare of the individual born as a result of such technology. Moreover, the intervention must also be consistent with the welfare of such a person. Secondly, principles of social justice and solidarity must be upheld and the intervention should not result in an intensifying of social divides or marginalising disadvantaged groups in society.

The United Nations Educational, Scientific and Cultural Organization has cautioned against recklessly applying gene editing, and emphasises the need to heed internationally agreed upon principles that affirm the values of human rights and human dignity as the prime concern for any medical research and intervention on human beings.[78] UNESCO has cautioned member countries on gene modifications that will pass onto future generations albeit the promise of scientific advancement for the benefit of humanity. A moratorium on genome editing of the human germline has been called for by the International Bioethics Committee of UNESCO for as long as the safety and effectiveness of these procedures remain unproven.[79]

---

75   See footnote 71 above.

76   Ibid.

77   See footnote 71 above. Nuffield Council on Bioethics *Genome Editing and Human Reproduction: Social and Ethical Issues* (2018): http://nuffieldbioethics.org/wp-content/uploads/Genome-editing-and-human-reproduction-FINAL-website.pdf (accessed on 20 March 2020).

78   United Nations Educational, Scientific and Cultural Organisation *UNESCO Cautions Against Reckless Application of Gene Editing* 30 November 2018: https://unesco.go.ke/unesco-cautions-against-reckless-application-of-gene-editing/ (accessed on 14 March 2020).

79   United Nations Educational, Scientific and Cultural Organisation *Report of the IBC on Updating its Reflection on the Human Genome and Human Rights* (2015): https://unesdoc.unesco.org/ark:/48223/pf0000233258 (accessed on 20 March 2020).

A case study on gene editing in China

He Jiankui, a Chinese scientist, caused a global outcry when he announced that his team at Southern University of Science and Technology in Shenzhen had made and implanted human embryos less susceptible to HIV by editing their DNA with the use of CRISPR gene editing system. His actions were condemned because gene editing technology was regarded as too premature to be used for reproductive purposes and there was a risk of introducing mutations with potentially harmful effects. In addition, because the babies were not at high risk of contracting HIV, the gene editing conferred little benefit. There were speculations and concerns that other scientists would follow in his footsteps.[80]

He was fired from his University in January 2019. The following December, a Chinese court sentenced him to three years in prison for illegal medical practice and a fine of 3 million yuan (US$430,000). Shorter sentences and fines were handed down to two colleagues who assisted him. They too have been banned from working with human reproductive technology ever again by the health ministry and from applying for research funding from the science ministry. Chinese scientists believe that the punishments are likely to deter others from similar conduct.[81]

Did He Jiankui infringe any international ethical norms? Why or why not?

Some questions on genetic issues

Should surplus embryos from artificial fertilisation be used for embryonic stem cell research? Why or why not?

---

80   D Cyranoski and H Ledford 'Genome-edited baby claim provokes international outcry' (2018) 563 *Nature* 607–608; doi:10.1038/d41586-018-07545-0 (accessed on 20 March 2020).
81   D Cyranoski 'What CRISPR-baby prison sentences mean for research' (2020) 577 *Nature* 154–155; doi:10.1038/d41586-020-00001-y (accessed on 20 March 2020).

CHAPTER 11

Use of human tissue

David McQuoid-Mason and Ames Dhai

By the end of this chapter readers will be able to:

1. Explain the ethical aspects in respect of the use of human tissue.
2. Explain the legal position regarding the removal of tissue from living persons.
3. Explain the legal position regarding the removal of tissue from dead bodies.
4. Explain the consent and authorisation procedures for the removal of tissue from dead persons.

11.1 Ethical aspects of using human tissue

Human tissue is now being used in an increasing variety of new ways. With rapid advances in science and technology, medical procedures that were thought about as science fiction in the past are a reality today. Despite this, the human body, both living and dead, is accorded the special respect and protection that has been granted it throughout history. For instance, Principle 6 of the Declaration of Istanbul on Organ Trafficking and Transplant Tourism (2018) states as follows:

> Organs for transplantation should be equitably allocated within countries or jurisdictions, in conformity with objective, nondiscriminatory, externally justified, and transparent rules, guided by clinical criteria, and ethical norms.[1]

Society, religion and the law prescribe duties and obligations to ensure that human bodies are treated with dignity and the dead are left undisturbed. However, people from different cultures have very different or even contradictory views on how tissue, body parts and/or the entire body should be treated or disposed of. Certain ritualistic acts, deemed essential from a traditional perspective by some cultures, may be scorned by others. It is important that the healthcare practitioner recognise and understand the deeply rooted religious and multiculturally diverse influences amongst patients and their families regarding the human body.

---

1   https://journals.lww.com/transplantjournal/Fulltext/2019/02000/The_Declaration_of_Istanbul_on_Organ_Trafficking.3.aspx

In recent times in post-colonial countries, the issue of legacy collections involving human tissue has become an important one affecting the past use and treatment of human bodies and tissue. For instance, in South Africa in 2002, the body of Saartjie Baartman was repatriated from France, where she was known as the 'Hottentot Venus', and reburied in the Eastern Cape on Women's Day.[2] It has been suggested that there should be a national audit of all legacy collections of human bodies and tissues in universities, museums and other institutions.[3]

Patients may assume that tissue removed from them during the course of medical management will be used only for diagnostic purposes for their illness and destroyed thereafter. Patients need to be informed if tissue is to be archived or stored for possible use in future diagnosis, research or study. In addition, consent for storage and future use is necessary.

11.1.1 Arguments for and against the buying and selling of human tissue

There are differing views on whether human tissue and body parts should be sold for commercial gain.

Arguments in favour of using a market system that allows the sale of tissue and organs include the following:[4]

(a) A financial incentive will help to match supply and demand, thereby addressing the shortage of organs and other tissues.

(b) Those whose tissues are scarce and therefore in demand as sources for treatment should be awarded.

(c) Efficient and easier procurement of tissues for commercial tissue banks will facilitate medical and scientific advancement and progress.

Arguments against the procurement of human tissue on a commercial basis include the following:[5]

(a) It interferes with the consent process.

(b) The poor and vulnerable may find themselves tempted by the financial incentives and thereby ignore the risks.

---

2   https://www.sahistory.org.za/people/sara-saartjie-baartman (accessed on 28 March 2020).
3   DJ McQuoid-Mason 'UKZN Anniversary Symposium on the Medico-Legal and Ethical Implications on Human Tissue Use' (2011) 4(1) *SAJBL* 13–14.
4   Nuffield Council on Bioethics *Human Tissue: Ethical and Legal Issues* (1995) 39–53.
5   M Slabbert and H Oosthuizen 'Establishing a market for human organs in South Africa' (2007) 28 *Obiter* 44 and 304; M Slabbert 'Ethics, justice and the sale of kidneys for transplantation purposes' (2010) 13(2) *PER* 2–31; M Slabbert 'This is my kidney, I can do what I want with it' (2009) 3 *Obiter* 499–517; M Slabbert 'Combat organ trafficking – reward the donor or regulate sales?' (2008) 73(1) *KOERS* 75–99.

(c) Altruistic desires may be undermined or deterred by a commercial system.

(d) Criminal or morally reprehensible methods of procurement might be encouraged.

An alternate to financial incentives is 'rewarded gifting',[6] which describes the offer of incentives for donation where the rewards are in kind and not money. The arguments for and against financial incentives apply equally to rewarded gifting.

Treating the body with dignity could denote that the body and its parts should not be commodified, owned by others or used for commercial gain. In addition, theft of body parts (e.g. as in organ trafficking) is ethically impermissible. An individual's body or body parts may not be used as a means to an end that he or she may not endorse.

11.1.2 Embryonic stem cell research – medical possibilities

Chronic debilitating degenerative diseases including those of the brain (Parkinson's and Alzheimer's disease), pancreas (diabetes), liver (hepatitis), joints (rheumatoid arthritis), heart, lungs and kidneys as well as spinal cord injuries cause immense suffering to patients, their families and society. They also shorten life spans and limit activity. Embryonic stem cell research may offer unique ways of investigating and possibly treating many of these diseases.[7]

Creating embryos using nuclei from individuals carrying genetic mutations predisposing them to particular diseases could be used to develop an improved understanding and treatment of the diseases. Embryonic stem cells could populate unhealthy or dead tissue, differentiate into different types of cells, regenerate diseased tissue and compensate for the loss of or restore normal functions. Moreover, embryonic stem cells could benefit patients requiring transplants. A further benefit of embryo stem cell research could be genetic therapy for genetic diseases as a result of combining cloning techniques with genetic manipulation.[8] Stem cell research could lead to the acceleration of the healing of burns and fractures. Cystic fibrosis, muscular dystrophy and other genetic diseases could be cured by using stem cells to deliver the missing protein or gene to target tissue.[9] The possible medical gains from embryonic stem cell research are immense and hence compelling argument can be made for work to proceed in this area.

---

6   Nuffield Council on Bioethics *Human Tissue: Ethical and Legal Issues* (1995) 39–53.
7   World Health Organization Advisory Committee on Health Research Genomics and World Health (2002) 107–173.
8   D Solter and J Gearhart 'Putting stem cells to work' (1999) 283 *Science* 1468–1470.
9   NM Fisk and P Braude 'Stem Cells' (2001) 3 *The Obstetrician and Gynaecologist* 211–212.

In law, the destruction of an embryo is not murder because the embryo is not regarded as a person.[10] Widely held philosophical and moral views hold that the status of a person requires further development such as a nervous system capable of sentience. At day 14, the primitive streak, the first sign of development of the nervous system, is observed. Based on this, some countries permit research for specified purposes on embryos of less than 14 days, and this has been adopted by South Africa and included in the National Health Act.[11]

Reproductive cloning has been banned in many countries. Some countries have banned all forms of cloning without making a distinction between reproductive and therapeutic cloning. In South Africa, the National Health Act allows for therapeutic cloning but not reproductive cloning.[12]

11.2 Legal aspects of using human tissue

The donation of human tissue is presently governed by Chapter 8 of the National Health Act.[13] The Act covers the removal of tissues, blood or gametes from the bodies of living persons for therapeutic and other uses and the removal of tissues from dead bodies and the donation of human bodies.

11.2.1 Removal of human tissue from living persons

The National Health Act governs the removal of tissue, blood or gametes from the bodies of living persons for therapeutic and other uses. 'Tissue' is defined as 'human tissue, and includes flesh, bone, a gland, an organ, skin, bone marrow or body fluid, but excludes blood or a gamete'.[14] 'Organ' is defined as 'any part of the body adapted by its structure to perform any particular vital function, including the eye and its accessories, but does not include skin and appendages, flesh, bone, bone marrow, body fluid, blood or a gamete'.[15] Although 'organ' is separately defined, it is also included in the definition of 'tissue'. 'Gamete' is defined as 'either of the two generative cells essential for human reproduction'.[16] It has been suggested that a foetus is the 'tissue' of the woman in whose womb it is.[17]

---

10   cf *Christian Lawyers' Association of South Africa v Minister of Health* 1998 (4) SA 1113 (T).
11   61 of 2003 s 57(4).
12   61 of 2003 s 57(1).
13   61 of 2003.
14   Section 1.
15   Ibid.
16   Ibid.
17   SA Strauss *Doctor, Patient and the Law* 3 ed (1993) 147.

The National Health Act and regulations[18] provide for the donation and use of tissue, blood and gametes removed or withdrawn from the body of a living person for medical and dental purposes. These purposes of the Act include (a) the training of students in health sciences; (b) health research; (c) the advancement of health sciences; (d) therapeutic purposes, including the use of tissue in any living person; or (e) the production of a therapeutic, diagnostic or prophylactic substance.[19] The regulations sometimes appear to be ignored by the courts.[20]

The Act does not apply to the preparation of the body of a deceased person for the purposes of embalming it, whether or not such preparation involves (a) the making of incisions in the body for the withdrawal of blood and the replacement thereof by a preservative; or (b) the repair of any disfigurement or mutilation of the body before its burial.[21]

The National Health Act provides that such tissue, blood, blood products or gametes obtained from the following persons may not be used for any of the above purposes: (a) a person who is mentally ill within the meaning of the Mental Health Care Act;[22] (b) tissue which is not replaceable by natural processes from a person younger than 18 years; (c) a gamete of a person younger than 18 years; and (d) placenta, embryonic or foetal tissue, stem cells and umbilical cord, excluding umbilical progenitor cells.[23] However, the Act provides that such tissue, blood, blood products or gametes may be used with the consent of the Minister of Health, and subject to any conditions mentioned in the consent.[24]

11.2.1.1   Consent to removal of tissue

The National Health Act states that a person may not remove tissue, blood, a blood product or gametes from the body of another living person for such medical or dental purposes as may be prescribed unless it is done (a) with the written consent of the person from whom the tissue, blood, blood product or gametes are removed granted in the prescribed manner; and (b) in accordance with prescribed conditions.[25] The removal of tissue, blood and gametes for any of the above purposes may be effected only with the consent of the donor or, in the case of a person under the age of 18 years, the consent of the parents

---

18   Regulations regarding the general control of human bodies, tissue, blood, blood products and gametes: GN R 180 of 2 March 2012; as amended by GN 392 of 26 April 2016.
19   Section 64(1).
20   See *S v Frederiksen* (33/2016) ZAFSHC 161 (14 September 2017), where the judge did not consider the regulations; B Venter and M Slabbert 'S v Frederiksen (33/2016 ZAFSHC: SACR 29 (FB) (14 September 2017): Human tissue in a freezer: a crime or not?' 2019 *De Jure* 109–114.
21   Section 64(2).
22   17 of 2002.
23   Section 56(2)(*a*).
24   Section 56(2)(*b*).
25   Section 55.

or guardian.[26] A person may not remove blood from the body of another living person unless written consent thereto has been granted by a person older than 18 years.[27]

11.2.1.2   Procedure for removal of tissue

The National Health Act states that tissue for transplantation from a living person to another living person may be removed only in a hospital or other authorised institution.[28] Such removal and transplantation of human tissue must be done with the written authority of (a) the medical practitioner in charge of clinical services in the hospital or authorised institution, or any other medical practitioner authorised by him or her; or (b) in the case where there is no medical practitioner in charge of the clinical services at that hospital or authorised institution, a medical practitioner authorised to give consent by the person in charge of the hospital or authorised institution.[29] The medical practitioners mentioned above may not participate in a transplant for which they granted authorisation in terms of the Act.[30]

11.2.1.3   Persons authorised to remove tissue

The National Health Act provides that only a registered medical practitioner or dentist may for the purposes of the Act remove any tissue from a living person, or use tissue so removed for any of the purposes in the Act or transplant tissue so removed into another living person.[31] Only a registered medical practitioner or dentist, or a person acting under the supervision or on the instructions of a medical practitioner or dentist, may for the purposes of the Act administer blood or a blood product to, or prescribe blood or a blood product for, a living person.[32]

It has been suggested, however, that the similar provisions of the repealed Human Tissue Act[33] did not confer an absolute discretion on the authorising doctor, the surgeon undertaking the removal or the donor and that, whether the removal of the tissue will be legal, will depend upon the boni mores of society – not just consent by the donor. Therefore, the courts should weigh up the interests of the donor against those of the recipient, and should take into account factors such as the following:

---

26   GN R 180 of 2 March 2012 reg 2(b).
27   GN 392 of 26 April 2016.
28   Section 58(1)(*a*).
29   Section 58(1)(*b*).
30   Section 58(2).
31   Section 59(1).
32   Section 59(2).
33   65 of 1983.

(a) The removal should not substantially imperil the life of the donor.

(b) The removal should be in accordance with scientifically approved methods.

(c) The advantage to the patient should be commensurate with the disadvantage suffered by the donor.[34]

11.3 Removal of human tissue from dead bodies

The National Health Act[35] has special provisions regarding the removal of human tissue from deceased persons and defines death as 'brain death'.[36] Whether or not a person is dead is a question of fact which will be resolved by expert medical evidence if there is a dispute.

The National Health Act provides that for the purposes of removing tissue, the death of the donor must be established by two doctors, one of whom must have been practising for five years – and both of whom may not be members of the transplant team.[37] Human bodies, tissue, blood, blood products or gametes may be donated to a prescribed institution (e.g. hospital, university or other institution involved in medical training or research) for any purpose provided for in the Act.[38]

11.3.1 Consent

In terms of the National Health Act, consent to the removal of tissue from a dead person may be given by (a) the deceased prior to his or her death (e.g. in a will document attested by two competent witnesses of 14 years or older, or orally before two competent witnesses);[39] or (b) the spouse, or designated relatives such as a major child, parent, guardian or any major brother or sister of the deceased after his or her death.[40]

A donation may be revoked before death by a donor before transplantation of the relevant organ into a recipient, in the same manner that it was donated in a will or other document, or by intentional destruction of such will or document.[41] It has been suggested that consent cannot be given by relatives or guardians if the

---

34   SA Strauss *Doctor, Patient and the Law* 3 ed (1993) 149.
35   61 of 2003 s 1.
36   Section 1.
37   Regulations regarding the general control of human bodies, tissue, blood, blood products and gametes: GN R 180 of 2 March 2012 reg 9.
38   Sections 56 and 64(1).
39   Section 62(1)(*a*).
40   Section 62(2).
41   Section 65.

deceased has forbidden it prior to his or her death, and a donation by the deceased cannot be revoked or vetoed by one relative against the consent of another.[42]

If the spouse or designated relatives cannot be traced, the Director-General of Health may donate specific tissue for transplantation purposes – provided that he or she is satisfied that the prescribed steps have been taken to trace the relatives concerned.[43]

11.3.2 Official authorisation

The National Health Act provides for the lawful removal of tissue from a dead body, and there must be official authorisation in writing in the prescribed manner by one of the following:

(a) The medical practitioner in charge of clinical services in a hospital or authorised institution in which the deceased died or of a mortuary where the body is; or

(b) Any other medical practitioner authorised by the medical practitioner in charge; or

(c) Where there is medical practitioner in charge of clinical services, a medical practitioner authorised by the person in charge such hospital or authorised institution.[44]

The National Health Act states that, despite anything to the contrary in any other law, a medical practitioner who conducts a post-mortem examination in terms of the Inquests Act[45] or for research purposes in terms of the Act[46] must remove or cause to be removed from a body such tissue as may be specified in an authorisation by the minister and must hand it over to the institution or person in possession of the authorisation.[47] However, such removal may not be effected if (a) the removal of the tissue is likely to affect the outcome of the examination; or (b) the body or tissue in question has been donated; or (c) if the removal would be contrary to a direction given by the deceased before his or her death.[48]

Where the body was donated in terms of a will or other document, authority may be given by the medical practitioner concerned on the face of the will or document if it appears to be legally valid.[49] Except where an entire body is

---

42   SA Strauss *Doctor, Patient and the Law* 3 ed (1993) 153.
43   Section 62(3).
44   Section 66(2).
45   58 of 1959 s 3.
46   National Health Act s 64(1)(*a*).
47   Section 67(3).
48   Section 67(4).
49   GN R180 of 2 March 2012.

donated, the donee of tissue has 24 hours after the death of the donor to remove the tissue donated.[50] After 24 hours, whether or not the tissue has been removed, the body may be claimed for burial or other purposes by the spouse, partner, major child, parent, guardian, major brother or major sister in the specific order mentioned.[51]

It has been suggested that the law as it stands is an obstacle to the donation of solid organs for transplantation purposes.[52]

11.3.3 Miscellaneous provisions

The National Health Act regulations state that a person requiring human tissue has exclusive rights over it provided he or she uses the body, tissue, blood or gamete for the purposes for which it was donated or supplied.[53] Hospitals, authorised institutions or prescribed institutions, or authorised persons may receive payments for the importation, export or acquisition for the supply to another person of tissue, gametes, blood or a blood product.[54] Such payments may not exceed an amount reasonably required to cover the costs of such importation, export, acquisition or supply of the tissue, gamete, blood or blood product in question.[55] Healthcare providers registered with a statutory health professions council may receive remuneration for any professional services rendered by them.[56]

The regulations[57] under the National Health Act provide that nobody shall publish or make known any fact without consent concerning the identity of (a) the deceased person whose body or any specific tissue thereof has been donated; (b) the donor of the body of a deceased person or any specific tissue thereof; (c) a living person from whose body any tissue, blood or gamete has been removed or withdrawn for any purpose; or (d) the person who has given his or her consent to the removal of any tissue, blood or gametes from a living person for such purpose.[58] No such publication shall be made before or after the death of the person concerned, unless:

(a) in the case of a recipient alive at the time of such publication, he or she had beforehand granted consent thereto in writing; or

---

50   Regulation 8(1).
51   Regulation 8(2).
52   M Slabbert 'The law as an obstacle in solid organ donations and transplantations' (2018) 81(1) *THRHR* 70.
53   Regulations regarding the general control of human bodies, tissue, blood, blood products and gametes in GN R180 of 2 March 2012 reg 26.
54   Section 60(1).
55   Section 60(2).
56   Section 60(3).
57   Regulations regarding the general control of human bodies, tissue, blood, blood products and gametes in GN R 180 of 2 March 2012.
58   GN R 180 of 2 March 2012 reg 24(1).

(b) in the case of a recipient who at the time of such publication has died:

    (i) the recipient before his or death had granted consent to such publication in writing; or

    (ii) the recipient had not before her or his death indicated he or she would not be prepared to grant such consent, and their spouse, partner, major child, parent, guardian, major brother or major sister had granted consent in writing before such publication.[59]

The National Health Act states that the following offences are punishable by imprisonment for a period not exceeding five years or both a fine and such imprisonment: (a) providing a blood transfusion service without a licence;[60] (b) being paid for donating, or selling or trading in, tissue, a gamete, blood or blood products except as provided for in terms of the Act;[61] (c) charging a fee for an organ or without ministerial permission transplanting organs into persons who are not South African citizens or permanent residents.[62]

The regulations[63] under the Act also mention that the following offences, inter alia, are punishable by a fine or imprisonment of up to 10 years or both a fine and imprisonment: where any person has (a) except in so far as it may be permitted by or under any other law, acquired, used or supplied a body of a deceased person or any tissue, blood or gamete of a living or deceased person in any other manner or for any other purpose than that permitted in the Act and the regulations; (b) refused or failed to comply to the best of his or her ability with any demand, requirement or order of a health officer or a health officer of blood transfusion services or any other person made or given in terms of any provision of the Act and the regulations; or (c) has hindered any person in the performance of his or her duties in terms of the Act and the regulations.[64]

Some questions on the use of human tissue

1. Given that there is a shortage of kidneys for transplantation, should South Africa change from an 'opt in' to an 'opt out' approach to organ donations, i.e. people's organs will be used for donation purposes unless they notify the authorities that they do not wish to donate their organs?

2. Should people be allowed to sell their organs? Why or why not?

---

59   Regulation 24(2).
60   Section 53(3).
61   Section 60(5).
62   Section 61(5).
63   GN R 180 of 2 March 2012.
64   Regulation 35.

CHAPTER 12

End-of-life issues

David McQuoid-Mason and Ames Dhai

By the end of this chapter readers will be able to:

1. Explain some of the ethical aspects of end-of-life decisions.

2. Explain the relationship between murder and euthanasia.

3. Describe the legal position regarding end-of-life decisions made by mentally competent patients.

4. Describe the role of palliative care during terminal illness

5. Describe the legal position regarding end-of-life decisions involving mentally incompetent patients.

6. Explain how 'living wills' operate.

7. Describe the arguments in favour of and against 'living wills'.

8. List the statutes dealing with death and dead bodies.

12.1 Ethical aspects of end-of-life decisions

Currently, there exists a growing range of life-saving or life-prolonging treatments which make it possible to extend the lives of patients who, through organ or system failure, might otherwise die. Modern techniques such as cardiopulmonary resuscitation, renal dialysis, artificial ventilation, and artificial nutrition and hydration have considerably benefited gravely ill patients. It is important, though, to remember that life has a natural end and the duty of the healthcare professional does not extend to sustaining life artificially for many years for patients for whom there is little hope of recovery.[1] Some treatments might result in a quality of life which raises questions as to whether it would be in the best interests of the patient to start or continue treatment. It is important to bear in mind that the dying process for patients should be a dignified one.[2]

---

1   HPCSA Guidelines for Good Practice in the Healthcare Professions Booklet 7: *Guidelines for the Withholding and Withdrawing of Treatment* (2016) para 1.1.

2   Ibid para 1.2.

The HPCSA states that any medical intervention where the healthcare professional's primary intention is to end the patient's life is both contrary to the ethics of healthcare and unlawful.[3] Thus, active euthanasia or the wilful act by a healthcare professional to cause the death of a patient is unacceptable even where this is requested by the patient or proxy. The duty of the healthcare professional is to alleviate the suffering of a terminally ill patient. This may be accomplished by withholding or withdrawing treatment, i.e. allowing the natural process of death to follow its course.[4] However, the patient has to be provided with the necessary medication and palliative care in order to alleviate the terminal phase of illness.

Practitioners often express concerns about increasing sedation and pain relief which could result in secondary complications that accelerate death. In situations like this it is recommended that the intention of the management is considered. Where the intention is to relieve suffering and not to accelerate death, this treatment would be both legally and ethically acceptable. This scenario is sometimes referred to as the 'doctrine of double effect'. It has been suggested that legally the term 'double effect' is a misnomer that conflates intention and motive. Legally, such conduct is accepted as lawful because society regards it as such. Although healthcare practitioners have the good motive to relieve suffering, legally they have the 'eventual intention' to end the patient's life, because they know that the patient will die once treatment is withheld or withdrawn.[5]

12.1.1   Consulting the family before withholding or withdrawing treatment

At times, the patient or family may request continued treatment against health advice that considers such treatment to be futile. The HPCSA recommends that the patient or the family is given the choice of transferring to another institution where such treatment is available.[6] If this option is refused and the health team considers treatment to be futile, and this is confirmed by an independent healthcare practitioner, the treating practitioner should go ahead and withhold or withdraw treatment.[7]

Although health practitioners should consult with family members before withholding or withdrawing treatment, 'consult' does not mean that the family members have to consent. For instance, if the prognosis is hopeless and treatment would be futile, and the family refuses to sanction the withholding or withdrawal of treatment, the health practitioners should explain to them that it would be

---

3   Ibid.

4   Ibid para 1.3.

5   DJ McQuoid-Mason 'Withholding or withdrawal of treatment and palliative treatment hastening death: The real reason why doctors are not held legally liable for murder' (2014) 104(2) *SAMJ* 102–103.

6   HPCSA Guidelines for Good Practice in the Healthcare Professions Booklet 7: *Guidelines for the Withholding and Withdrawing of Treatment* (2016) para 2.6.

7   Ibid.

unethical to engage in hopeless treatment and proceed to withhold or withdraw such treatment. The healthcare practitioners may suggest that the family seek legal advice, but the courts are unlikely to sanction futile treatment.

12.1.2 Futility

The notion of futility, while discussed in the HPCSA documents, has not been defined by the HPCSA. The World Medical Association (WMA) has defined 'futile treatment' as treatment that offers no reasonable hope of recovery or improvement, or from which 'the patient is permanently unable to experience any benefit'. It is important to remember that interventions that have 'utility' and benefit the patient could in different circumstances be characterised as 'futile'.[8] Have and Janssens state that 'futile', in the literal sense, could mean 'useless', 'ineffective', 'vain' or 'serving no purpose'.[9] In the healthcare setting, futility can be viewed from the perspective of being 'quantitative', 'qualitative' or both.

12.1.2.1 Quantitative futility

Where futility is quantitative, treatment is unlikely to work because it will have no or very minimal effect, i.e. it is unlikely that the treatment will produce the desired effect on the patient, based on existing scientific knowledge and accepted professional standards. For there to be quantitative futility, the medical treatment must have been found to be useless in the last 100 cases. This could be through personal experience, experiences shared with colleagues or consideration of reported empirical data.[10]

12.1.2.2 Qualitative futility

Qualitative futility will arise when a treatment that has an effect on the patient will not necessarily benefit the patient, bringing into question whether such effect is worth achieving at all. An example of qualitative futility is when treatment results in preserving permanent unconsciousness. The notion of qualitative futility has resulted in considerable debate as it involves a judgement about the quality of life and is hence controversial.[11]

---

8   WMA *Handbook of Medical Ethics* (2015): https://www.wma.net/wp-content/uploads/2016/11/Ethics_manual_3rd_Nov2015_en.pdf (accessed on 23 April 2020); cf DJ McQuoid-Mason 'Emergency medical treatment and 'do not resuscitate' orders: When can they be used?' (2013) 103(4) *SAMJ* 223–225.

9   TH Have and R Janssens 'Futility, limits and palliative care' in HT Have and D Clark (eds) *The Ethics of Palliative Care: European Perspectives* (2002) 212–231.

10 LJ Schneiderman, NS Jecker and AR Jonsen 'Medical futility: Its meaning and ethical implications (1990) 112 *Annals of Internal Medicine* 949–954.

11 TH Have and R Janssens 'Futility, limits and palliative care' in HT Have and D Clark (eds) *The Ethics of Palliative Care: European Perspectives* (2002) 212–231.

It is unethical to extend the life of a dying patient by providing futile treatment for financial gain.[12]

12.2 Murder, euthanasia and physician-assisted dying

Murder is the unlawful and intentional killing of another person, while euthanasia or 'mercy killing' is aimed at allowing hopelessly ill or injured people to die with dignity in order to prevent further suffering.[13] Terminology in the context of euthanasia has evolved to include physician-assisted dying. Physician-assisted dying comprises both physician-assisted suicide (PAS) and euthanasia. In PAS, a patient self-administers lethal drugs supplied by a doctor, and with euthanasia, a doctor administers lethal drugs to a patient at the patient's request. It is important to note the difference between the two with respect to the doctor's role. With PAS, while the doctor facilitates access to lethal medications, the patient plays an active role in terminating his or her own life. So, in PAS, the doctor's role is facilitatory, as compared to euthanasia, where the doctor's role is active.[14]

Both PAS and euthanasia are regarded as murder in South African law (e.g. the administration of a lethal injection).[15] 'Passive euthanasia' occurs where a health professional or member of a patient's family withdraws or withholds treatment from a patient who is suffering from a terminal injury or illness or one that is so serious that the prospects of recovery are nil. Such conduct may not be regarded as murder (e.g. withdrawing feeding from a persistent vegetative state patient).[16]

While still used by the legal fraternity, it is important to point out the problem with the use of the terms 'active' and 'passive' euthanasia. When a decision is made to withhold or withdraw life-sustaining treatments and change the trajectory of management to palliative care, this is only done when a diagnosis of medical futility is arrived at and hence death is the inevitable end result as life runs its natural course. The result of instituting palliative care is that of alleviation of pain and suffering during this period and not death. The intention is to try to make the patient as comfortable as possible in the final stages of life and that he

---

12 Health Professions Council of South Africa Booklet 7: *Guidelines for the Withholding and Withdrawing of Treatment* (2016) para 9.5; cf DJ McQuoid-Mason 'Is it ethically and legally justified for doctors to provide futile medical treatment In patients or their proxies are prepared to pay for it? What should doctors do?' (2017) 107(2) *SAMJ* 108–109.

13 SA Strauss *Doctor, Patient and the Law* 3 ed (1993) 336; M Slabbert and C van der Westhuizen 'Death with dignity in lieu of euthanasia' (2007) 2 *SA Public Law* 366–384.

14 A Dhai 'Physician-assisted dying and palliative care: Understanding the Two' (2015) 8(2) *SAJBL* 2–3.

15 *S v Hartmann* 1975 (3) SA 532 (C); cf *Minister of Justice and Correctional Services v Estate Late James Stransham-Ford* 2017 (3) SA 152 (SCA) para 54. For a general discussion of euthanasia, see Carstens and Pearmain 200–210.

16 *Clarke v Hurst NO* 1992 (4) SA 630 (D).

or she lives in dignity until the very end. When death does occur, it is as part of the natural process or because of the side effects of the treatment to alleviate pain and suffering and not passive mercy killing.[17]

12.2.1 Case studies

In a case where a patient had been in a persistent vegetative state for a period of four years from which there was no prospect of any improvement in his condition and no possibility of recovery, his wife applied for a court order to appoint her as curatrix in order that she could authorise the withdrawal of treatment. She also wanted a court order stating that such withdrawal would not amount to murder. The court appointed the wife as curatrix and gave her the power to withhold agreement to treatment, including nasogastric feeding, and stated that if she did authorise the withholding of treatment she would not be acting unlawfully.[18]

In cases of active euthanasia, even though a person's motive for killing is good, his or her act or omission constitutes murder.[19] Where, however, a person's mental state is so disturbed that he or she acts automatically and involuntarily, the person will not be guilty of murder. For example, where the accused person's mother was suffering from incurable disease, causing unbearable pain, the accused tried all types of medical assistance but none of them alleviated her condition. The accused also tried to persuade a friend to give his mother a fatal injection but the friend refused. Eventually the accused could stand it no longer and in a severe emotional outburst shot his mother in the head and killed her. The court held that the accused person's obsession with 'helping' his mother led to an irresistible impulse to kill her. He had acted automatically and involuntarily, and was therefore acquitted.[20]

Recently, a High Court granted an order allowing a person who was experiencing 'intractable suffering' to commit suicide with the assistance of a medical doctor and stated that the doctor's conduct would not be unlawful on constitutional grounds.[21] The evidence before the court was that the applicant was a highly qualified lawyer who had terminal stage 4 cancer and had tried a number of traditional and other forms of medication, as well as palliative care, but none of these had alleviated his suffering. In his application, he stated that he was fully mentally competent and had only a few weeks left to live. The judge heard

---

17   A Dhai 'Physician-assisted dying and palliative care : Understanding the two' (2015).

18   *Clarke v Hurst NO* 1992 (4) SA 630 (D).

19   *S v Hartmann* 1975 (3) SA 532 (C).

20   *R v Davidow* 1995 (unreported); cf SA Strauss *Doctor, Patient and the Law* 3 ed (1993) 339. See also, *S v McBride* 1979 (4) SA 313 (W).

21   *Stransham-Ford v Minister of Justice and Correctional Services and Others* 2015 (4) SA 50 (GP).

the application, but two hours before he was due to make his order, the applicant died of natural causes. At the time the judge made his order, neither he nor the applicant's lawyers knew that he had passed away. The judge gave his reasons for his judgment after he had learnt of the applicant's death, but decided not to recall his order as he thought that is was matter of great public importance.[22] The appeal court subsequently overruled his judgment on three grounds: (a) the applicant had died before the High Court had given judgment and 'his cause of action ceased to exist'; (b) there was 'no full and proper examination' of the current local and international legal position; and (c) the order was based on incorrect and restricted facts.[23] However, the appeal court left the door open by concluding that 'it cannot be said that in the current state of our law [assisted suicide] is in all circumstances unlawful'.[24] Thus, the original legal position remains that 'active doctor-assisted euthanasia' or 'physician-administered euthanasia' is murder.[25]

12.3 Palliative care

Palliative care, as defined by the World Health Organization, is:

> [an] approach that improves the quality of life of patients and their families facing problems associated with life-threatening illness, through the prevention and relief of suffering, the early identification and impeccable assessment and treatment of pain and other problems, physical, psychosocial and spiritual'.[26]

The intention of palliative care management is neither to hasten nor postpone death but to affirm life and uphold dying as a normal process. It does this by allowing for the provision of relief from pain and other distressing symptoms. It integrates the psychological and spiritual aspects of patient care and offers a support system to help patients live as actively as possible until death by using a team approach to address the needs of patients and their families. Support is provided to families to help them to cope during the patient's illness and in their bereavement, including counselling when required. In this way, it serves to enhance quality of life and positively influence the course of the illness. Management with palliative care should begin early in the course of the illness, together with other therapies, such as chemotherapy or radiation therapy that are

---

22 *Stransham-Ford v Minister of Justice and Correctional Services and Others* 2015 (4) SA 50 (GP).
23 *Minister of Justice and Correctional Services v Estate Late James Stransham-Ford* 2017 (3) SA 152 (SCA) para 5.
24 Ibid para 54.
25 DJ McQuoid-Mason 'Assisted suicide and assisted voluntary euthanasia: *Stransham-Ford* High Court case overruled by the Appeal Court – but the door is left open' (2017) 107(5) *SAMJ* 381–382.
26 WHO definition of palliative care: http://www.who.int/cancer/palliative/en/ (accessed on 5 April 2020).

used to prolong life. Palliative care management includes those investigations needed to understand and manage distressing clinical complications better.[27]

While there remains opposition to physician-assisted dying on grounds of personal morality, it is also essential that the advances in all aspects of palliative care over the past few decades are taken into account. Palliative care is capable of relieving much of the suffering that once accompanied the dying process and the case for legalising physician-assisted dying should be less strong today than it was in the past. It is also essential that the process of physician-assisted dying is understood.

With regard to drugs used in PAS, 9–10 grams of a barbiturate (about 50 times the dose used clinically) is administered. Drugs used in euthanasia are similar to those used in judicial executions in the United States. These are usually a short-acting anaesthetic agent plus pancuronium. The patient is completely paralysed by the pancuronium and then dies of asphyxia. There is no available evidence as to whether the terminally ill patient who is administered euthanasia regains consciousness. However, post-mortem toxicology reports of executed prisoners have shown that drug levels had fallen to a point at which they may have regained a degree of consciousness by the time of death. Because of complete paralysis, official observers would not be able to detect this.[28]

PAS and euthanasia are not without medical complications. There were difficulties in administering the lethal drugs in 10% of PAS and 5% of euthanasias in a Dutch study. Other complications included vomiting and muscle spasms during the process in 7% of PAS and 3% of euthanasias; a long time for death (up to 7 days) in 15% of PAS and 5% of euthanasias. Similar reports of a long interval between ingestion and death have been recorded in Oregon. Six patients who attempted PAS were reported to have re-awoken. None re-attempted PAS.[29]

Vulnerability in this context must also be considered. Not only is it linked to socio-economic factors and other issues like elder abuse and possible coercion by family members, but also to feelings of dependency, loss of independence, inability to communicate and psychological distress.[30] Clinical depression cannot be ignored, whatever the socio-economic status of the patient. One-third of patients who were being prospectively monitored as part of a PAS research project

---

27   Ibid; see also, HPCSA Guidelines for Good Practice in the Healthcare Professions Booklet 17: *Ethical Guidelines on Palliative Care* (2019).
28   LG Koniaris, TA Zimmers, DA Lubarsky and JP Sheldon 'Inadequate anaesthesia in lethal injection for execution' (2005) 5(9468) *Lancet* 1412–1414.
29   DA Jones 'Evidence of the adverse impact in assisted suicide and euthanasia' (2015) 351 *BMJ* H443: http://www.bmj.com/content/351/bmj.h4437/rr-10 (accessed on 1 November 2015).
30   HM Chochinov, KG Wilson, M Enns and S Lander 'Depression hopelessness and suicidal ideation in the terminally ill' (1998) 39(4) *Psychosomatics* 366–370; I Finlay and R George 'Legal physician-assisted suicide in Oregon and The Netherlands: Evidence concerning the impact on patients in vulnerable groups – another perspective on Oregon's data' (2011) 37 *Journal of Medical Ethics* 171–174.

in Oregon and who died after ingesting the lethal drugs, had been suffering from clinical depression. This condition had neither been diagnosed nor referred for expert psychiatric or psychological assessment and treatment.[31] Evidence from research confirms a strong correlation between depression and hopelessness amongst those requesting physician-assisted dying.[32]

While it is important to recognise the patient's right to dignity and the entwining of this right with the right to autonomy as entrenched in the Constitution of South Africa when considering physician-assisted dying, other core matters like the need for advocating for quality palliative care and the importance of taking the social context in the country into account require equal consideration.[33]

12.4 Mentally competent patients

Patients who are legally competent to consent to medical treatment also have legal capacity to refuse it.[34] The courts generally recognise that a mentally competent patient who requests the withdrawal or withholding of medical treatment – even if it may result in death – may do so.[35] It is not regarded as 'doctor-assisted suicide' or 'practitioner-administered suicide'.[36] Although such patients may consent to withdrawal of treatment or the withholding of treatment so that the underlying illness or injury causes their death, they may not consent to active euthanasia as this would be unlawful and could result in the person killing them being convicted of murder.[37]

The National Health Act[38] provides that patients must be informed of their right to refuse health services and of the implications, risks and obligations of such refusal.[39] This means that a refusal of medical treatment by a patient must be an 'informed' refusal. Therefore, if such refusal may result in the patient's death, the patient must be informed not only of the implications and the risks involved in the decision, but also that he or she should take measures regarding his or her estate (e.g. such as making or updating their will) in case he or she dies.

---

31   L Ganzini, ER Goy and K Dobscha 'Prevalence of depression and anxiety in patients requesting physicians' aid in dying: A cross sectional survey' (2008) 337 *BMJ* 1682.

32   KA Smith, TA Harvath, ER Goy and L Ganzini 'Predictors of pursuit of physician-assisted death' (2015) 49(3) *Journal of Pain and Symptom Management* 555–561.

33   A Dhai 'Physician-assisted dying and palliative care: Understanding the two' (2015).

34   *Minister of Justice and Correctional Services v Estate Late James Stransham-Ford* 2017 (3) SA 152 (SCA) para 31.

35   Ibid.

36   Ibid.

37   *Minister of Justice and Correctional Services v Estate Late James Stransham-Ford* 2017 (3) SA 152 (SCA) paras 36 and 40.

38   61 of 2003.

39   Section 6(1)(*d*).

12.5 Mentally incompetent patients

People who have legal authority to consent to medical treatment of mentally incompetent patients also have legal capacity to consent to the withdrawal or withholding of treatment from them – even if it amounts to passive euthanasia.[40] Mentally incompetent patients are unable to understand the nature and effect of the withdrawal or withholding of medical treatment, and therefore may not give a valid consent or refusal of consent regarding medical treatment.

In the case of mentally ill patients, the Mental Health Care Act[41] prescribes the persons who are legally competent to consent to treatment of mentally disabled persons, while the National Health Act provides that if patients cannot give consent, their spouse or partner may do so, or if they are not available, their parent, grandparent, adult child or brother or sister, or any other person authorised by law to do so.[42] The National Health Act also allows patients who might become mentally incompetent during a medical procedure to appoint a proxy in advance (in writing) who can make decisions on their behalf while they are incompetent to do so.[43] This is a form of 'substituted judgement' which occurs when an incompetent patient has not made his or her treatment wishes known while he or she was still competent, and an appointed person, usually a member of the family, is authorised to make the necessary treatment or refusal of treatment choice on behalf of the patient when the latter becomes incompetent.[44]

12.6 'Living wills'

Previously competent patients can also provide for decision making in advance of their becoming incompetent by using advance directives such as 'living wills'. A 'living will' is an advance directive that states that if at any time a person suffers from an incurable disease or injury which cannot be successfully treated, life-sustaining treatment should be withheld or withdrawn and the patient left to die naturally. A 'living will' takes the form of a written document in which the maker states that he or she is of sound mind, and which is signed by the person making it in the presence of two witnesses who also sign the will in the presence of the maker and each other.[45]

---

40 cf *Clarke v Hurst NO* 1992 (4) SA 630 (D).
41 Act 17 of 2002.
42 Section 1, definition of 'user'.
43 Act 61 of 2003 s 7(1)(*a*)(i).
44 cf *Clarke v Hurst NO* 1992 (4) SA 630 (D); *Airedale NHS Trust v Bland* [1993] 1 All ER 821 (HL), where the courts authorised the 'substituted judgment'.
45 SA Strauss *Doctor, Patient and the Law* 3 ed (1993) 344–347.

12.6.1 Ethical aspects of 'living wills'

The living will furthers the ethical principle of autonomy. However, some healthcare practitioners are reluctant to recognise 'living wills' because they fear that the patient might have changed his or her mind, or because legal opinion is divided with regard to the validity and acceptance of the living will currently in law. Nonetheless, if there is clear evidence that the 'will' reflects the patient's current wishes, the practitioner should respect them.[46] Furthermore, the HPCSA states that patients should be given the opportunity and be encouraged to indicate their wishes regarding further treatment.[47] The World Medical Association Declaration of Venice on Terminal Illness also requires doctors to recognise the rights of patients to develop written advance directives.[48] In addition, the National Patients' Rights Charter[49] states that patients should inform healthcare practitioners concerning their wishes regarding death.

Patients should place in writing their directives for future care in possible critical circumstances (e.g. permanent coma or terminal illness) which can be conveniently done in an appropriately drafted 'living will' which may be used for this purpose. It is also recommended that patients should be given the opportunity to reconsider their directives from time to time and to alter instructions, should they wish to do so. While legal opinion in the country is divided with regard to the validity of the 'living will', ethical guidance for the professions from the HPCSA is unequivocal as to the recognition and acceptability of the document.[50] According to HPCSA: 'Where a patient lacks the capacity to decide, healthcare practitioners must respect any valid advance refusal of treatment'.[51]

---

46 Strauss *Doctor, Patient* 344–7; DJ McQuoid-Mason 'Living wills' *Continuing Medical Education* (January 1993) 59–64.

47 Health Professions Council of South Africa Booklet 7: *Guidelines for the Withholding and Withdrawing of Treatment* (2016) para 2.3.

48 World Medical Association *Declaration on Terminal Illness* (1983) revised at Pilanesburg, South Africa (2006) Principle 8.

49 National Patients' Rights Charter: https://www.safmh.org.za/documents/policies-and-legislations/Patient%20Rights%20Charter.pdf (accessed on 11 June 2020).

50 HPCSA Guidelines for Good Practice in the Healthcare Professions Booklet 7: *Guidelines for the Withholding and Withdrawing of Treatment* (2016) para 2.3.

51 Ibid para 8.2.1.

12.6.2 *Concerns about and advantages of 'living wills'*

12.6.2.1 Concerns

The following concerns about 'living wills' have been expressed:[52]

(a) The patient, when drafting the 'living will', may have done so without knowing the exact circumstances that would exist when the will is required to be activated.

(b) Under normal circumstances it cannot be expected that a person who is healthy when making the decision about a 'living will', will take into account all the factors that would have influenced the decision if it was made at a time of actual illness or injury.

(c) The document may be too specific and hence fail to cover all circumstances.

(d) The document may be too general and hence cause problems of inter-pretation.

(e) Problems could arise as to the exact time at which the document should come into force, what the criteria should be and who should decide that the criteria have been met.

(f) The attending practitioner may have difficulty in ascertaining whether the document has been revoked since being written and hence difficulties may arise about accepting the document at face value.

Some other practical concerns are:

(a) 'living wills' are often not available in emergency situations;

(b) 'living wills' need to be updated in line with advances in medical technology; and

(c) people sometimes forget that they have made a 'living will'.

The above difficulties can be overcome by patients keeping copies of 'living wills' in their wallets or ensuring that their doctor has a copy of their most recent one.

12.6.2.2 Advantages

The advantages of living wills are as follows:[53]

(a) Knowing the wishes of a loved one makes it easier for proxies to make decisions.

---

52   SA Law Commission *Euthanasia and the Artificial Preservation of Life* Working Paper 53, Project 86 (1994) 163–164.
53   Ibid.

(b) Patients feel secure that they will not be unnecessarily kept alive during the terminal phase of an illness or will not suffer extreme pain and suffering in situations where the prognosis is hopeless.

(c) Patients are secure in the knowledge that where they have little chance of regaining mental competence after an accident, they will not be resuscitated.

(d) The psychological well-being of many elderly persons who witness the deaths of their friends and spouses on a regular basis is assured by the knowledge that their deaths will not be unnecessarily prolonged.

12.6.3 The SA Law Commission's recommendations on euthanasia and end-of-life decisions

In 1994, the SA Law Commission proposed a Euthenasia Act which was never implemented. The proposed Act would:

(a) define the meaning of a 'terminal illness';

(b) recognise a written advance directive regarding the cessation of medical treatment in cases of terminal illness;

(c) recognise an 'enduring power of attorney' authorising a person to make decisions concerning medical treatment or its cessation in the event of terminal illness;

(d) recognise that a power of attorney endures even if the patient becomes mentally incompetent;

(e) recognise a court order as a remedy in the absence of an advance directive or power of attorney in the case of terminally ill patients; and

(f) recognise instances in which the head of a medical institution may, in the absence of a directive from the patient, or the patient's agent, or of a court order, decide to discontinue the treatment of a terminally ill patient.[54]

The proposed Euthenasia Act defined 'terminal illness' as an illness or injury which in the opinion of at least two competent medical practitioners:

(a) will inevitably result in the death of the person named (the patient) and which is causing the patient severe suffering; or

(b) is causing the patient to be in a persistent, irreversible, unconscious condition with the result that no meaningful existence is possible for the patient.[55]

---

54   SA Law Commission *Euthanasia and the Artificial Preservation of Life* Working Paper 53, Project 86 (1994) 54–58.

55   Section 1 Draft Euthanasia Act, SA Law Commission *Euthanasia* (1994) 54.

In a subsequent paper in 1997, the Law Commission recommended that doctor-assisted suicide should be legalised.[56] Doctor-assisted suicide has since been condemned as unethical by the World Medical Association's Declaration of Venice on Terminal Illness,[57] but might be recognised in future in South Africa if an appropriate persuasive case is brought to court – although the courts would prefer parliament to pass a law in this regard.[58]

12.7 The Constitution and assisted voluntary euthanasia

The Constitution provides for a right to privacy,[59] right to freedom and security of the person,[60] and a right to respect for and protection of dignity[61] which may outweigh the right to life[62] in euthanasia cases.[63] This was the basis of the High Court decision allowing 'doctor-assisted euthanasia'[64] that was overruled by the appeal court.[65] Either parliament or the Constitutional Court will finally have to determine the issue.[66]

12.8 Death and dead bodies

12.8.1 Post-mortems and inquests[67]

As has been mentioned, the National Health Act defines death as 'brain death'.[68] The main law relating to post-mortems and inquests is to be found in the Inquests Act.[69] Certain aspects of post-mortems are also regulated by the National

---

56 Section 5(1) Draft End of Life Decisions Act, 1997 SA Law Commission *Euthanasia and the Artificial Preservation of Life* Paper 71 Project 86 (1997) 99–100.

57 World Medical Association *Declaration on Terminal Illness* (1983) revised at Pilanesburg, South Africa (2006) Preface para 1.

58 *Minister of Justice and Correctional Services v Estate Late James StranshamFord* 2017 (3) SA 152 (SCA) para 54; cf DJ McQuoid-Mason 'Assisted suicide and assisted voluntary euthanasia: Stransham-Ford High Court case overruled by the Appeal Court – but the door is left open' (2017).

59 Constitution s 14.

60 Section 12(1).

61 Section 10.

62 Section 11.

63 See L Jordaan 'The right to die with dignity: A consideration of the constitutional arguments' (2009) 72 *THRHR* 192–216, 374–393; cf *In re Quinlan* 429 US 922 (1976) (right to privacy); *Cruzan v Director, Missouri Dept of Health* 110 S Ct 2841 (1990) (right to bodily integrity).

64 *Stransham-Ford v Minister of Justice and Correctional Services and Others* 2015 (4) SA 50 (GP).

65 *Minister of Justice and Correctional Services v Estate Late James Stransham-Ford* 2017 (3) SA 152 (SCA).

66 cf DJ McQuoid-Mason 'Assisted suicide and assisted voluntary euthanasia: Stransham-Ford High Court case overruled by the Appeal Court – but the door is left open' (2017).

67 See generally, CW van Wyk and M Slabbert 'Post-mortems, burials, anatomy' WA Joubert and JA Faris (eds) *The Law of South Africa* 20(2) 2 ed (2008) paras 250–274.

68 61 of 2003 s 1.

69 58 of 1959.

Health Act),[70] the Correctional Services Act,[71] the Births and Deaths Registration Act,[72] the Occupational Injuries and Diseases in Mines and Works Act,[73] the Health Professions Act[74] and the Dissolution of Marriages on the Presumption of Death Act.[75]

12.8.2 Burials[76]

The law relating to burials is governed by the different provincial ordinances and some parliamentary statutes[77] such as the Births and Deaths Registration Act, the National Heritage Resources Act,[78] the Commonwealth War Graves Act[79] and the National Health Act.

12.8.3 Anatomy[80]

The law relating to anatomy, in particular organ and tissue donations and transplants, is regulated by the National Health Act.[81]

Some questions on death and dying

Consider the following scenario and decide what the healthcare practitioner should do:

> A patient who is terminally ill has made a living will in which he states that he does not want to be kept alive if the prognosis for his illness is hopeless. The patient lapses into a permanent vegetative state but his family request that he be kept alive. Can the practitioners involved in the patient's management rely on the living will to override the wishes of the patient's family? Why or why not?

---

70   61 of 2003.
71   111 of 1998.
72   51 of 1992.
73   78 of 1973.
74   56 of 1974.
75   23 of 1979.
76   See generally, CW van Wyk and M Slabbert 'Post-mortems, burials, anatomy' WA Joubert and JA Faris (eds) *The Law of South Africa* 20(2) 2 ed (2008) paras 281–314.
77   See M Slabbert 'Burial or cremation – who decides' (2016) 49(2) *De Jure* 230–241.
78   25 of 1999.
79   8 of 1992.
80   See generally, CW van Wyk and M Slabbert 'Post-mortems, burials, anatomy' WA Joubert and JA Faris (eds) *The Law of South Africa* 20(2) 2 ed (2008) paras 317–349.
81   See above Chapter 8.

CHAPTER 13

HIV and AIDS

David McQuoid-Mason and Ames Dhai

By the end of this chapter readers will be able to:

1. Discuss some of the ethical challenges associated with the HIV and AIDS epidemic.

2. Explain how people living with HIV and AIDS are protected against unfair discrimination.

3. Describe the rights of people living with HIV and AIDS to access healthcare.

4. Explain when people who intentionally infect others with HIV may be held criminally liable.

5. Explain when people who negligently or intentionally infect others with HIV may be held civilly liable.

6. Explain how HIV may legally affect medical personnel and hospitals.

7. Describe the challenges associated with disclosure of HIV status to children.

13.1   Introduction

Since the start of the HIV and AIDS epidemic, an estimated 74.9 million people have become infected with HIV, and 32 million people have died of AIDS-related illnesses. In 2018, 770 000 people died of AIDS-related illnesses. This is 55% less than the peak of 1.7 million in 2004 and 1.4 million in 2010. Most people living with HIV live in low- and middle-income countries, and an estimated 68% live in sub-Saharan Africa, of which 20.6 million live in East and southern Africa, which saw 800 000 new HIV infections in 2018.[1]

Thus, HIV and AIDS have overwhelmed the African continent over the past decades. From a global perspective, sub-Saharan Africa bears the brunt of the HIV epidemic,[2] and this figure is growing by the day. The epidemic is fuelled

---

1   https://www.avert.org/global-hiv-and-aids-statistics (accessed on 29 March 2020).
2   AA Van Niekerk and LM Kopelman (eds) (2005) *Ethics and AIDS in Africa: The Challenge to Our Thinking* (2005) 53–70.

by the many ethical, social and political complexities that make up Africa. In turn, the pandemic has also resulted in the many ethical, social and political complexities with which Africa, including South Africa, grapples.

13.2   HIV infection: Ethical complexities and challenges

When the first cases of AIDS were discovered among homosexual men in the United States, there was the initial misunderstanding that AIDS was a disease that affected only homosexuals. However, today the perception has shifted to AIDS being a 'black' disease or 'African epidemic',[3] leading to discriminatory attitudes, especially towards people in sub-Saharan Africa.

AIDS management has thus far been associated with significant trade-offs. AIDS is usually singled out for special attention and focus, over and above other life-threatening diseases like tuberculosis and malaria, despite the link between AIDS and these other diseases being apparent. Not only does AIDS constitute a public health crisis, but it also severely threatens economic livelihood,[4] with infection with HIV and AIDS being the greatest threat to life, freedom and the pursuit of happiness and prosperity.[5]

Gender inequality is still pervasive and studies have demonstrated that women with violent or controlling male partners are at increased risk of HIV infection. An important influence on sexual behaviour and HIV risk is the unequal distribution of sexual power between men and women, and the subordination of women's needs and rights. Norms around intimate partner violence perpetuate coercive sex and sex without condoms. In sub-Saharan Africa, four in five new infections are among girls aged 15–19 years, and young women aged 15–24 years are twice as likely as men to be living with HIV.[6]

The interactive and synergistic effects of poverty, instability, gender inequality, insufficient education and sexual oppression directly determine the vulnerability of women to infection with HIV.[7] More women than men in Africa are tested for HIV as a result of women attending antenatal and family planning clinics. Hence, it is not unusual for more women to be aware of their HIV status as compared to men. The challenge faced by healthcare professionals is whether or not to inform the woman's partner of her HIV status. While compelling arguments based on utilitarian grounds underscore the importance of breaching the chain of

---

3   See generally, AIDS Law Project and AIDS Legal Network *HIV/AIDS and the Law: A Resource Manual* 2 ed (2001).

4   N Nattrass *The Moral Economy of AIDS in South Africa* (2004) 13–40.

5   K de Cock, D Mbori-Ngacha and E Marum 'Shadow on the continent: public health and HIV/AIDS in Africa in the 21st century' (2002) *Lancet* 360.

6   https://www.avert.org/global-hiv-and-aids-statistics (accessed on 29 March 2020).

7   SS Abdool Karim and Q Abdool Karim (eds) *HIV/AIDS in South Africa* (2005) 143–182.

transmission of HIV necessitating partner notification, it is questionable whether this could be justified in the background context of the disempowered woman, where such disclosure could have devastating psychosocial consequences both for her and her family.[8]

Moreover, fear and disgrace have resulted in an HIV and AIDS stigma which has been a pervasive dimension of the disease since the beginning of the pandemic. In 1998, when Gugu Dlamini, a young woman in South Africa, revealed her HIV status, she was stoned to death.[9] This attitude, even today, is pervasive, albeit covertly. The reality is that people are afraid to speak openly of their HIV status. Fear, stigma and shame are powerful deterrents to health-seeking behaviours, especially among those suspecting that they may already be infected with HIV.

Healthcare practitioners, as patients' fiduciaries, have a primary responsibility to their patient. Their true ethics are exposed in the way they balance their own interests against those of the patient.[10] Within the socio-political context of the disease, there has been a strong emphasis on human rights issues, especially in relation to discrimination. However, discrimination against individuals with HIV or AIDS remains pervasive, even within the scientific community, where the risk of infection has resulted in a reluctance to treat them. Besides moral arguments, scientific evidence has not been able to support such a position.[11]

13.3   Protection against unfair discrimination

The Constitution provides for the right to equality before the law and equal protection of the law,[12] and prevents people from being unfairly discriminated against on the grounds of sexual orientation or disability, etc.[13] The Constitution also applies to people living with HIV and AIDS, and protects them against unfair discrimination. While HIV infection itself may not constitute a 'disability', which is a listed ground in the Constitution, illnesses arising from full-blown AIDS could constitute a 'disability', like any other illness which makes it impossible for a person to hold down a job. If a person can show that he or she has been discriminated against on one of the listed grounds in the Constitution, it will be presumed that the discrimination was unfair. If the grounds for the discrimination are not listed in Constitution, the presumption will not apply, but the aggrieved person may still prove that the discrimination was unfair.

---

8   See below para 13.7.
9   See generally, the *SA Health Review* (1999).
10   ED Pellegrino 'Altruism, self-interest and medical ethics'. (1987) 259 *JAMA* 1939–1940.
11   CP Szabo, A Dhai and M Veller 'HIV-positive status among surgeons – an ethical dilemma' (2006) 96 *SAMJ* 1072–1075.
12   Constitution s 9(1).
13   Constitution s 9(3) and (4).

'lhe courts have held that people living with HIV or AIDS may not be unfairly discriminated against. For example, it has been held that it is unfair discrimination to unjustifiably refuse to employ a person who is HIV infected.[14] The same would apply if a person who was HIV infected, and whose condition did not affect his or her capacity to work, was dismissed from employment merely because of the HIV status.[15]

The Promotion of Equality and Prevention of Unfair Discrimination Act[16] goes further than the Constitution and lists discrimination on the grounds of HIV and AIDS as one of the listed grounds when unfairness will be presumed once the patient proves that he or she has been discriminated against. As has been mentioned above, this does not apply in the case of the provisions in the Constitution. According to the Constitution, people living with HIV and AIDS would not be able to rely on a presumption of unfairness unless they can show that they were suffering from a disability (one of the listed grounds). However, if they can show that they have acquired full-blown AIDS, which has become a disability (one of the listed grounds), unfairness would be presumed once they have established that they have been discriminated against.

It would be unfair discrimination to refuse to treat patients infected with HIV- or AIDS-related illnesses if there were no reasonable and justifiable reason for doing so.[17] Therefore, medical aid schemes are no longer allowed to exclude people living with HIV or AIDS from membership or to make them pay higher premiums.

13.4   Access to healthcare

The Constitution provides that everyone has a right to healthcare services (including reproductive healthcare).[18] People living with HIV or AIDS have a right of access to healthcare like everyone else. Given the extent of the HIV and AIDS pandemic in South Africa, it can be argued that there is a special duty on the state to improve the range of healthcare services available to people living with HIV or AIDS. Children have a right to basic healthcare services[19] – not just a right of access to healthcare services. Therefore, children living with HIV or AIDS may not be denied basic healthcare services.

---

14   *Hoffmann v South African Airways* 2001 (1) SA 1 (CC).
15   See N Arendse 'Employment, HIV and AIDS: Proposals for law reform' (1993) 9 *SA Journal on Human Rights* 89–104.
16   4 of 2000.
17   MA Dada and DJ McQuoid-Mason (eds) *Introduction to Medico-Legal Practice* (2001) 31–32.
18   Constitution s 27(1)(*a*).
19   Constitution s 28(1)(*c*).

The Constitutional Court has held that there is a duty on the state to provide pregnant mothers with antiretroviral treatment to prevent mother-to-child transmission of HIV.[20] It has been suggested that there is also a constitutional duty on the state to provide antiretroviral drugs to rape survivors, because such persons qualify for 'emergency medical treatment'.[21]

13.5   HIV and AIDS and the criminal law

13.5.1   Assault

Assault is the unlawful and intentional use of force on another person or making such person believe that force will be used on them.[22] Thus, this would apply where a person unlawfully and intentionally infects or threatens to infect a person with a disease or illness. A person who unlawfully and intentionally infects a person or threatens to infect a person with HIV will be guilty of assault if the victim contracts the disease but has not died. For example, if a person knowingly suffering from HIV or AIDS does not warn a sexual partner that he or she has the disease and has unprotected sex with such partner, the person will be guilty of assault if the partner becomes infected with the disease and is still alive.[23]

13.5.2   Murder

Murder is the unlawful and intentional killing of another human being.[24] Therefore, if the assault on the victim by the person living with HIV or AIDS results in the victim becoming infected with HIV and dying from an AIDS-related illness, the assailant may be found guilty of murder. In cases of reckless behaviour, where a person unlawfully and recklessly infects another with HIV, not caring whether or not that other person contracts the disease and dies, the person concerned will also be guilty of murder. In such a case, the person has the legal or eventual intention to kill the person infected – rather than the direct intention to do so.[25]

---

20   *Minister of Health v Treatment Action Campaign (Case No 2)* 2002 (5) SA 721 (CC).

21   DJ McQuoid-Mason, A Dhai and J Moodley 'Rape survivors and the right to emergency medical treatment to prevent HIV infection' (2003) 93 *SAMJ* 41.

22   cf J Burchell *Principles of Criminal Law* 3ed (2006) 667.

23   MA Dada and DJ McQuoid-Mason *Introduction to Medico-Legal Practice* (2001) 29–30.

24   J Burchell *Principles of Criminal Law* 3ed (2006) 667.

25   See above para 4.3.

13.5.3 Attempted murder

Furthermore, a person who unlawfully and intentionally or recklessly exposes another to HIV without infecting them may be guilty of attempted murder. In 2013, an HIV-positive AIDS counsellor who was convicted of attempted murder for having unprotected sex with his unsuspecting girlfriend was sentenced to six years in prison. The judge stated the following:

> It was sufficient for a conviction on the count of attempted murder to establish that the appellant, knowing that he was HIV-positive, engaged in sexual intercourse with the complainant, whom he knew to be HIV-negative, without any preventative measures.[26]

13.5.4 Culpable homicide

Culpable homicide is the unlawful, negligent killing of another human being.[27] Therefore, a person who unlawfully and negligently infects another with HIV, which results in the latter's death, may be found guilty of culpable homicide.[28]

Negligence means that a reasonable person in the position of the wrongdoer would have foreseen the likelihood of infecting the other person with HIV and would have taken steps to prevent such infection from occurring – but the person concerned failed to take such steps.[29] For instance, a person living with HIV or AIDS who has sexual intercourse with a person without using a condom and without warning that person, with the result that the person contracts the disease and dies, will be guilty of culpable homicide.[30]

In criminal prosecutions for infecting others with HIV, it is difficult to prove causation, because there may be no evidence regarding the status of the victim before the alleged assault. To overcome this, in some American and Australian states, the crime of 'knowingly and wilfully exposing another to HIV or AIDS' has been created. In such circumstances a crime is committed even if the victim does not become infected.[31] Zimbabwe has passed a similar law.[32]

---

26   SAPA *HIV+ man loses appeal over unprotected sex*: https://www.iol.co.za/news/hiv-man-loses-appeal-over-unprotected-sex-1561786 (accessed on 29 March 2020).
27   J Burchell *Principles of Criminal Law* 3ed (2006) 667.
28   MA Dada and DJ McQuoid-Mason *Introduction to Medico-Legal Practice* (2001) 29.
29   See above para 4.3.
30   MA Dada and DJ McQuoid-Mason *Introduction to Medico-Legal Practice* (2001) 29.
31   M Kirby 'AIDS and the law' (1993) 9 *SA Journal on Human Rights* 15–16.
32   Criminal Law Amendment Act 1996 s 3.

13.6   HIV and AIDS and the civil law

As has been previously mentioned, there are two types of civil actions:

(a) Intentional or negligent acts or omissions which result in physical injuries or death and a claim for pecuniary loss

(b) Intentional acts or omissions which result in infringements of a person's dignity, privacy or reputation that cause sentimental damages.[33]

A person who negligently infects a person who does not die cannot be charged with assault, because the person's action is not intentional, but he or she may be sued civilly. Thus a woman patient was able to recover damages when she was infected by paramedics who had attended to an HIV-positive patient who was bleeding at the scene of an accident, and negligently did not take the necessary precautions to ensure that the plaintiff was not infected by the HIV-infected blood of the other patient when they treated her.[34]

13.6.1   Actions for pecuniary loss

In actions for pecuniary loss (losses that can be accurately measured in terms of money) arising from physical injuries or death, infected persons or their dependants must prove intention or negligence by the wrongdoer. The requirement of intention or negligence in civil cases is the same as in criminal actions.

In cases where a person living with HIV or AIDS has negligently infected another, the test is whether a person in the position of the infected person would have foreseen the possibility of harm and taken steps to guard against the other person becoming infected (e.g. by avoiding exchanging body fluids; using a condom; informing the other party about the disease; informing recipients of blood or semen or organs; subjecting him- or herself to a blood test after high-risk activities; or monitoring the foetus of a mother suffering from HIV or AIDS). Persons who are not living with HIV but who negligently infect others, such as healthcare personnel, including paralegals, with infected fluids may also be held liable.[35]

It would be a good defence for persons living with HIV or AIDS if the person infected by him or her knew that such person had HIV or AIDS and had consented to the risk of infection (e.g. by not insisting on the use of a condom). The damages awarded against persons living with HIV or AIDS would be reduced if the person infected by them was contributorily negligent (e.g. by

---

33   See above para 4.3.

34   *Franks v MEC for the Department of Health for the Province of KwaZulu-Natal* [2010] ZAKZPHC 1: http://www.saflii.org/za/cases/ZAKZPHC/2010/1.html (accessed on 29 March 2020).

35   Ibid.

sharing a needle for drug injections, sharing razors, sharing toothbrushes or using untested blood).[36]

Where people living with HIV or AIDS cause the death of persons infected by them, the dependants of the latter (e.g. widows and children), may sue for loss of support, while the deceased's estates may sue for funeral and hospital expenses.[37]

13.6.2 Actions for sentimental damages

Where a person has intentionally infringed the dignity, reputation or privacy of another person, the latter will be entitled to claim sentimental damages. A person's privacy may be invaded where his or her HIV status is disclosed to third parties without his or her consent.[38] A person's privacy may also be invaded if his or her blood is tested for HIV without his or her consent.[39]

In South Africa, there is a move towards mass testing of people as a strategy towards HIV prevention. Other prevention strategies include wide-scale male circumcision (of both adults and infants)[40] and a shift in terminology from voluntary counselling and testing (VCT) to HIV counselling and testing (HCT). In addition, discussion and debate continue with regard to routine and compulsory testing for HIV in pregnant women. However, in all situations, ethical and legal principles and rules, and constitutional rights in respect of consent and confidentiality still apply. Moreover, circumcisions should not be viewed as a panacea for HIV transmission, and caution should prevail in respect of risk-taking behaviour.

The requirement of a court order to authorise HIV testing of employees in terms of the Employment Equity Act[41] does not apply to anonymous or voluntary HIV status testing of employees.[42]

13.7 Legal aspects regarding HIV and medical personnel and hospitals

Medical personnel who negligently or intentionally infect others with HIV may be held criminally or civilly liable depending on the circumstances. If medical personnel infect others with HIV while they are acting in the course and scope of

---

36   MA Dada and DJ McQuoid-Mason *Introduction to Medico-Legal Practice* (2001) 30.
37   Ibid.
38   *Jansen van Vuuren v Kruger* 1993 (4) SA 842 (A).
39   *C v Minister of Correctional Services* 1996 (4) SA 292 (T).
40   cf DJ McQuoid-Mason 'Is the mass circumcision drive in KwaZulu-Natal involving neonates and children less than 16 years of age legal? What should doctors do?' (2013) 103(5) *SAMJ* 283–284.
41   55 of 1998.
42   *Irvin and Johnson Ltd v Trawler and Line Fishing Union* 2003 (3) SA 212 (LC).

their employment, their employers as well as themselves will be liable to persons who are infected with the illness.[43] Hospitals, doctors and blood banks will be liable for the wrongs of their employees and servants acting in the course and scope of their employment.

Medical personnel or hospitals that negligently test the blood or body fluids of people living with HIV or AIDS and do not take 'universal precautions' in situations where their staff or patients may be subject to the risk of HIV or AIDS will be liable to people infected as a result of such negligence. According to the National Health Act, there is a duty on healthcare providers to protect healthcare personnel from disease transmission.[44] This provision imposes a duty on hospitals working under conditions where medical personnel or staff are at risk concerning HIV to take proper precautions to protect staff and patients from the danger of transmission of HIV (e.g. through infected body fluids or contaminated needles and equipment).[45]

13.7.1   HIV and consent

Hospitals and medical personnel should not test the blood of patients without their consent and providing individual pre- and post-test counselling, as this would be regarded as an interference with the patient's personality rights, more particularly with their right to privacy.[46] If a medical practitioner knows that a person is infected with HIV and that the person will not allow the doctor to inform a fellow healthcare practitioner directly involved in the care of the patient, or a sexual partner, then there is an ethical duty on the doctor to do so. The doctor should first attempt to obtain the consent of the patient by counselling the person before making any such disclosure.[47]

State health employees cannot refuse to treat HIV- or AIDS-related diseases. HIV is a 'communicable disease' like cholera, chicken pox, etc. and must be reported to the Regional Director of Health. It has not been made a 'notifiable disease' because of the fear of driving it underground. It could be argued that mentally ill patients infected with HIV are a danger to others and should be reported to the police.

In terms of section 130(1) of the Children's Act,[48] a child may be tested for HIV only if (a) it is in the best interests of the child and with informed consent

---

43   *Franks v MEC for the Department of Health for the Province of KwaZulu-Natal* [2010] ZAKZPHC 1: http://www.saflii.org/za/cases/ZAKZPHC/2010/1.html (accessed on 29 March 2020).
44   Section 20(3)(*b*).
45   MA Dada and DJ McQuoid-Mason *Introduction to Medico-Legal Practice* (2001) 31.
46   *C v Minister of Correctional Services* 1996 (4) SA 292 (T).
47   cf *Jansen van Vuuren v Kruger* 1993 (4) SA 842 (A).
48   38 of 2005 s 130(1).

from the child or the person legally able to give consent on the child's behalf; or (b) if the test is necessary to establish whether, during a medical procedure, a healthcare practitioner (HCP) may have contracted HIV because of contact with any substance from the body of the child that may transmit HIV; or (c) when the court has authorised the test to establish whether any other person may have contracted HIV because of contact with any substance from the body of the child that may transmit HIV.

Generally, testing is considered to be in the child's best interests if it advances the child's physical and emotional welfare, such as enabling the child to access appropriate treatment, and encouraging risk reduction.[49]

For the child's consent to be ethically and legally valid, the child must not only have pertinent knowledge of the illness, but must understand and appreciate the benefits, harms, risks and social implications of testing. This includes the ability to foresee the possible outcomes and implications of testing.[50] Cognitive maturity, emotional stability and willingness to accept support are necessary for this. Emotional stability will allow for the child to cope with a positive test result.[51]

Factors to be considered when assessing capacity to give informed consent include (a) the child's behaviour, mental state and ability to engage with the counseling process; (b) the child's ability to get across to the HCP a basic understanding of HIV, testing and its implications; (c) the ability of the child to think rationally through concerns; (d) the emotional state of the child; and (e) the child's voluntariness to test.[52]

13.8 HIV and confidentiality

People living with HIV or AIDS have the same right to confidentiality as anyone else[53] – unless their condition poses a threat to the life or health of endangered third parties or it is in the public interest to invade their right to privacy.[54] The court has pointed out that disclosure of an individual's HIV status, in

---

49   K Grant, R Lazarus, A Strode, H van Rooyen and M Vujovic *Legal, ethical and counselling issues related to HIV testing of children. HIV counselling and testing of children: Implementation guidelines* (2012): http://www.hsrc.ac.za/uploads/pageContent/3295/HIV%20counselling%20and%20testing%20 of%20children%20-%20Implementation%20gui.pdf (accessed on 5 May 2020); HE van Rooyen, AE Strode and CM Slack 'HIV testing of children is not simple for health providers and researchers: Legal and policy frameworks guidance in South Africa' (2016) 106(5) SAMJ 451–453. doi:10.7196/SAMJ.2016v106i5.10484 (accessed on 5 April 2020).

50   DJ McQuoid-Mason and AM Dhai 'Consent' in A Dhai and D McQuoid-Mason *Bioethics, Human Rights and Health Law. Principles and Practice* (2011) 69–91.

51   See footnote 32 above.

52   Ibid.

53   See above para 7.2.

54   *NM v Smith* 2007 3 SA 250 (CC) 263.

South Africa, should be protected against the potential intolerance and discrimination that may result from such disclosure.[55] Wrongful publication of a person's HIV status is a breach of the right to privacy.[56]

13.8.1 Children and confidentiality in respect of their HIV status

Special provisions in the National Health Act[57] deal with children and the confidentiality of their HIV status.[58] Disclosures concerning their status may only be made (a) by persons carrying out their powers and duties in terms of the Act or any other law; (b) when it is necessary for the purposes of carrying out the provisions of the Act; (c) for the purposes of legal proceedings; or (d) in terms of a court order.[59]

In addition, children who are legally able to consent, or persons authorised by the Act to consent on their behalf, may consent to disclosure of information about their HIV status. Children may consent to disclosure of their HIV status if they are (a) 12 years of age or older; or (b) under the age of 12 years and are of sufficient maturity to understand the benefits, risks and social implications of such disclosures.[60]

If the child is under the age of 12 years and is not of sufficient maturity to understand the benefits, risks and social implications of such a disclosure, the following may consent to disclosures concerning his or her HIV status:

(a) The parent or caregiver[61]

(b) A designated child protection organisation arranging the placement of the child[62]

(c) The superintendent or person in charge of a hospital, if the child has no parent or caregiver, and there is no designated child protection organisation arranging the placement of the child[63]

(d) A children's court, if consent is unreasonably withheld and disclosure is in the best interests of the child, or the child or the parent or caregiver of the child is incapable of giving consent.

---

55   Ibid.
56   *NM v Smith* 2007 3 SA 250 (CC) 264.
57   61 of 2003.
58   Section 133.
59   Section 133(1).
60   Section 133(2)(*a*).
61   Section 133(2)(*b*).
62   Section 133(2)(*c*).
63   Section 133(2)(*d*).

13.9 Does the patient have a right to know the practitioner's HIV status?

A highly contentious issue with regard to informed consent and patient autonomy is whether it would be necessary to inform the patient of the practitioner's HIV status where the latter is HIV positive. Does the patient have a right to know the practitioner's HIV status? If so, what about the practitioner's rights to autonomy and confidentiality? While the initial focus regarding risk in the healthcare setting was protective of the practitioner, awareness of the emergence of the HIV-positive practitioner has broadened the scope of such concerns to include patient safety.[64] Since the beginning of the AIDS crisis, there have been only a few possible cases of transmission from the practitioner to the patient and this was, in the main, in the much-publicised Florida (USA) case.[65] This seminal case shifted concerns towards practitioner–patient transmission. However, analysis of the case reveals problems with infection control and universal precautions rather than practitioner–patient transmission.

Estimates of the chance of a patient contracting HIV from invasive procedures have been determined by the US Centers for Disease Control (CDC) as 1:263 000 to 2.6 million from dental surgery in the decade before 1991, without universal precautions being applied.[66] Research into transmission rates from known HIV-positive practitioners to patients established a zero transmission rate both in the case of surgeons and dental workers.[67] Besides, with effective antiretroviral treatment now available, the perceived risks to patients would be further reduced.[68]

The HPCSA in its latest guidelines on ethical practice provides that restrictions that cannot be scientifically justified should not be imposed on HIV-infected healthcare practitioners. However, universal precautions should always be used when undertaking invasive procedures in order to minimise transmission from healthcare practitioners to patients. It further states that patients should be made aware by healthcare practitioners that HIV infection can affect everybody, including healthcare practitioners. The latter are not obliged to disclose their HIV status to an employer.[69]

---

64 CP Szabo, A Dhai and M Veller 'HIV-positive status among surgeons – an ethical dilemma' (2006) 96 *SAMJ* 1072–1075.

65 EM Beltrami, IT Williams, CN Shapiro CN and ME Chamberland 'Risk and management of blood-borne infections in health care workers' *Clinical Microbiol Review* (2000) 13 385–407.

66 Centers for Disease Control 'Recommendation for preventing transmission of human immunodeficiency virus and hepatitis B virus to patients during exposure-prone invasive procedures' (1991) 40 *Morb Mortal Wkly Rep* (RRO8) 385–407.

67 B Lutz 'Prevention of transmission of blood-borne pathogens to patients during invasive procedure' (1991) 8(3) *AIDS Information Exchange* 2–11.

68 TC Porco, JN Martin, KA Page-Shafer, E Cherlebois, RM Grant and DH Osborne 'Decline in HIV infectivity following the introduction of highly active antiretroviral therapy' (2004) 18(1) *AIDS* 81–88.

69 Health Professions Council for South Africa Guidelines for Good Practice in the Health Care Professions Booklet 6: *Ethical guidelines for good practice with regard to HIV* (2016) para 11.

13.10 HIV and children – special considerations

All aspects of life, including physical, psychological and social, are affected when a child is infected with HIV. They therefore require holistic care. Attending to their psychosocial well-being is an integral part of their management. Children generally are vulnerable, and being infected with HIV increases their vulnerability. Not only does this add to the burdens and challenges in an already troubled healthcare system in the country, but it also enforces additional responsibilities, duties and obligations on healthcare practitioners involved in their care. In addition, poverty and other social challenges prevalent in the country, which result in lack of access to healthcare and adequate nutrition and education, add to the hurdles faced by these individuals. The healthcare team also needs to take into consideration social harms like stigmatisation, ostracisation and discrimination if they are to be managed holistically.[70]

Disclosure of the child's HIV status is therefore complex as challenges arise both from the ethico-regulatory requirements with regard to privacy, confidentiality, disclosure to third parties (as described above in para 13.8) and from the perspective of whether, when and how to inform children and adolescents that they are infected with HIV.[71]

13.10.1 Disclosure of status to children

Children are living longer since the initiation of antiretroviral (ARV) use in children. They reach a level of cognitive development which allows them to understand their HIV diagnosis and participate in treatment decisions. The reality is that children now reach a level of physical and emotional development leading to sexual activity and transmission risks.[72] However, they are limited in terms of sexual experience, and hence may be uninformed in terms of safe sexual practices. In addition, if they are infected during the perinatal period and they are not adherent to ARVs, there is potential risk of transmitting resistant virus.[73]

Disclosure requires that they be informed that they have a chronic, potentially life-threatening, possibly stigmatising, sexually transmissible illness. Challenging questions that arise are: when and how to inform? What exactly should be said and how would the psychosocial effects be managed? When, if ever, is full disclosure not appropriate? How should the rights of the child be

---

70   Department of Health National HIV Counselling and Testing Policy Guidelines (2015): https://www.health-e.org.za/wp-content/uploads/2015/07/HCT-Guidelines-2015.pdf (accessed on 5 April 2020).

71   A Dhai and S Mahomed 'HIV infection in children and adolescents: Ethical, legal and social issues' (ELSI) 'Special Edition on HIV Infection in Children and Adolescents' (2019) *Springer Nature* 309–322.

72   R Klitzman, S Marhefka, C Mellins and L Wiener 'Ethical issues concerning disclosure of HIV diagnoses to perinatally infected children and adolescents' (2008) 19(1) *J Clin Ethics* 31–42.

73   See footnote 43 above.

balanced against the rights of the parents? How should healthcare practitioners proceed in this situation?

Generally, parents prefer delaying the process until the child reaches 10 to 12 years of age. Children under 10 years of age have less fully developed cognitive abilities to understand abstract concepts of having a chronic illness, particularly if they do not feel ill.[74] A reasonable approach would be to disclose to the child gradually with age-appropriate information until the child develops the cognitive and emotional maturity to process full disclosure.[75]

Difficulties that children may face include that they may not be adequately prepared to handle the implications of disclosure, resulting in psychological harms; they could have internalised societal conceptions of what it means to be HIV positive and its associated stigma, ostracisation and discrimination before getting to know their status and they would therefore need to go through a process of change from a prior identity of being HIV negative to a new one of being HIV positive after they are informed of the real cause of their illness; and they would also be faced with the need for a similar process regarding their parents' identities. Resultant social harms include that they could become secretive about their illness and might withdraw or keep their distance from others who are known to be HIV infected to avoid any indication that they are different from their uninfected peers, leading to isolation, poor self-esteem and mental health problems such as depression.[76]

Adding to the disclosure dilemmas is the presence of a third party, i.e. a partner when the child becomes sexually active. The sexual partner's well-being is also of consequence to the treating HCP who is bound to uphold the specific ethico-regulatory obligations as mandated in the HPCSA guidelines.[77] Hence, arriving at the best interests of the child in this context is complex. The Department of Health *Guidelines on Disclosure* recommend that for disclosure to be optimum, it must be embarked on as a process, must be prepared, health promoting, age appropriate, occur within a supportive and enabling environment, and managed according to the complexity of the circumstances.[78] The child and

---

74   Department of Health *Disclosure Guidelines for Children and Adolescents in the context of HIV, TB and non-communicable diseases* (2016): http://www.google.com/url?sa=t&rct=j&q=&esrc=s&source =web&cd=1&ved=2ahUKEwjhg8z8hoDhAhURgHMKHSvUB44QFjAAegQIChAC&url=http%3A%2F%2 Fwww.health.gov.za%2Findex.php%2Fhiv-aids-tb-and-maternal-and-child-health% 3Fdownload% 3D1696%3Ahiv-disclosure-guideline-for-children-and-adolescent-2016-1&usg=AOvVaw0ZMC-L54QyA1iKej-iXypy (accessed on 5 April 2020).

75   Ibid.

76   Klitzman et al 2008.

77   Health Professions Council of South Africa Ethical Guidelines for Good Practice with Regard to HIV (2016): https://www.hpcsa.co.za/Uploads/editor/UserFiles/downloads/ethical_rules/Booklet%206% 20Gen.pdf (accessed on 5 April 2020).

78   See footnote 74 above.

parents/guardians/caregivers must have opportunities to ask questions which need to be answered truthfully. The practitioner must be empathic and sensitive to the psychological and emotional well-being of the child and should have a non-judgemental attitude towards risk behaviour.

The Department of Health Guidelines[79] recommend that all children from three years of age should start the process of preparation for disclosure as follows:

(a)   Under 2 years – non-disclosure

(b)   3-9 years – partial disclosure that is age-appropriate and teaches the children about their body and illness without using the terms HIV and AIDS

(c)   10 years and above – full disclosure that is age appropriate and takes into account the child's cognitive and emotional preparedness to process the information received. Information will include issues around sexuality and avoiding risks.

Some questions on HIV and AIDS

Consider the following questions and decide whether the person concerned is legally liable:

1.   An HIV-positive woman allows men to have unprotected sex with her.

2.   A man intentionally infects a number of women with HIV through unprotected sex because he wants to avenge the fact that he was infected by a woman.

3.   A rural woman does not tell her husband that she has tested positive for HIV because she fears that he will kill her.

---

79   See footnote 74 above.

CHAPTER 14

Resource allocation

Ames Dhai and David McQuoid-Mason

By the end of this chapter readers will be able to:

1. Discuss some of the questions which need to be answered when considering allocation of scarce resources or rationing decisions in healthcare.
2. Know the different levels at which resource allocation decisions are made in a country.
3. Describe the principle of justice in the context of resource allocation and rationing.
4. Describe aspects of the law and its application to resource allocation decisions.
5. Describe some models of resource allocation.

14.1 Introduction

Resource scarcity is not common only to the developing world. The issue of distributing scarce resources in an equitable and efficient manner is one which poses ethical dilemmas worldwide. Amongst some of the reasons for this is that there is a wide and steadily increasing gap between the needs and desires for healthcare services and the availability of resources to provide for these needs.[1]

Resources devoted to health and healthcare are finite – often there are not enough to go around. Public health systems, like the National Health System (NHS) in the United Kingdom, operate on a budget which is determined as a percentage of gross national product. In South Africa, the public sector operates along the same lines but is administered at a provincial rather than national level. There is also a private sector where patients pay for medical services out of their own pockets or through a medical aid scheme. Given that this requires substantial income, private medical care is often available only to those people that can afford it in South Africa.

---

1 World Medical Association *Medical Ethics Manual* 3 ed (2015) 65–83.

In order to eliminate these discrepancies, the government is introducing a national health insurance (NHI) scheme 'designed to pool funds to provide access to quality affordable personal health services for all South Africans based on their health needs, irrespective of their socio-economic status'.[2]

South Africa's plans for universal healthcare coverage in the form of the NHI have been in the pipeline for some time. Historically, in 2011, the Green Paper was published for comment.[3] This was followed by a Draft White Paper in 2015 and a White Paper, the National Health Insurance Policy (NHIP) in 2017. The NHIP underpins the establishment of a unified health system in the country based on the principles of social solidarity, progressive universalism, equity and health as a public good and a social investment, thereby underscoring the values of justice, fairness and equity.[4] The NHIP has been critical in the drafting of the National Health Insurance Bill which was released on 18 June 2018 for public comment.[5] Universal healthcare coverage is being promoted globally and is in line with the United Nation's Sustainable Development Goal 3.[6]

Once a budget for healthcare has been allocated, it must be spent in a manner which will advance access to healthcare and address the most pressing health needs of the population. In resource-poor developing countries, this gives rise to a number of questions. For instance, should the state spend more money on building primary healthcare clinics in rural areas or sophisticated district hospitals? Should the state spend more money on antiretroviral treatments and less on vaccination programmes for children? In the clinical situation, choices have to be made between patients to determine who gets treatment (e.g. who receives kidney dialysis).[7] Practitioners who exercise control over these resources must decide which patients will have access to them and which will not, even though those who are denied the treatments may suffer morbidity or even die as a result.[8] Making these decisions will inevitably result in trade-offs, something which is unavoidable when needs outstrip the resources to provide for them. When making these decisions, it is important to take heed of the WMA Declaration of Lisbon on the Rights of the Patient, which states as follows:

---

2   South African Government *National Health Insurance*: https://www.gov.za/about-government/ government-programmes/national-health-insurance-0 (accessed on 30 March 2020).

3   Department of Health *Policy on National Health Insurance* (2011): http://pmg-assets.s3-website-eu-west-1.amazonaws.com/docs/110812nhi_0.pdf (accessed on 6 April 2020).

4   Department of Health *National Health Insurance Policy* (2017): https://cdn.mg.co.za/content/ documents/2017/06/29/whitepaper-nhi-2017compressed.pdf (accessed on 6 April 2020).

5   Department of Health *National Health Insurance Bill* (2018): https://www.gov.za/sites/default/ files/41725_gon635s.pdf) (accessed on 6 April 2020).

6   United Nations Development Project *Sustainable Development Goals* (2015): http://www.undp.org/ content/dam/undp/library/corporate/brochure/SDGs_Booklet_Web_En.pdf (accessed on 6 April 2020).

7   cf *Soobramoney v Minister of Health KwaZulu-Natal* 1998 (1) SA 765 (CC).

8   Ibid.

In circumstances where a choice must be made between potential patients for a particular treatment that is in limited supply, all such patients are entitled to a fair selection procedure for that treatment. That choice must be based on medical criteria and made without discrimination.[9]

14.2 Levels at which resource allocation decisions are made

According to the World Medical Association's Medical Ethics Manual, resource allocation takes place at three levels.[10] The choices made at these levels raise major ethical concerns because they have a significant impact on the health and well-being of individuals and communities:

(a) *Resource allocation at the macro level:* At this level, national governments decide how much of the overall budget should be allocated to health. This includes funding for healthcare expenses, capital and operating expenses for hospitals and other institutions, research, education of health professionals and remuneration of staff.

(b) *Resource allocation at the meso level:* This level includes hospitals, clinics, healthcare agencies, etc., and the local authorities determine how to distribute their resources in line with their specific needs.

(c) *Resource allocation at the micro level:* At this level, individual practitioners decide on individual patient management, for example which tests to order, whether to refer or not, or whether or not to hospitalise a patient. Sometimes hard choices have to be made at this level, where compassion and justice will conflict.

Practitioners who are involved in formulating general policies that affect their own patients face additional conflicts in allocating resources. This occurs in hospitals and other institutions where practitioners hold administrative positions or serve on committees where policies are recommended or determined, for example managed care committees. Whatever roles practitioners have in allocating scarce health resources, they need to be reminded that they also have a role in advocating for expansion of these resources so patient needs can be met.[11]

---

9   WMA Declaration of Lisbon on the Rights of the Patient. 1(e). *Adopted by the 34th World Medical Assembly, Lisbon, Portugal, September/October 1981 and amended by the 47th WMA General Assembly, Bali, Indonesia, September 1995 and editorially revised by the 171st WMA Council Session, Santiago, Chile, October 2005 and reaffirmed by the 200th WMA Council Session, Oslo, Norway, April 2015:* https://www.wma.net/policies-post/wma-declaration-of-lisbon-on-the-rights-of-the-patient/ (accessed on 8 April 2020).

10   World Medical Association *Medical Ethics Manual 3ed* (2015) 65–83.

11   Ibid.

14.3 The principle of justice and resource allocation

The principle of justice is an important factor in resource allocation decisions. Using this principle, a more social approach to the distribution of resources is employed, where the needs of others and not just the individual patient are taken into account.[12] The justice principle requires that where choices have to be made between patients for particular treatments, decisions must be based on sound medical criteria without discrimination – all patients are entitled to fair selection procedures.

14.3.1 Distributive justice

Trade-offs in resource allocation or rationing raise questions around distributive justice. Distributive justice is defined as 'fair, equitable, and appropriate distribution determined by justified norms that structure the terms of social cooperation'.[13] Problems of distributive justice arise when there is scarcity and competition. There are two complementary aspects to distributive justice – substantive justice and procedural justice.

Substantive justice deals with the content of principles that govern the distribution of benefits and burdens in society. Substantive justice principles are most frequently used in debates between socialism and capitalism. Procedural justice deals with fairness in the process of decision making. A focus on procedural justice is especially helpful when there is no reasonable prospect of consensus on substantive principles to guide resource allocation in situations where priorities need to be set.

Priority setting ranks services according to their importance and hence determines the distribution such that both winners and losers are created.[14] Priority setting, which occurs at macro, meso and micro levels of decision making, needs to be impartial and treat people as equals, with the aims being that of promoting health maximisation, fair distribution and protection against poverty.[15] Accordingly, ethical priority setting would require that health outcome inequalities associated with personal characteristics are to be avoided because they would be irrelevant, unfair and unacceptable. These criteria include treating people differently according to their gender, race, ethnicity, religion, sexual

---

12   World Medical Association *Declaration on the Rights of the Patient* (2005): http://www.wma.net/e/policy/l4.htm (accessed on 10 May 2009).
13   TL Beauchamp and JF Childress 'Justice' in *Principles of Biomedical Ethics* (eds) 7th ed (2013) 249–301.
14   OF Norheim 'Ethical priority setting for universal health coverage: Challenges in deciding upon fair distribution of health services' (2016) 14 *BMC Medicine* 14–75.
15   MK Wynia, D Cummins, D Flemming, K Karjens, A Orr, J Sabin, I Saphire-Bernstein and R Witlen 'Improving fairness in coverage decisions: Performance expectations for quality improvement' (2004) 4(3) *American Journal of Bioethics* 87–100.

orientation, social status or area of residence.[16] Moreover, in South Africa this would entail an infringement of section 9 of the Bill of Rights of the Constitution that prohibits unfair discrimination on these and other grounds. For priority setting to be fair, there must be transparency in the processes and governments need to make explicit the range of and reasons for the services they offer. Broad and inclusive stakeholder involvement with mechanisms for critical assessment and revision are necessary.[17]

For cost effectiveness, a measure of health benefits is needed[18] which takes into account the net health outcomes of services to be provided and the resources required to achieve these outcomes, a clearly consequentialist approach.[19] Cost-effective analysis is used to compare different approaches to the same problem and is often presented as a comparison of the cost of preserving quality-adjusted life years (QALYs) or averting disability-adjusted life years (DALYs).[20] Declining cover for services that are relatively ineffective could prevent harms from the dangers of such therapies, and paying for them will reduce the pool of resources available for other, more effective services.[21]

Triage is derived from the French word *trier* and it literally means 'to sort'.[22] Limited resources are prioritised to achieve the greatest possible benefit for all. The likelihood of recovery and length of survival after discontinuing the treatment or being discharged from hospital are taken into account. For example, during the Covid-19 pandemic, the South African Medical Association (SAMA) stated that appropriate risk taking, futility of treatment, co-morbid conditions and other relevant factors should be taken into account when allocating medical interventions. SAMA recommends that frailty rather than age be considered when making these decisions.[23] Essential services and in particular healthcare workers at the frontline assume heightened personal risk while responding to their duty of care. The principle of reciprocity entails that fitting and proportional returns be made to those making contributions. Hence, it requires frontline

---

16 OF Norheim 'Ethical priority setting for universal health coverage: Challenges in deciding upon fair distribution of health services' (2016).

17 Ibid.

18 OF Norheim 'Ethical perspective: Five unacceptable trade-offs on the path to universal health coverage' (2015) 4(11) *Int J Health Policy Manag* 711–714.

19 Ibid 87–100.

20 World Health Organization *Making fair choices on the path to universal health coverage* (2014): http://apps. who.int/iris/bitstream/10665/112671/1/9789241507158_eng.pdf?ua=1 (accessed on 1 October 2017).

21 MK Wynia et al 'Improving fairness in coverage decisions: Performance expectations for quality improvement' (2004).

22 Life Healthcare *The importance of triage* (2019): https://www.lifehealthcare.co.za/news-and-info-hub/latest-news/the-importance-of-triage-management/) (accessed on 8 April 2020).

23 South African Medical Association *SARS-CoV-2 (COVID-19) Guidance for Managing Ethical Issues*: https:// www.samedical.org/files/covid19/doctor_resource/SAMA_Ethics%20Guidance%20_COVID-19%20 Ethics_2020%207%20Apr.pdf (accessed on 25 April 2020).

workers to be prioritised for personal protective equipment, medical interventions like ICU care, ventilator allocation and vaccinations when developed. This would also impact positively on the principle of utility whereby there would be a constant supply of healthcare workers to care for the sick. Therefore, during triage, healthcare workers at risk ought to be given priority when triage decisions are made.

The Critical Care Society of South Africa (CCSSA) recommends using the clinical frailty scale (CFS) to assess the patient. The CSF ranges from 1 to 9 as follows:

1. Very fit – those amongst the fittest for their age, and very active and motivated

2. Well – no active disease or symptoms, but not as active as in category 1

3. Managing well – medical problems present, but well controlled. Not regularly active

4. Vulnerable – not dependent on others for daily help, but symptoms limit activities

5. Mildly frail – more evident slowing and need help in high-order IADLS (e.g. finances, transport, etc.)

6. Moderately frail – need help with all outside activities, keeping house, bathing and dressing

7. Severely frail – completely dependent for personal care, but stable and not at high risk for dying (within 6 months)

8. Very severely frail – completely dependent, approaching the end of life and not able to recover from a minor illness

9. Terminally ill – life expectancy of less than 6 months.

Patients with a CFS score of less than 5 are to be offered a management plan excluding ICU. The lower the score, the higher the likelihood of benefit from ICU care.[24]

14.3.2 Justice and resource allocation: other approaches

There are other approaches to justice when determining resource allocation decisions. These include the following:

---

24   Critical Care Society of South Africa *Allocation of scarce critical care resources during the COVID-19 public health emergency in South Africa* (2020): https://criticalcare.org.za/wp-content/uploads/2020/04/Allocation-of-Scarce-Critical-Care-Resources-During-the-COVID-19-Public-Health-Emergency-in-South-Africa.pdf (accessed on 6 April 2020).

(a) To each, an equal share

(b) To each, according to need

(c) To each, according to effort

(d) To each, according to contribution

(e) To each, according to merit

(f) To each, according to free market exchange.[25]

While there is no obvious barrier to the acceptance of any of these approaches, when faced with competing interests and trade-offs due to scarcity of resources, it is recommended that the principles of procedural justice are drawn upon to assist with decision making in a fair and just manner.

The principles of distributive justice have been incorporated into legal instruments such as the Bill of Rights of the Constitution of South Africa,[26] and in the context of healthcare, the National Health Act.[27]

14.4 Resource allocation and the law

14.4.1 The constitutional right of access to healthcare

In South Africa, the allocation of healthcare resources is provided for in the Constitution.[28] The Constitution states that everyone has the right to access to healthcare services (including reproductive healthcare), the right to sufficient food and water, and the right to social security, including, if they are unable to support themselves and their dependants, appropriate social assistance.[29] It goes on to say that the state must take reasonable legislative and other measures, within its available resources, to achieve the progressive realisation of each of these rights.[30] Finally, it states that no one may be refused emergency medical treatment.[31]

The clause dealing with access to healthcare and other social rights is not absolute – the realisation of these rights depends on the amount of resources available. This is different from the clauses dealing with children's rights in the Constitution, where children have the right to healthcare and not simply the right of access to healthcare.[32]

---

25 TL Beauchamp and JF Childress 'Justice' in *Principles of Biomedical Ethics* (eds) 7th ed (2013) 249–301.

26 Constitution of the Republic of South Africa, 1996 Chapter 2.

27 National Health Act 61 of 2003.

28 Constitution of the Republic of South Africa 1996 s 27.

29 Constitution s 27(1).

30 Constitution s 27(2).

31 Constitution s 27(3).

32 Constitution s 28.

The provisions of the Constitution dealing with access to healthcare impose an important duty on South African legislators and decision makers to provide healthcare within available resources. If they make the wrong decisions concerning resource distribution, the general population may suffer the consequences of the unrealised right to healthcare and other services. The courts are generally reluctant to interfere with the decisions of the policy makers and administrators of healthcare services unless they violate the provisions of the Constitution, as happened when the government embarked on an AIDS denial policy and refused Nevirapine for pregnant mothers and their babies, who required it to prevent transmission of HIV to the neonates.[33]

It is submitted that decision makers who intentionally, recklessly or negligently waste limited resources should be held legally liable by the courts.[34]

14.4.2 Legislative measures to improve equity of resource distribution in South Africa

14.4.2.1 The Pharmacy Amendment Act[35]

The Pharmacy Amendment Act provides that pharmacies can be owned by people other than pharmacists, thus expanding access to pharmaceutical services in underresourced areas. It also stipulates that generic substitution of medicines should be encouraged and it prevents doctors from dispensing medication unless they are licensed to do so.

14.4.2.2 Medical, Dental and Supplementary Health Services Amendment Act

The Medical, Dental and Supplementary Health Services Amendment Act[36] introduced the requirement of community service for doctors. The purpose of community service is to increase the number of doctors in underserviced areas. In 2000, community service was extended to pharmacists and in 2002 to other healthcare practitioners including dieticians and occupational therapists. Nurses were included in community service in 2006 by the new Nursing Act.[37]

---

33   *Minister of Health v Treatment Action Campaign* (Case 2) 2002 (5) 721 (CC).

34   DJ McQuoid-Mason 'Establishing liability for harm caused to patients in a resource-deficient environment' (2010) 100(9) *SAMJ* 573–575; DJ McQuoid-Mason 'With the clinical independence of doctors in hospitals faced with a shortage of resources: What should doctors do?'(2014) 104(11) *SAMJ* 741–742; DJ McQuoid-Mason 'Public health officials and MECs should be held liable for harm caused to patients through incompetence, indifference, maladministration or negligence regarding the availability of hospital equipment' (2016) 106(7) *SAMJ* 681–683.

35   88 of 1997.

36   18 of 1995.

37   33 of 2005.

14.4.2.3 National Health Act

The National Health Act[38] is concerned with ensuring that healthcare is provided to vulnerable groups. It provides for equitable distribution and rationalisation of healthcare with special attention to the women, children, the elderly and people with disabilities.

One of the main distributive measures mandated by the National Health Act is the 'certificate of need' requirement. This aims to even out the resource distribution between the public and private health sectors, and to ensure that healthcare practitioners are spread equally between urban and rural areas. The 'certificate of need' will achieve this aim by ensuring that new healthcare facilities are opened only in areas of great need. The provision has proved very controversial and is not yet in force.

14.4.2.4 National Health Insurance Bill

In 2019 the National Health Insurance Bill was published to establish a comprehensive national health insurance (NHI) scheme for the country.[39] The aim of the scheme is to ensure that people using healthcare services do not suffer financial hardship by providing universal health coverage. This means that every South African will have a right to access free comprehensive healthcare at accredited health facilities such as clinics, hospitals and private healthcare practitioners.

The services will be delivered closest to where people live or work. NHI began being implemented in phases over a 14-year period that started in 2012. The government will establish a single fund that will buy services on behalf of the entire population. Funding for NHI will be through a combination of mandatory prepayment sources and general taxes.[40]

14.5 Some models of resource allocation

The question arises as to how resources should be allocated. The answer is that the allocation should be just and equitable, as well as ethically and legally valid. In the South African context, the allocation must also take into account the needs of large sections of the population who were historically disadvantaged. In short, resources must be distributed equally amongst everybody, whilst also considering the heritage of our past.[41]

---

38 61 of 2003.
39 National Health Insurance Bill B-11 (2019): https://www.gov.za/documents/national-health-insurance-bill-b-11-2019-6-aug-2019-0000 (accessed on 30 March 2020).
40 South African Government *National Health Insurance*: https://www.gov.za/about-government/government-programmes/national-health-insurance-0 (accessed on 30 March 2020).
41 A Hassim, M Heywood and J Berger (eds) *Health and Democracy – A Guide to Human Rights, Health Law and Policy In Post-apartheid South Africa* (2007) 35.

14.5.1 *Vertical and horizontal equity*

Resource allocation can be considered in terms of vertical and horizontal equity. Vertical equity recognises that different groups have different starting points and therefore require differential treatment.[42] Horizontal equity dictates that 'equal people must be treated equally'.[43] Generally, health systems aim to achieve both vertical and horizontal equity. This may be done by promoting healthcare under the banner of 'universal access' or 'access for all', whilst recognising vertical equity by having people pay for healthcare according to their ability to do so.

The proposed NHI for South Africans[44] is a good example of vertical and horizontal equity. Vertical equity will occur because premiums will be in the form of a tax calculated according to individual income declared – this means that those who are in a position to make a more substantial contribution than others will do so. Horizontal equity will be achieved by making health services available free to all South Africans.[45]

14.5.2 *Geographical equity*

Past distribution of healthcare resources on the basis of geographical location accounts for the fact that some areas of South Africa are presently severely under-serviced with healthcare services. Furthermore, remote areas seem to face critical resource shortages or have greater unfulfilled healthcare needs than other areas. The result is that people who are ill in remote areas do not seek healthcare resources because they are 'too far away'.[46] Often, rural areas are underresourced whilst large urban centres have an abundance of state and private healthcare facilities.

In order to remedy the geographical inequalities inherent in health resource distribution under apartheid, the South African healthcare sector was restructured in 1994. Currently, there is one Department of Health – as opposed to the 14 different health authorities overseeing predominantly specialist and private care during apartheid. The National Department of Health is the umbrella body for the nine provinces and 53 health districts which cover the entire country.[47]

---

42   D McIntyre and L Gilson 'Redressing disadvantage – Promoting vertical equity within South Africa' (2000) 8 (3) *Health Care Analysis* 235–258.

43   D McIntyre and L Gilson 'Putting equity in health back onto the social policy agenda – Experience from South Africa' (2002) 54 *Social Science and Medicine* 1637–1656.

44   See above para 14.4.

45   cf South African Government *National Health Insurance*: https://www.gov.za/about-government/government-programmes/national-health-insurance-0 (accessed on 30 March 2020).

46   YM Dambisya and SI Modipa. 'Capital flows in the health sector in South Africa: Implications for equity and access to health care' *Equinet Discussion Paper* 76 (2009) 2: http://www.equinetafrica.org/bibl/docs/DIS76pppDAMBISYA.pdf (accessed on 21 May 2010).

47   YM Dambisya and SI Modipa 'Capital flows in the health sector in South Africa: Implications for equity and access to health care' *Equinet Discussion Paper* 76 (2009) 4: http://www.equinetafrica.org/bibl/docs/DIS76pppDAMBISYA.pdf (accessed on 21 May 2010).

One of the main focuses is on the provision of primary healthcare through the district health system, with priority given to rural and historically underserviced areas. Improving access in such areas will help to promote geographical equity in resource distribution. It is hoped that geographical equity will be achieved by the NHI scheme if it ensures that health 'services will be delivered closest to where people live or work'.[48]

14.5.3 Ability to pay

Another method by which scarce health resources are distributed in South Africa is based on the 'ability to pay'. There are glaring inequalities inherent in this method of resource distribution, given the social and economic history of the country. The 'ability to pay' method is exemplified by the private healthcare sector in South Africa. The private sector caters for less than 20% of the population, but uses the majority of resources available – both financial and human.[49]

Pro-equity initiatives (policies and initiatives which try to promote equity) have been instituted. Pro-equity initiatives aimed at increasing access to private health services include the Government Employees Medical Scheme (GEMS) which increases coverage of medical aid and regulation of the private sector through laws and policies like the National Health Act.[50]

Although the examples above seek to address inequalities in resources allocated on an 'ability to pay' basis, some decisions which seem to be a hindrance have also been taken. For instance, in 1994 a moratorium was placed on the building of private hospitals. This theoretically freed up resources with which to build and equip public facilities. The moratorium was subsequently lifted, resulting in a proliferation of private hospitals in South Africa, whilst the number of public hospitals has remained relatively stagnant.[51] For instance, by 2007 Gauteng province had 112 private hospitals and only 28 public hospitals.[52] Again it is hoped that the introduction of the NHI scheme will help to reduce these discrepancies by compelling the public and private health sectors to work together to achieve free universal health services for all South Africans.[53]

---

48   cf South African Government *National health insurance*: https://www.gov.za/about-government/ government-programmes/national-health-insurance-0 (accessed on 30 March 2020).

49   YM Dambisya and SI Modipa 'Capital flows in the health sector in South Africa: Implications for equity and access to health care' *Equinet Discussion Paper* 76 (2009) 4: http://www.equinetafrica.org/bibl/ docs/DIS76pppDAMBISYA.pdf (accessed on 21 May 2010).

50   61 of 2003.

51   YM Dambisya and SI Modipa 'Capital flows in the health sector in South Africa: Implications for equity and access to health care' *Equinet* Discussion Paper 76 (2009) 10: http://www.equinetafrica.org/bibl/ docs/DIS76pppDAMBISYA.pdf (accessed on 21 May 2010).

52   Ibid.

53   cf South African Government *National Health Insurance*: https://www.gov.za/about-government/ government-programmes/national-health-insurance-0 (accessed on 30 March 2020.)].

14.6 Conclusion

When it comes to healthcare resources, a just distributive balance is difficult to achieve. Not only do resources need to be spread equitably amongst the population, but efficiency of resource use is also of great importance. Balancing equity and efficiency in the public sector is not easy. For instance, a sophisticated ultrasound scanner is no good in a primary care clinic if the clinic staff does not have the expertise to use it. While such a scarce resource remains unused in a clinic, its value depreciates. The scanner would be used more efficiently if it were to be placed in a facility which did not possess such equipment but did have the ability to operate it.

An important factor is that the health needs of populations are always in flux. If a contagion like Covid-19 were to spread rapidly throughout South Africa, this would drastically change the resource requirements of the population. The ability to accommodate equitable, efficient, cost-effective and quick responses to such changes is vital if social justice in the healthcare sector of South Africa is to be achieved. This can best be done if the public and private sectors work together to ensure the delivery of quality healthcare services to all South Africans, which is one of the aims of the NHI scheme.[54]

Some questions on resource allocation

1. How would you define a trade-off in the healthcare context? Discuss some examples and explain why you consider them to be such.

2. Discuss the concepts of vertical and horizontal equity and explain with examples how these would apply in the healthcare context.

3. Explain how the different concepts of justice would apply in healthcare provision.

---

54   cf MP Matsoso and R Fryatt 'National health insurance: The first 18 months' (2013) 103(3) *SAMJ* 156–158.

CHAPTER 15

Business ethics – the healthcare context

Ames Dhai and David McQuoid-Mason

By the end of this chapter readers will be able to:

1. Define perverse incentives, conflicts of interests and improper financial gain.
2. Identify some of the situations for potential conflict of interest in the healthcare context.
3. Explain how to avoid conflicts of interest in healthcare practice.
4. Describe some acceptable business models in healthcare practice.

15.1 Introduction

If healthcare practitioners are to act in the best interests of their patients, they should try to avoid potential conflicts of interest and maintain professional autonomy and independence when dealing with patients. However, because of the changing socio-economic environment in the country and its impact on the provision of healthcare, undesirable business practices in the healthcare sector have started emerging, undermining the trust inherent in the practitioner–patient relationship.

Medical practice has become rapidly industrialised and commodified over the past few years. It is important to recognise that healthcare cannot be a commodity in the free market. This is because it is not a transaction. There is no relationship between the seller and buyer. The practitioner–patient relationship is embedded in the healthcare interaction. Moreover, a commodity is proprietary and is owned by the seller. This is not the case in healthcare, where medical knowledge is gained because of the social contract whereby society sanctions the training of healthcare practitioners. Hence, medical knowledge is not owned by the practitioner[1] and the practitioner–patient relationship can be appropriately explained as a fiduciary one to benefit the patient.

---

1   ED Pellegrino 'The commodification of medical and health care: The moral consequences of a paradigm shift from a professional to a market ethic' (1999) 24 *J Med Philos* 243–266.

As a result, the Health Professions Council of South Africa (HPCSA) has compiled guidelines for practitioners on the avoidance of undesirable business practices, over-servicing, perverse incentives and related matters.[2] In addition, the HPCSA published its *Policy Document on Business Practices* to determine what may be regarded as acceptable business practices in the healthcare sector in order to protect the public.[3]

A conflict of interest arises when a secondary interest opposes or interferes with a primary one. In the healthcare context, the secondary interest could be financial gain for the practitioner and the primary interest would be his or her patient. Practitioners who allow themselves to become involved in conflict-of-interest situations may be guilty of unethical conduct. This chapter draws substantially from the HPCSA's Booklet 11: *Guidelines on Over-servicing, Perverse Incentives and Related Matters.*[4]

15.2 Definitions

For the purposes of this chapter, a health establishment may be defined as follows:

> [A]n institution, facility, building or place where persons receive treatment, diagnostic or therapeutic interventions or other allopathic or complementing health services and it includes facilities such as a clinic, mobile clinic, hospital, community health centre, maternity home or unattached delivery suite, convalescent home, consulting room, dispensary of health-related treatment or aids and appliances, first aid station, orthopaedic workshop, dental laboratory or workshop, ambulance, unattached operating theatre, sanatorium, laboratory, pharmacy, occupational health clinic, radiological clinic, and health spa or hydro.[5]

Perverse incentives, improper financial gain or other valuable consideration are defined as follows:

> [M]oney or any form of compensation, reward or benefit which is not legally due or which is given on the understanding that the recipient will engage or not engage in certain behaviour which is illegal, contrary to ethical professional rules or may adversely affect the interests of a patient or groups of patients. This is done to procure advantage, benefit, reward or payment for the person offering or giving the incentive.[6]

---

2   See generally, HPCSA Guidelines for Good Practice in the Healthcare Professions Booklet 11: *Guidelines on Over-servicing, Perverse Incentives and Related Matters* (2016).

3   See generally, Health Professions Council of South Africa *Policy Document on Business Practices* (2016): https://www.hpcsa.co.za/Uploads/Professional_Practice/CPD/Policy%20on%20Business%20 Practices%20final%20-%202016.pdf (accessed on 30 March 2020).

4   HPCSA Guidelines for Good Practice in the Healthcare Professions Booklet 11: *Guidelines on Over-servicing, Perverse Incentives and Related Matters* (2016).

5   See generally, HPCSA Guidelines for Good Practice in the Healthcare Professions Booklet 11: *Guidelines on Over-servicing, Perverse Incentives and Related Matters* (2016) para 2.7.

6   Ibid para 2.15 read with para 2.9.

15.3 Conflict of interest situations

Some examples of situations in which conflicts of interest could arise are (a) managed healthcare; (b) over-servicing; (c) manufacturing of health-related products by healthcare practitioners; (d) advertising; (e) preferential use of prescriptions; (f) referrals to health establishments in which health practitioners have interests; (g) over-servicing by using technological equipment; (h) financial interest in hospitals; (i) preferential rental agreements; (j) payment of commissions; (k) charging, receiving or sharing of fees; (l) funding of continuing professional development (CPD); and (m) attendance at conferences.

Practitioners should avoid allowing conflict of interest situations to arise in these circumstances to ensure that their conduct is professional and ethical at all times.

15.3.1 *Managed healthcare*

With the growing focus on managed healthcare initiatives, tools such as formularies, disease management programmes, contracts, utilisation review programmes, clinical guidelines and quality assurance programmes appear to be receiving increased attention.

Most medical schemes offer managed care options, which restrict the choice of patients and healthcare providers to varying degrees. Such medical schemes tend to be less expensive than the traditional fee-for-service options. Practitioners not only have to be informed of the implications of managed care for their practices, but also have obligations to educate their patients on the implications of their managed healthcare cover. Patient welfare should always take precedence over the personal interests of healthcare practitioners.

15.3.2 *Over-servicing*

'Over-servicing' is defined by the HPCSA as:

> the supply, provision, administration, use or prescription of any treatment or care (including diagnostic and other testing, medicines and medical devices) which is medically and clinically not indicated, unnecessary or inappropriate under the circumstances or which is not in accordance with the recognised treatment protocols and procedures, without due regard to both the financial and health interests of the patient.[7]

---

7   See generally, HPCSA Guidelines for Good Practice in the Healthcare Professions Booklet 11: *Guidelines on Over-servicing, Perverse Incentives and Related Matters* (2016) para 2.14.

It would be unethical to provide a service or direct the provision of a service or procedure on a patient where this is not indicated or scientifically proven, or has been scientifically shown to be ineffective, harmful or inappropriate through evidence-based reviews.[8] This would also apply when patients are referred to other healthcare practitioners unnecessarily.

15.3.3 Manufacturing of health-related products by healthcare practitioners

As a precaution to avoid conflicts of interest, the HPCSA states that healthcare practitioners shall not manufacture or participate in the manufacture, for commercial purposes or trade, of orthodox medicine, complementary medicine, veterinary medicine, a medical device, a scheduled substance or a health-related product. The only time they can do so is where this would form an integral part of the normal scope of practice of the healthcare practitioner. In respect of the latter, the practitioner will have to obtain explicit permission from the HPCSA.[9]

15.3.4 Advertising

The HPCSA defines 'advertising' as:

> any written, pictorial, visual or other descriptive matter or verbal statement or reference to the matter which appears in any newspaper, magazine, pamphlet or other publication, or is distributed to the public or is brought to the notice of members of the public to attract patients to a health establishment or health-related service.

Promoting the sale of orthodox medicine, complementary medicine, veterinary medicine, medical devices, scheduled substances or health-related products in a similar manner would also be included in the definition.[10]

Advertising could unfairly promote the practice of a particular healthcare practitioner or a healthcare facility for the purpose of financial gain or other valuable consideration that could lead to a conflict of interest.[11] Advertising is discouraged, and advertising that is misleading, non-objective or is not factual will be regarded as unethical.

---

8   HPCSA Guidelines for Good Practice in the Healthcare Professions Booklet 11: *Guidelines on Over-servicing, Perverse Incentives and Related Matters* (2016) para 3.1.1; see also Ethical Rules of Conduct for Practitioners registered under the Health Professions Act 56 of 1974, GN R717, 4 August 2006 rule 7.

9   Ibid rule 23.

10   Ibid rule 7.

11   Ibid rule 3.

15.3.5 Preferential use of prescriptions

Where financial gain or other valuable consideration is derived from preferential usage or preferential prescription, or the advocacy of preferential use of a health establishment, health service, drug or device, a conflict of interest would arise. Such practices should be avoided as they would be regarded as unethical.[12]

15.3.6 Referrals to health establishments in which health practitioners have interests

Patients may be referred to health establishments in which practitioners have an interest, usually of a financial nature. The interest could be a personal one or may be related to a close family member or business associate. It would be necessary for the practitioner to declare to and obtain approval from the HPCSA for such a practice. Moreover, the interest must be discussed with the patient and the patient must agree and consent to the referral. Failure to do so will constitute unethical conduct.[13]

15.3.7 Over-servicing by using technological equipment

Where health practitioners own and use technological equipment, this may be done if such use forms an integral part of their scope of profession and practice.[14] Obviously, the practitioner should have received appropriate training in the use and management of such equipment.[15] However, if equipment is used for procedures, tests and other applications that are not indicated, not scientific or not based on evidence, such use would be construed as over-servicing and hence unethical. The equipment should not be used to make a profit. Fees for the use of the equipment must be market related.[16]

15.3.8 Financial interest in hospitals

Practitioners may have direct or indirect financial interest or shares in a hospital or any other healthcare institution. This is allowed by the HPCSA under the following conditions:

(a) Such interests or shares are purchased at market-related prices in arm's-length transactions.

---

12   Ibid rule 23.
13   Ibid rule 24.
14   Ibid para 3.6.1.
15   Ibid para 3.6.2.
16   Ibid para 3.6.3.

(b) The purchase transaction or ownership of such interest or shares does not impose conditions or terms upon the practitioner that will detract from the good, ethical and safe practice of his or her profession.

(c) The returns on investment or payment of dividends are not based on patient admissions or meeting particular targets in terms of servicing patients.

(d) Such practitioner does not over-service patients, and to this end establishes appropriate peer review and clinical governance procedures for the treatment and servicing of his or her patients at such hospital or healthcare institution.

(e) Such practitioner does not participate in the advertising or promotion of the hospital or healthcare institution, or in any other activity that amounts to such advertising or promotion.

(f) Such practitioner does not engage in or advocate the preferential use of such hospital or healthcare institution.

(g) The purchase agreement is approved by the HPCSA based on the criteria listed in paragraphs (a) to (f) above.

(h) Such practitioner annually submits a report to the HPCSA indicating the number of patients referred by him or her or his or her associates or partners to such hospital or healthcare institution and the number of patients referred to other hospitals in which he or she or his or her associates or partners hold no shares.[17]

A failure to comply with any of the above conditions may result in disciplinary action by the HPCSA for unethical conduct.

15.3.9 Preferential rental agreements

Some private establishments and practitioners have 'agreements' regarding referrals to and/or use of the facilities at particular health establishments. Such 'agreements' may include the use of rooms by practitioners at the establishments at a minimal rental or at no cost.

The HPCSA views as unethical rentals in lease agreements between practitioners and health establishments that are not market related or are at preferential rates.[18] To avoid this conflict of interest from arising, practitioners should not enter into lease agreements with health establishments or services that wish to rent their consulting rooms at rates conditional on the practitioner achieving a certain turnover or targets, such as the admission of a specific

---

17   Ibid rule 23A.
18   Ibid para 3.8.1.

number of patients at a private healthcare facility.[19] Furthermore, practitioners should not rent consulting rooms from health establishments or services under financial arrangements that are not openly available to other similarly qualified healthcare practitioners.[20]

Practitioners should not enter into a contract to work in a particular health establishment or service on the understanding that the practitioner generates a particular amount of revenue for the health establishment or service.[21] However, a health establishment or service that equips a theatre, ward or other facility for a practitioner according to his or her specifications may enter into a contractual agreement with the practitioner on condition that turnover targets for the practitioner are not stipulated by the health establishment or service.[22]

15.3.10 Payment of commissions

It is unethical for practitioners to accept or pay commission or any financial or other gain in return for the purchase, sale or supply of any goods, substances or materials used by the healthcare professional in his or her practice.[23]

15.3.11 Charging, receiving or sharing of fees

It is unethical for practitioners to receive any financial gain or other valuable consideration for:

(a) referring patients to the other health professionals;
(b) participating in drug trials or other research trials;
(c) seeing medical representatives;
(d) services not personally rendered, unless those services have been rendered by a partner, shareholder or *locum tenens*.[24]

---

19   Ibid para 3.8.2.
20   Ibid para 3.8.3.
21   Ibid para 3.12.1.
22   Ibid.
23   HPCSA Guidelines for Good Practice in the Healthcare Professions Booklet 11: *Guidelines on Over-servicing, Perverse Incentives and Related Matters* (2016) paras 3.9.1 and 3.9.2; see also Ethical Rules of Conduct for Practitioners registered under the Health Professions Act 56 of 1974, GN R717, 4 August 2006 rule 7.
24   HPCSA Guidelines for Good Practice in the Healthcare Professions Booklet 11: *Guidelines on Over-servicing, Perverse Incentives and Related Matters* (2016) paras 3.10.1 to 3.10.4; see also Ethical Rules of Conduct for Practitioners registered under the Health Professions Act 56 of 1974, GN R717, 4 August 2006 rule 7.

It is also unethical to charge a patient for an appointment not honoured by the patient.[25] In addition, it is unethical to share fees with any person or healthcare professional who has not taken a commensurate part in the service for which the fees are charged.[26]

15.3.12 Funding of continuing professional development (CPD)

Historically there has been a close collaboration between practitioners and the pharmaceutical and health supply industry that extended particularly to CPD. With healthcare to a large extent being self-governing, practitioners should ensure that their participation in such collaborative efforts is in keeping with their ethical duties towards patients and society.[27]

Continuing professional development activities should address the educational needs of the targeted healthcare group, especially when sponsored by the private sector.[28] Funds for the CPD activities should preferably be in the form of an educational grant payable to the healthcare provider organisation arranging the activity to prevent conflicts of interests arising.[29] Professional associations, their branches and groups are usually involved in obtaining the funding for these activities, and they should not be in a position of conflict of interest by virtue of any relationship with the funding body. The organisers may acknowledge financial or other aid received but should not identify any specific products. It is recommended that generic names of products should be used rather than trade names in the course of continuing professional development activities.[30]

Travel or lodging costs or other expenses should not be paid by the industry directly to the individual healthcare practitioners to attend a CPD event. Indirect funding or scholarships for CPD events may be permissible in instances where such sponsorships are paid to the organisers of the CPD events, who in turn will identify, through a transparent selection process, deserving candidates. Factors such as historically disadvantaged individuals, status, gender, geographical location in terms of rural and inaccessible locations, young practitioners and developing practitioners should be taken into consideration when identifying the deserving candidates.[31]

The organisers may extend reasonable honoraria and imbursements for travel, lodging and meal expenses to speakers. The principal event should at all times centre on education and not on meals, entertainment or other hospitality, the cost

25   Ibid.
26   Ibid.
27   Ibid para 3.13.1.
28   Ibid para 3.13.2.
29   Ibid para 3.13.4.
30   Ibid para 3.13.3.
31   Ibid para 3.13.5.

of which should not exceed that level at which the recipients might reasonably be expected to incur for themselves under similar circumstances.[32]

15.3.13 Funding of international conference attendance

Conferences and workshops expose practitioners to new knowledge and insights into their respective professions and disciplines. According to the HPCSA, it is permissible for companies to sponsor delegates to attend international conferences, either directly or through professional associations or societies, with the proviso that a fair and transparent process should be followed in the election and sponsoring of delegates to attend such events. Preference should be given to new practitioners and educators and those from disadvantaged backgrounds when determining sponsorship and funding allocations. The sponsorships should be specific to educational events and conferences and not for holiday purposes.[33]

15.3.14 Product promotions

Product promotions may sometimes give rise to conflicts of interest. Accordingly, it is necessary for a distinction to be made between education and training and product promotion. Practitioners cannot earn CPD points for attending product launches or other product promotion events. No travel, lodging or other expenses for healthcare practitioners should be paid for attendance at product promotion events or product launches. However, modest meals may be provided.[34]

15.3.15 Dual practice

Healthcare practitioners employed in the public service place their undivided attention, time and skills at the disposal of the public service as employer. Practitioners engaging in 'remunerative work outside public service' (RWOPS) must do so in line with the approval of the executing authority in order to place the health and well-being of their patients as their first priority.[35] Practitioners abusing RWOPS must be reported to the HPCSA.[36]

---

32   Ibid.
33   Ibid para 3.13.6.
34   Ibid para 3.13.7.
35   Ibid para 3.14.1.
36   Ibid para 3.14.2.

15.4 Acceptable business models

Current legislation allows for a number of desirable business models. Acceptable business models are solo practices; partnerships/groups/organisations; associations; personal liability companies (incorporated practices – inc.); and franchises (subject to compliance with the ethical rules – see below). These practice models are allowed to outsource their administration or establish a company to manage their administration conditional to such arrangements not violating the ethical rules of HPCSA. Any other type of business model will need to be submitted to the HPCSA for review and approval.[37]

The HPCSA defines a franchise as follows: A franchise is a system in which one organisation ('Franchisor') grants the right to produce, sell or use a developed product, service or brand to another organisation or person or group of persons ('Franchisee'). Royalties based on either turnover or contractually agreed to be paid by the Franchisee. The Franchisee agrees to comply with the Franchisor's policies in respect of buying, marketing, and management. The Franchisor may offer advertising and back-up services.

When practitioners engage in franchise arrangements of healthcare services, they may potentially transgress ethical rules because inherent in the franchise is the sale of exclusive rights to the franchisee. In addition, franchises are usually dependent on advertising of the franchise. The following ethical rules could potentially be breached in a franchise: advertising, canvassing and touting (rule 3); naming of practice (rule 4); information on professional stationery (rule 8); fees and commissions (rule 7); partnership (rule 8); professional secrecy (rule 16); professional appointments (rule 18); consulting rooms (rule 20); exploitation (rule 22); and performance of professional acts (rule 30).[38]

15.5 Corporates and healthcare practitioners

According to the HPCSA, a person who is not registered in terms of the Act does not qualify to share in the profits or income of a professional practice. In addition, direct or indirect corporate ownership of a professional practice by a person other than a registered practitioner in terms of the Act is not permissible. The following are examples of what would constitute a transgression under this stipulation: transferring any part of income generated from patients in the practice to such person; giving shares or a similar interest in the professional

---

37   HPCSA Policy Document on Business Practices (2016) s 2.1: https://www.hpcsa.co.za/Uploads/Professional_Practice/CPD/Policy%20on%20Business%20Practices%20final%20-%202016.pdf (30 March 2020).
38   Ibid paras 2.1 and 3.1.

practice to such a person; and paying a fee, which is not market related, from the income of profits from the practice to a service provider.[39]

Corporates get involved when they provide services like administration and rental to a professional practice. There must be an official agreement that has been objectively negotiated and takes into consideration market-related or fair remuneration or fee payable by the practice to the corporate entity. Practitioners must avoid potential conflicts of interests and must maintain professional autonomy, independence and commitment to the HPCSA's professional and ethical norms.[40] For example, a practitioner renting rooms at a private hospital is not allowed to get into an arrangement which allows for no rental or below market-related rental, conditional to a certain number of patients being admitted by that practitioner into the hospital every month.

Regarding employment of practitioners, generally this is not allowed by persons not registered in terms of the Act. However, there are specific categories of exemptions from this prohibition. They are: the public service; universities and training institutions; mining companies; non-profit organisations (NPOs) and non-government organisations (NGOs). NPOs and NGOs are subject to approval of the relevant boards.

The HPCSA stresses that all employing institutions should be accredited by them. In addition, the practitioner's clinical independence cannot be violated by the employing body who should not force the practitioner to violate the HPCSA's ethical rules. Any other institution, agent or person could, however, lodge an application with HPCSA for permission to employ a registered practitioner.[41]

Some questions on business ethics in the context of healthcare

1. A practitioner is approached by a pharmaceutical company which plans to do a clinical trial on a new intervention for diabetes. She is asked to refer potential participants to the trial site. She will be paid R500 for each patient referred. Would this be a perverse incentive? Why or why not?

2. With the use of examples, describe how conflict of interest situations may arise in the healthcare context and discuss how these could be avoided.

---

39   Ibid para 2.2.
40   Ibid para 2.3.
41   Ibid para 2.4.

CHAPTER 16

Human health and the environment

Ames Dhai and David McQuoid-Mason

By the end of this chapter readers will be able to:

1. Describe legal aspects of human health and the environment.

2. Explain some ways in which human health and environmental health are interrelated.

3. Discuss the importance of environmental education in healthcare practice.

4. Explain the importance of environmental bioethics.

5. Understand the HPCSA's guidelines on protecting and preserving the environment.

16.1 Introduction

One theory of bioethics follows the classical application of bioethical analysis to problems facing healthcare practitioners and policy makers in clinical practice and policy. The other is more expansive and places people within the context of their environment pointing to wider bioethical considerations concerning the relation of the environment to human health and vice versa.[1] Thus it has been said that it is necessary to 'reunite the bioethical twins that have been separated since birth'.[2] The latter approach suggests that it is time to reconsider the orientation of bioethics to include all life forms – not simply human life.

Global environmental problems have led to resource depletion, global warming and unprecedented levels of species extinction. Climate change threatens ecosystems and creates new forms of injustice by undermining the foundation of fundamental rights and deepening inequalities. Developing countries are particularly vulnerable while being the least able to adjust to the costs of adapting to it. Moreover, the poorest countries are often those that are most affected by

---

1   VR Potter *Bioethics Bridge to the Future* (1971); VR Potter and PJ Whitehouse 'Deep and global bioethics for a liveable third millennium' (1998) 12 *The Scientist* 9.

2   W Reich 'The word "bioethics": Struggle over its earliest meanings' (1995) 5 *Ken Inst Eth J* 31.

uncontrolled global warming.[3] Environmental concerns must be consistent with contemporary ethical requirements, including respect for human rights and equal consideration for all human beings. The reality is that not all human populations are equal in the face of the climate challenge. Respecting human rights is aligned with a principle of international solidarity to allow for the the global management of climate change.[4] Hans Jonas, the German philosopher, developed the 'imperative of human responsibility' principle in the late 1970s precisely for ecological issues: 'Act so that the effects of your actions are compatible with the permanence of genuine human life on Earth'.[5] Concerns for sustainability of the ecosystem in the very long term and responsibilities towards future generations must be integrated into contemporary social life.[6]

16.2 Legal aspects of human health and the environment

The Constitution[7] and several statutes and national standards are concerned not only with the environment but also with the health and well-being of the people of South Africa. These include the National Environmental Management Act (NEMA),[8] the National Environmental Management: Waste Act (NEMWA),[9] the National Environmental Management: Air Quality Act,[10] and the South African National Standards on Health Care Waste Management

16.2.1 The Constitution

The Constitution states that everyone has the right to an environment that is not harmful to their health or well-being,[11] and that the state must take reasonable legislative and other measures that prevent pollution and ecological degradation.[12] The Constitution imposes a duty on the provinces and local governments to ensure that the right to a clean and healthy environment is fulfilled.[13]

---

3   M Jafari 'Challenges in climate change and environmental crisis: Impact of aviation industry on human, urban and natural environments' (2013) 3(3) *International Journal of Space Technology Management and Innovation* 24–46.

4   B Feltz 'The philosophical and ethical issues of climate change' (2019) July-Sept *The UNESCO Courier* 7–9.

5   Ibid.

6   Ibid.

7   Constitution of the Republic of South Africa, 1996.

8   107 of 1998.

9   59 of 2008.

10   39 of 2004.

11   Section 24(1).

12   Section 24(2).

13   Section 152(1)(*b*) and (*d*).

16.2.2 The National Environmental Management Act (NEMA)

The National Environmental Management Act[14] echoes the Constitution in its preamble and states:

> Whereas many inhabitants of South Africa live in an environment that is not harmful to their health and well-being everyone has the right to an environment that is not harmful to his or her health or well-being; and everyone has the right to have the environment protected, for the benefit of present and future generations, through reasonable legislative and other measures that prevent pollution and ecological degradation.

The Act states that environmental management 'must place people and their needs at the forefront of its concern, and serve their physical, psychological, developmental, cultural and social interests equitably'.[15] Both the Constitution and NEMA are not only concerned with the environment but also with the health and well-being of South Africans.

NEMA requires national government departments, such as the Department of Health, to prepare environmental management plans at least every four years.[16] When preparing their environmental implementation plans or environmental management plans, and before submitting them, the relevant departments must take into consideration environmental implementation plans and environmental management plans already adopted, in order to achieve consistency among such plans.[17]

16.2.3 The National Environmental Management: Waste Act (NEMWA)

The National Environmental Management: Waste Act[18] controls the licensing process for specified waste activities, including medical waste, in South Africa. The purpose of the Act is, amongst others, (a) to protect health and the environment by providing reasonable measures for the prevention of pollution and ecological degradation and for securing ecologically sustainable development; (b) to provide for national norms and standards for regulating the management of waste by all spheres of government; (c) to provide for specific waste management activities; and (d) to provide the national waste information.[19]

---

14   107 of 1998.
15   Section 2(2).
16   Section 11(2).
17   Section 11(4).
18   59 of 2008.
19   Ibid.

16.2.4 The National Environmental Management: Air Quality Act

The National Environmental Management: Air Quality Act[20] aims to protect the quality of air in the South Africa by the prevention of air pollution and environmental degradation by regulating emission standards for incinerators being used in medical waste disposal. The purpose of the Act is, amongst others, (a) to reform the law regulating air quality in order protect the environment by providing reasonable measures for the prevention of pollution and ecological degradation; (b) to provide for national norms and standards regulating air quality monitoring, management and control by all spheres of government; and (c) to provide for specific air quality measures.[21]

16.2.5 The South African National Standards on Health Care Waste Management

The South African National Standards on Health Care Waste Management[22] deal with all aspects of medical waste management from generation to disposal of waste and also include a guide to the training of staff. According to the Standard on the Management of Health Care Waste, medical waste must be separated at source of generation according to the risks it poses and temporarily stored in colour-coded containers. In addition, each health facility must ensure that their workers are trained in the identification and separation of various types of medical waste and contract their final treatment and disposal to an authorised company which should in return hand the facility a certificate of safe disposal.[23]

16.3 Environmental bioethics in education

Environmental bioethics involves ethical reflection on the connectivity of all life systems. In this context, the various approaches to environmental ethics cover such diverse issues as Darwinian principles, microbial life, emerging infectious diseases in the broader framework of global warming, ecological destruction and population pressures (e.g. density and shifts). These perspectives represent a particular niche in the broader applications of environmental ethics and environmental philosophy and can be appropriately placed in health sciences bioethics programmes.

Problems such as global warming, new and emerging infectious disease, pollution and consumerism can no longer be considered as separate from

---

20   39 of 2004.
21   Ibid.
22   South African National Standards SANS 10248-3 Management of Health Care Waste (2011).
23   Ibid.

bioethics. When the interrelatedness of all life forms is considered, the conclusion is that humans are parts of larger systems. This conclusion should lead people to consider what obligations and duties they have to protect and sustain the biotic community. As the Earth is an essential resource for all forms of life, the damage it sustains impacts not only on human health but also on the health of non-human animals, plants, soil, water and air. Destruction of the planet leads to interruptions in the basic biological structure of diversity. It disturbs Darwinian evolution and permanently damages the biotic community.

Environmental education forms a necessary component of contemporary learning. The *Porto Alegre Declaration on University, Ethics and the Environment* supports this view, stating as follows:

> The 21st Century university ought both to bridge and to blend the sciences and humanities into an integrated whole. To speak effectively on environmental issues, the university should abandon the dogma that science deals with a domain of objective facts and the humanities with a domain of subjective values. Scientific inquiry is directed by our values and the revelations of science often inform, expand and transform our values in unexpected ways.[24]

16.4 The importance of environmental bioethics

Bioethics is a multidisciplinary field of activity. In environmental bioethics this is particularly evident in that it involves knowledge beyond environmental ethics. Disciplines such as the sciences (e.g. clinical medicine and healthcare, microbiology, ecology, climatology, chemistry, as well as environmental law) are also involved. This means that people must learn to think differently. For example, 'philosophers and theologians must learn a great deal about science and technology'.[25] Likewise, scientists must learn about philosophy and theology. The resolve to address the magnitude of environmental problems cannot fall on a single discipline. Rather it should be multidisciplinary but voiced as a single consensus of like-minded environmentally sensitive individuals. This is necessary because:

> [o]ur modern age may soon end due to ecological collapse ... in order to survive, humanity must go beyond the attitudes, values, and practices of the present age and develop an integrated scientific, ethical, aesthetic, and religious worldview.[26]

---

24   JB Callicott and FJR da Rocha (eds) *Earth Summit Ethics* (1995) 221.

25   J Lutzenberger 'Science, technology, economics, ethics and environment' in JB Callicott and FJR da Rocha (eds) *Earth Summit Ethics* (1995) 43.

26   D Orr *Ecological Literacy, Education and the Transition to a Post Modern World* (1992) 193–220.

This implies that human concerns must be expanded beyond a strong anthropocentric axiology.[27] As a result, the following questions should be considered which challenge conventional education that excludes environmental concerns:[28]

(a) What kind of a world do we have?

(b) What kind of a world do we want?

(c) What must we do to get it?

16.4.1 What kind of a world do we have?

The kind of a world we have is one in which:

(a) species are disappearing at an exponential rate;

(b) human arrogance and ignorance has led us to alter our physical environment to the extent that the patterns of the seas, lakes and marine creatures have changed. Climate change has and will continue to alter the ways in which all life forms currently exist. There is no doubt that the potential range and magnitude of climate change-associated risks is a global research priority;[29]

(c) the degradation of the Earth has resulted in increasing infectious diseases and the corresponding challenge to treat infectious diseases effectively because of mounting drug resistance.

Below are some of ways in which the question can be answered.

16.4.2 What kind of world do we want?

There are many different answers to this question, such as the following:

(a) In the context of infectious diseases, new emerging ones (e.g. Covid-19) and drug resistance are natural responses to an unbalanced world of human making and we need to be prepared for them and try to avert them.

(b) For every application of technology, there will be unknown consequences that people must be wary of.

(c) The numbers and density of human population and its drive towards materialism should be moderated.

---

27   BF Norton 'Environmental ethics and weak anthropocentrism' in C Pierce and D van de Veer (eds) *People, Penguins, and Plastic Trees* 2 ed (1995) 182–192.

28   K Malone 'Environmental education researchers as environmental activists' (1999) 5 *Env Edu Res* 163–177.

29   See generally, World Health Organization *Protecting Health from Climate Change: Global Research Priorities* (2009).

(d) The environment should not be 'commodified' but rather protected and respected.

(e) The power behind the construction of ideologies and their influence in the media should be cautiously received and, where possible, resisted.

(f) 'Sustainable development' requires that people understand the difference between what they need and what they desire.

(g) The value of every life form should be respected.

16.4.3 What must we do to get it?

To answer this final question requires a change in thinking by people to looking beyond themselves to the biotic community as a whole. Humans need to reallocate and clarify their felt preferences and enlighten themselves by adopting a more environmentally sensitive worldview. To inform felt preferences requires a great amount of time and political will. Time appears to be short when faced with the increasing numbers and potential of harmful micro-organisms, climate change, faltering biological diversity, and alterations in the atmosphere, oceans and earth that give rise to grave problems. Political will is another impediment, because of the many competing claims for the prioritisation of other interests. This means that it is unlikely that the problems raised by environmental bioethics will be placed above all such other claims.

At the same time, without the aesthetic values, resources and physical environment that influence all human beings, people will not be able to realise their full potential, so to do nothing is hardly a moral option.

16.5 Broadening perspectives

It has been said that biomedical ethics should be reconceived in a social context because moral justification in traditional biomedical ethics assumes that 'real life moral problems come sorted and labelled and ready for the manipulation of rules, principles or theories' and disregards

> the extent to which moral concepts and norms derive their meaning and their force from the social and cultural surroundings in which they are embedded; neglects the ways in which moral problems are generated and framed by the practices, structures, and institutions within which they arise; and ignores the means by which social and cultural ideologies, and the power relationships they entrench, can both perpetuate moral inertia and effect moral change.[30]

---

30 B Hoffmaster *Bioethics in Social Context* (1984) 2–3.

Human beings are merely one link in the chain of creation and what humans do, or do not do, has an impact on the whole dynamic system of life. Environmental bioethics allows people to explore the reasons behind the human impact on the planet and provides individuals with a different way of seeing their ethical responsibilities.

16.6 Ethical principles in relation to the environment and climate change

Climate change impacts health substantively. Some consequences such as food and water insecurity, land degradation and natural disasters have significant effects on health. In November 2017, UNESCO adopted a Declaration of Ethical Principles in Relation to Climate Change. The Declaration is based on the following six ethical principles:[31]

(a) *Prevention of harm:* Responsible and effective policies to mitigate and adapt to climate change must be implemented to prevent harm.[32]

(b) *Precautionary approach:* The adoption of measures to prevent or mitigate the adverse effects of climate change must not be postponed on the grounds of a lack of definitive scientific evidence.[33]

(c) *Equity and justice:* The response to climate change must be such that everyone benefits. Those who are unjustly affected by climate change must be allowed access to judicial and administrative proceedings, including redress and remedy.[34]

(d) *Sustainable development:* New paths for development must be adopted to sustainably preserve our ecosystems, while building a more just and responsible society that is more resilient to climate change. Special attention has to be paid in situations where the humanitarian consequences of climate change can be striking, such as food, energy, water insecurity, the oceans, desertification, land degradation and natural disasters.[35]

(e) *Solidarity:* People and groups most vulnerable to climate change and natural disasters must be supported, particularly in the least developed countries (LDCs) and small island developing states (SIDS). Co-operative action in certain areas like technology development and transfer, knowledge sharing and capacity building must be established or strengthened where already established.[36]

---

31 UNESCO *Declaration of Ethical Principles in Relation to Climate Change* (2017): https://unesdoc.unesco.org/ark:/48223/pf0000260889 (accessed on 9 April 2020).
32 Article 2.
33 Article 3.
34 Article 4.
35 Article 5.
36 Article 6.

(f) *Scientific knowledge and integrity in decision making:* The interface between science and policy to aid decision-making optimally must be strengthened. Relevant long-term strategies, including risk prediction must be implemented. The independence of science must be promoted. Scientific finding must be widely disseminated to as many people as possible for the benefit of all.[37]

16.7 The Health Professions Council of South Africa and environmental health

The Health Professions Council of South Africa (HPCSA) has developed Guidelines[38] for the proper disposal of healthcare waste by healthcare practitioners so that the environment can be preserved and protected. This is viewed as an essential element of good professional practice. Proper disposal of healthcare waste forms part of practitioners' ethical and professional obligations to their patients and to the community, and assists practitioners to meet the HPCSA's mandate to protect the public and the requirements of the South African Constitution[39] regarding the preservation and protection of the environment.[40]

The HPCSA defines 'healthcare waste' as:

> any undesirable or superfluous by-product, emission, residue or remainder generated by [or] in the course of health care by healthcare professionals, healthcare facilities and other non-healthcare professionals, which is discarded, accumulated and stored with the purpose of eventually discarding it, or is stored with the purpose of recycling, re-using or extracting a usable product from such matter.[41]

Healthcare waste includes infectious waste; pathological waste, including body fluids, secretions and surgical specimens; sharps, especially contaminated ones; pharmaceutical waste; chemical waste; heavy metals; radioactive waste; genotoxic waste; cytotoxic agents; and pressurised containers.[42]

Healthcare waste may be hazardous because it contains infectious, radioactive or toxic (including genotoxic, immunotoxic and cytotoxic) materials, hazardous chemicals or pharmaceuticals, and could be responsible for traumatic injury and other forms of physical hazard.[43] Irresponsible and illegal dumping of hazardous

---

37   Article 7.
38   HPCSA Guidelines for Good Practice in the Healthcare Professions Booklet 12: *Guidelines for the Management of Health Care Waste by Health Care Practitioners* (2016).
39   Constitution of the Republic of South Africa, 1996 s 24.
40   HPCSA Guidelines for Good Practice in the Healthcare Professions Booklet 12: *Guidelines for the Management of Health Care Waste by Health Care Practitioners* (2016) para 1.
41   Ibid para 2.
42   Ibid para 3.
43   Ibid para 4.

healthcare waste in South Africa, as intermittently reported in the media, is a matter of serious concern for the HPCSA. It states that healthcare waste is a significant danger to society for the following reasons:[44]

(a) When hazardous healthcare waste is not managed safely, particularly in its disposal, the risk of needle-stick injuries may increase. There may be transmission of infectious agents and unsuspecting individuals may be exposed to unnecessary and entirely preventable risks. It may be difficult to quantify the severity of the risk associated with such exposures. It is important that such exposures are prevented.[45]

(b) Groundwater may get contaminated and may result in the spread of *E. coli* infection when healthcare waste enters the normal domestic waste stream. This is because it will end up being disposed of in municipal landfill sites or buried.[46]

(c) Generally, smaller landfill sites lack fencing and security resulting in unwanted tip-face picking and scavenging. When healthcare waste is disposed of on such sites, people scavenging on the sites are exposed to risk.[47]

(d) Unacceptably high financial and human resource burdens are placed on health authorities to manage the problem.[48]

(e) Burning of healthcare waste leads to environmental pollution, especially through the formation of dioxins. The HPCSA recommends that waste should be incinerated but stresses that incineration should only be used where it meets specifications that avoid secondary pollutant emissions.[49]

The HPCSA states the following in respect of the management of healthcare waste:[50]

(a) Heathcare practitioners have the responsibility to put a healthcare waste management system in place or to have access to such a system.

(b) Healthcare practitioners should only use accredited waste service providers.

---

44   Ibid para 5.
45   Para 5.1.
46   Para 5.2.
47   Para 5.3.
48   Para 5.4.
49   Para 5.5.
50   These duties are either a synopsis of or a direct quote from those listed in the HPCSA Guidelines for Good Practice in the Healthcare Professions Booklet 12: *Guidelines for the Management of Health Care Waste by Health Care Practitioners* (2016) para 6.

(c) Healthcare practitioners should deal comprehensively with measures for waste minimisation, segregation, packaging, labelling, storage and removal under circumstances that do not pose a threat to human health or the environment, both for routine circumstances and in the event of an accident resulting in contamination with healthcare waste.

(d) Healthcare practitioners who are in private practice are required to provide demonstrable evidence of compliance with an acceptable protocol for the management of healthcare waste, including 'an audit trail of the management of waste generated by the practice'.

(e) Healthcare practitioners employed in healthcare institutions must insist that the management comply with the provisions of these HPCSA *Guidelines*, and if such institutions do not, the practitioners should report the matter to the HPCSA and the Department of Health for appropriate action.

(f) Healthcare practitioners who are responsible for the management of healthcare facilities must ensure that such facilities have a waste management policy with sufficient resources and suitably trained team members to implement safe management of healthcare waste generated by such facilities and their staff.

(g) Healthcare practitioners should aim at all times to minimise the amount of healthcare waste generated in the process of healthcare delivery and to ensure that they are familiar with methods to minimise, segregate and store healthcare waste safely.

(h) Healthcare practitioners should, where necessary, keep up to date with the latest scientific knowledge on the safe management of healthcare waste by undergoing further training in waste management.

(i) Healthcare practitioners should regard all medical sharps as hazardous healthcare waste whether or not contaminated with infectious agents and make use of sharps containers that are suited for the purposes of disposing of sharps. They should ensure that:

    (i) sharps containers do not puncture easily, are stable and are durable enough to withstand a fall onto a hard surface;

    (ii) sharps containers are not filled beyond their capacity and are maintained upright throughout their use during handling, storage and transport;

    (iii) sharps that contain cytotoxic, genotoxic or radioactive waste are treated as required in their waste categories and not mixed with general sharps items;

    (iv) sharps containers that are designed, manufactured and intended for single-use purposes are not re-used.

(j) Healthcare practitioners have an obligation to report evidence of unsafe disposal or management of healthcare waste by other persons, including other healthcare practitioners, to the HPCSA and the Department of Health, should such unsafe practice come to their attention.

(k) Healthcare practitioners should consult the *Code of Practice of the South Africa Bureau of Standards on the Handling and Disposal of Waste Material within Health Care Facilities*[51] or updates, should it be amended, as a supplement to the HPCSA Guidelines for the management of healthcare waste by healthcare practitioners.

The HPCSA Guidelines also suggest that provincial and local government health authorities should, wherever possible, make their facilities for the management of healthcare waste available to independent healthcare practitioners in their areas.

Some questions on human health and the environment

1. Investigate climate change from the perspective of environmental ethics, then discuss climate change in the context of an emerging infectious disease. What are some of the problems which will arise and how do you think they can be successfully managed?

2. How would you describe the role of the HPCSA with respect to protection of the environment? Which law does the HPCSA draw from in this regard?

---

51 South African Bureau of Standards *Code of Practice of the South Africa Bureau of Standards on the Handling and Disposal of Waste Material within Health Care Facilities* (SABS 0248) (1993); see Annexure to HPCSA Guidelines for Good Practice in the Healthcare Professions Booklet 12: *Guidelines for the Management of Health Care Waste by Health Care Practitioners* (2016).

CHAPTER 17

The ethics of research

Ames Dhai

By the end of this chapter readers will be able to:

1. Explain the need for ethics in research from the historical perspective.

2. Explain the need for responsible conduct of research from the ethical perspective.

3. Explain the framework that regulates ethical research.

4. Explain the South African legal structures pertaining to research.

5. Define clinical research.

6. Apply the principles in ethics to research and research ethics review.

7. Explain the concepts of justice, vulnerability and group harms in research.

8. Explain how to avoid scientific misconduct in research.

17.1 History

Prior to the 19th century, research into disease was done by individuals working alone. Such people would carefully gather facts and then write books or pamphlets or present their observations and clinical experiences to gatherings of their peers. A classic example in Britain in the 18th century would be Edward Jenner, who over some 20 years studied vaccination with cowpox as a preventive inoculation against smallpox.[1] In France, the recommendations of the surgeon-general of Napoleon's army, Baron Larrey, improved the treatment of military casualties on the battlefield thereby saving the lives of many thousands of soldiers of all armies ever since.[2] Also from the military in the early 19th century, a United States Army surgeon, William Beaumont, said that individuals should consent to participate in research not just be used.[3] At the beginning of the 20th century, the Kingdom of Prussia introduced protection for vulnerable individuals by requiring consent from individuals before participating in research, a requirement that was

---

1   TA Kerns *Jenner on Trial* (1997) 5–17.
2   See generally, HI Dible *Napoleon's Surgeon* (1970).
3   H Beecher *Research and the Individual Human Subject* (1970) 219–220.

extended to include children in Germany by the beginning of the 1930s. Sadly, this protection disappeared once the Nazis took power in Germany.[4]

Prior to World War II, ethics concerned the behaviour between professionals. During the war, the concept that all people participated in a struggle to overcome a foe – something common to all nationalities – came to the fore. This included people in the military, at home, in hospitals or in prisons, a concept that gave medical researchers wide latitude in research involving people.

At the end of World War II, the Nuremberg Trials exposed the terrible excesses of Nazi medical research on concentration camp prisoners. As a reaction in 1947, two American doctors, Andrew Ivy and Leo Alexander, together with unnamed prosecutors in the Nuremberg Trials legal team, drew up a code of conduct called the Nuremberg Code. In summary, the 10 points of the code say that voluntary consent from people is essential prior to their participation in medical research, that such people may withdraw from the research at any time and that there should be potential benefit and minimal harm to them.[5]

Some 17 years later, this was followed by a research code of the World Medical Association that evolved into the Declaration of Helsinki in 1964.[6] This declaration is the ethical core of clinical research and has been revised several times. Currently the 2013 revision is in force. The declaration, which is an expansion of the Nuremberg Code, makes it clear that a physician's primary duty is to a patient under care.

The next important development was an article by Beecher,[7] in which he wrote of his concern for the rights of patients involved in medical research and described, anonymously, 22 experiments that he held were unethical because effective treatment was withheld; treatment was continued in the presence of side effects; known harmful treatment was given to study the mechanism of side effects; and extra procedures were done without the patient's consent.[8]

Beecher recommended the setting up, within organisations undertaking medical research, of committees to examine proposed research for the protection of participants. From his article grew the present-day research ethics committee system that screens research.

---

4   BA Brody 'A historical introduction to the requirement of obtaining informed consent from research participants' in L Doyal and JS Tobias (eds) *Informed Consent in Medical Research* (2001) 7–14.

5   See above Chapter 2.

6   Ibid.

7   HK Beecher 'Ethics and clinical research' (1966) 274 *N Engl J Med* 1354–1360.

8   Ibid.

17.2 The ethical and regulatory environment

Some of the key international ethical codes and declarations like the Nuremberg Code and the Declaration of Helsinki that influenced South African regulations regarding clinical research were discussed previously.[9] Other key international texts that have directed the development of these regulations and guidelines include the following:[10]

(a) ICH Guidelines for Good Clinical Practice, ICH Harmonised Tripartite Guideline

(b) Council for International Organizations of Medical Sciences (CIOMS) *International Guidelines for Ethical Review of Epidemiological Studies*

(c) CIOMS and World Health Organization (WHO) *International Ethical Guidelines for Biomedical Research Involving Human Subjects*

(d) WHO *Operational Guidelines for Ethics Committees that Review Biomedical Research.*

Research ethics committees (RECs), called institutional review boards (IRBs) in the United States, operate according to published guidelines, of which there are many around the world.

In South Africa, research ethics guidelines are published by the National Department of Health,[11] the Health Professions Council (HPCSA)[12] and the Medical Research Council (MRC).[13] The National Health Act[14] makes prior approval of health research by an REC compulsory. Review and approval of research by a South African REC registered with the National Health Research Ethics Council (NHREC) is necessary even if the research has been reviewed and approved by an REC or IRB outside the country. The National Health Act also requires that research is conducted in accordance with the Constitution.[15] What is remarkable about the latter requirement is that the South African

---

9   See above Chapter 2.

10   These references can be found in South African National Department of Health *Ethics in Health Research: Principles, Processes and Structures* (2015): https://www.ul.ac.za/research/application/downloads/DoH%202015%20Ethics%20in%20Health%20Research%20Guidelines.pdf (accessed on 10 April 2020).

11   Ibid; cf National Department of Health *Clinical Trials Guidelines* 2 ed (2006): http://www.kznhealth.gov.za/research/guideline2.pdf (accessed on 10 April 2020).

12   HPCSA Guidelines for Good Practice in the Healthcare Professions Booklet 13: *General Ethical Guidelines for Health Researchers* (2016); Booklet 14: *Ethical Guidelines for Biotechnology Research in South Africa* (2016).

13   South African Medical Research Council Guidelines on the Responsible Conduct of Research (2018): https://www.samrc.ac.za/sites/default/files/attachments/2018-06-27/ResponsibleConductResearchGuidelines.pdf (accessed on 10 April 2020).

14   61 of 2003.

15   Constitution of the Republic of South Africa, 1996.

Constitution is the only one in the world that entrenches informed consent to participate in medical research.[16] The Constitution states that everyone has the right 'not to be subjected to medical or scientific experiments without their informed consent'. The word 'experiments' may be seen as confusing and is taken from the International Covenant on Civil and Political Rights of the United Nations,[17] but is regarded as meaning research.

17.2.1 Definition of health research

'Health research' is defined in the National Health Act[18] as including any research that contributes to the knowledge of:

(a) the biological, clinical psychological or social processes in human beings;

(b) improved methods for the provision of health services;

(c) human pathology;

(d) the causes of diseases;

(e) the effects of the environment on the human body;

(f) the development or new application of pharmaceuticals, medicines and related substances; and

(g) the development of new applications of health technology.

This definition of health research is quite broad and most research will therefore require review by a research ethics committee. Research itself is defined as the systematic search or inquiry for knowledge.[19] Studies could range from projects designed to understand normal or abnormal physiological or psychological functions, to social phenomena. Clinical research also includes studies that evaluate diagnostic, therapeutic or preventative interventions and variations in services or practices. Research activities may include invasive or non-invasive procedures. Some examples are surgical interventions, removal of body tissues or fluids, administration of chemical substances or forms of energy, dietary modifications, daily routine or service delivery, alteration of the environment, observation, administration of questions or tests, and review of records.[20]

The proposed research must demonstrate scientifically sound methodology and a good probability of providing answers to the research question posed. The protocol should include knowledge of relevant literature derived from systematic review and where appropriate, relevant information from laboratory and

---

16   Constitution s 12(2)(c).

17   United Nations Organization *International Convention on Civil and Political Rights* (1966) article 7.

18   61 of 2003 s 1.

19   National Department of Health *Ethics in Health Research: Principles, Processes and Structures* (2015).

20   Ibid.

animal studies. In terms of the South African guidelines, the local principle investigator must be a South African-based researcher, i.e. one who is ordinarily permanently resident in South Africa.[21]

17.2.2 The National Health Act and research

Chapter 9 of the National Health Act deals with research and ethics in research.

17.2.2.1 Informed consent

According to the National Health Act,[22] notwithstanding anything to the contrary in any other law, research or experimentation on a living person may be conducted only in the prescribed manner, and with the written consent of the person after he or she has been informed of the objects of the research or experimentation and any possible positive or negative consequences of the research on his or her health. Where the potential participant is a child (i.e. less than 18 years of age), consent from the parent or guardian and from the child are required. The National Health Act provides for child participation in research. The Children's Act[23] is silent in this regard.

17.2.2.2 The National Health Research Ethics Council

The National Health Research Ethics Council (NHREC) is a statutory council that was established in terms of the National Health Act.[24] The functions of the NHREC are to:

(a) determine guidelines for the functioning of health research ethics committees;

(b) register and audit health research ethics committees;

(c) set norms and standards for conducting research on humans and animals, including norms and standards for conducting clinical trials;

(d) adjudicate complaints about the functioning of health research ethics committees and hear any complaint by a researcher who believes that he or she has been discriminated against by a health research ethics committee;

(e) refer to the relevant statutory health professional council matters involving the violation or potential violation of an ethical or professional rule by a healthcare provider;

---

21   Ibid.
22   61 of 2003 s 71.
23   38 of 2005.
24   61 of 2003 s 72.

(f) institute such disciplinary action as may be prescribed against any person found to be in violation of any norms and standards, or guidelines, set for the conducting of research in terms of the Act; and

(g) advise the national department and provincial departments on any ethical issues concerning research.[25]

17.2.2.3 Clinical trials

Section 72 of the National Health Act defines clinical trials as 'a systematic study involving human subjects that aims to answer specific questions about the safety or efficacy of a medicine or method of treatment'.[26] Hence, according to this definition, clinical trials are not limited to the study of drugs only, but include other methods of treatment as well (e.g. behavioural interventions). All clinical trials have to be registered with the South African National Research Registry which is based at the National Department of Health. Clinical trials are allocated a central registration number which must be attached to the ethics application on submission.

17.2.3 Oversight of research ethics committees

There is oversight of RECs in various countries. In South Africa, the National Health Act requires that RECs register with the National Health Research Ethics Council (NHREC) which has the authority to audit RECs and, if necessary, discipline their members.[27] Another organisation with which many South African RECs register is the United States Office of Human Research Protections (OHRP), an institution that has oversight over United States federal funds, the source of support for many South African–United States collaborative research studies.[28] If the OHRP grants what is known as a federal-wide assurance (FWA) to an REC then decisions by that REC are accepted for United States federal research funding.

17.2.4 Review methods for clinical research

Currently, three methods requiring three different committee structures are used for review:

---

25 National Health Act 61 of 2003 s 72(6).
26 Ibid s 72(7).
27 Ibid s 72(2).
28 Office of Human Research Protections; see http://www.hhs.gov/ohrp/.

(a) Research ethics committees (RECs)

(b) Data and safety monitoring committees – these oversee ongoing clinical trials with respect to treatment efficacy, safety and futility. Where efficacy, harm or futility is clearly evidenced, premature termination can be recommended on ethical grounds prior to the end of the trial.

(c) The regulatory authority (i.e. the South African Health Products Regulatory Authority) – this is responsible for reviewing the study design and in doing so reviewing important ethical questions.

17.3 Research ethics review

RECs consist of healthcare professionals, other professionals such as bioethicists, lawyers, laypersons, philosophers, ministers and scientists. They meet regularly to examine the risks and benefits inherent in a proposed investigation to decide if a research project is ethical or not.

17.3.1 Composition of RECs

An REC should consist of a reasonable number of members who collectively have the qualifications, experience and understanding of the social priorities of the communities being researched. Hence, membership should include academics together with laypeople to ensure that reviewers are not limited to individuals who are socially and culturally removed from the populations being researched. RECs need to be independent, multidisciplinary, multisectoral and pluralistic. All REC members should have documented proof of research ethics training, refreshed at least once within the period of appointment, and once every three years (4.4.2).[29] To this end, the South African National Health Department guidelines recommend that the REC membership should consist of the following:[30]

(a) 'At least nine members with a quorum being a simple majority;

(b) Where the number of members is more than 15, the quorum may be 33%;

(c) At least one layperson;

(d) At least one member with knowledge of, and current experience in, the professional care, counselling or health-related treatment of people. Such a member might be e.g. a medical practitioner, psychologist, social worker or nurse;

---

29 National Department of Health *Ethics in Health Research: Principles, Processes and Structures* (2015) para 4.4.2.

30 Ibid para 4.4.1.2.

(e) At least one member with professional training and experience in qualitative research methodologies;

(f) Members with professional training and experience in quantitative research methodologies;

(g) A member with expertise in bio-statistics;

(h) A member with expertise in research ethics; and

(i) At least one member who is legally qualified'.

It is a requirement that REC members receive initial and continued education in research ethics and are kept aware of current issues and developments in the broad area of ethics and science. Moreover, researchers should produce evidence of appropriate research ethics training within the previous three years (see para 2.3.8).[31]

17.3.2 REC procedures

According to the National Health Department's Guidelines,[32] RECs must establish and record working procedures with regard to the following:

(a) Frequency of meetings

(b) Processes for declaration of conflicts of interest

(c) Preparation of the agenda and minutes

(d) Distribution of the necessary documents prior to meetings

(e) Presentation of research protocols

(f) Presentation of all documents and other materials used to inform potential research participants

(g) Quorum and methods of decision making

(h) Requirements for submission of research projects for ethical approval

(i) Registration of applications

(j) Timely review and notification of decisions

(k) Written notification of decisions to researchers

(l) The recording in writing of decisions and reasons for the decisions made by the REC

(m) Confidentiality of the content of protocols

(n) Confidentiality of the REC's proceedings

---

31 National Department of Health *Ethics in Health Research: Principles, Processes and Structures* (2015) para 2.3.8.

32 Ibid para 4.5.

(o) Reporting of adverse events

(p) Reporting of amendments to protocols

(q) Access to documents

(r) Regular monitoring

(s) Complaints procedures

(t) Protections for whistleblowers

(u) Procedures for easy and adequate access to members of the REC

(v) Fees charged, if any

(w) Post approval reviews and annual re-certification

(x) Processes for expedited reviews.

17.3.3 The review process

While detailed working of RECs differ, the principles remain the same. A formal request for ethics clearance is made using an application form, a research plan (protocol) or both. This is considered at a committee meeting run according to the National Health Department's Guidelines mentioned. The ethical considerations presented in the ethics protocol application should be a real engagement with the ethical issues and not just a rote checklist. In considering the protocol, the REC may have to consult or seek assistance from experts. The REC would have to be satisfied that the expert would not have a conflict of interest in relation to the research project under consideration.

Furthermore, RECs also need to ensure that no member of the committee adjudicates on research in which that member has any conflict of interest with the proposed research, researcher or sponsor. Such members should be requested to recuse themselves when the proposal is being considered during the meeting. Typical decisions are approved, minor revisions needed, major revision and resubmission required, or not approved.[33] Should it be necessary, RECs may invite an applicant to attend a meeting to discuss their application.

How does an REC come to a decision? In brief, an analysis of benefits and risks to prospective participants is done though discussion by committee members. Low benefit–high risk applications are seldom approved. Protocols that are generally approved are low benefit–low risk, high benefit–low risk, and high benefit–high risk applications. The analyses are based on the knowledge and experience of REC members with the emphasis on the right of individual

---

33   P Cleaton-Jones and M Vorster 'Workload of a South African university-based health research ethics committee in 2003 and 2007' (2008) 1 *SAJBL* 38–43.

participants rather than the rights of society. Coupled with this is attention to the four principles of autonomy (respect for an individual), beneficence (potential benefit), non-maleficence (absence of harm) and justice (fair sharing of benefit and risk).

An applicant is informed of the outcome of his or her application during or after the meeting. The latter is usually the case. Should revisions be necessary there will be some guidance and perhaps the details of an REC member to contact for help. Communications between RECs and sponsors should be directed through the principal investigator.

17.3.4 Expedited reviews

The norm usually is to review research protocols at predetermined meetings of the full or quorate committee. However, the National Department of Health Guidelines[34] allow for expedited reviews to research that pose no more than minimal risk of harm. RECs should establish procedures and determine the classes of research to which an expedited review procedure would apply.

17.3.5 Rapid reviews

The National Department of Health Guidelines describe a major incident as any sudden event that occurs where local resources are constrained, making urgent response difficult.[35] Unusual and sudden demands on local resources could have ethical implications for patient care. Research in these contexts could be critical for advancing emergency healthcare interventions and treatments.

While the guidelines emphasise that patients in these contexts would be extremely vulnerable, RECs are cautioned not to be overly restrictive, and recommend that the ethics clearance process must occur rapidly and that related research proposals should be processed quickly without compromising rigour. For example, minimal risk studies could undergo rapid expedited review, while more than minimal risk studies could undergo rapid full committee review. RECs should innovate in developing such rapid review processes in line with the Department of Health.[36] The Covid-19 pandemic is an example of a such a context where rapid review was necessary.

---

34   National Department of Health *Ethics in Health Research: Principles, Processes and Structures* (2015) para 4.5.1.5.
35   Ibid para 3.4.1.
36   Ibid.

Regarding consent in major incident research, the guidelines state that proxy consent may be ethically permissible 'where no statutory proxy is available if the risk of harm to knowledge ratio justifies it'.[37] The REC may approve delayed consent (also referred to as deferred consent) in certain circumstances.[38]

The minimum conditions for research involving adults who are incapacitated are described by the guidelines as follows:[39]

Research involving incapacitated adults should be approved only if:

(a) The research, including observational research, is not contrary to the best interests of the individual;

(b) The research, including observational research, places the incapacitated adult at no more than minimal risk (i.e. the 'everyday risk standard' which means the risk is commensurate with 'daily life or routine medical, dental or psychological examinations and in social or education settings activities' – referred to as 'negligible risk' in some guidelines); or

(c) The research involves greater than minimal risk but provides the prospect of direct benefit for the incapacitated adult. The degree of risk must be justified by the potential benefit; or

(d) The research, including observational research, involves greater than minimal risk, with no prospect of direct benefit to the incapacitated adult, but has a high probability of providing generalisable knowledge; i.e. the risk should be justified by the risk–knowledge ratio;

(e) Greater than minimal risk must represent no more than a minor increase over minimal risk;

(f) The legally appropriate person is a person listed as a treatment proxy in the National Health Act[40] or the Mental Health Care Act[41] gives permission for the person to participate; and

(g) Where appropriate, the person will assent to participation. Note that the incapacitated person's refusal or resistance to participate, as indicated by words or behaviour, takes precedence over permission by a proxy.

---

37   Ibid para 3.2.4.3.
38   Ibid.
39   Ibid para 3.2.4.4.
40   61 of 2003 s 7.
41   17 of 2002 s 27(1)(*a*).

The sequence of legally appropriate treatment proxies are specified in the National Health Act[42] as: the spouse or partner; parent; grandparent; adult child; brother or sister. The Mental Health Care Act[43] provides, in no particular sequence, that legally appropriate proxies are spouse; next of kin; partner; associate (defined as 'a person with a substantial or material interest in the well-being of a mental health care user or a person who is in substantial contact with the user'); and parent or guardian.

The Guidelines describe the approach to be taken when reviewing research involving patients who are highly dependent on medical care.[44] Because of their medical vulnerability, and the fact that their decision-making and communication skills may be compromised, special attention needs to be paid when considering their participation. The Guidelines[45] also allow for the REC to approve delayed consent in particular circumstances in this context. However, it is emphasised that this does not mean that consent is waived. Clear and full justification for delayed consent must accompany the research proposal. It is also important to consider carefully the individual circumstances of the patient so as to avoid violating personal or cultural values.

The Guidelines[46] stipulate that the following criteria need to be satisfied when RECs approve delayed consent:

(a) '[T]he research is based on valid scientific hypotheses that support a reasonable possibility of more benefit than that offered by standard care; and

(b) [P]articipation is not contrary to the medical interests of the patient; and

(c) [T]he research interventions pose no more risk of harm than that inherent in the patient's condition or alternative methods of treatment; and

(d) [T]he research is based on valid scientific hypotheses that support a reasonable possibility of more benefit than that offered by standard care; and

(e) [A]s soon as reasonably possible, the participant and her relatives or legal representatives will be informed of the participant's inclusion in the research; be requested to give delayed consent; and advised of the right to withdraw from the research without any reduction in quality of care'.

---

42   61 of 2003 s 7.
43   17 of 2002 s 27(1)(*a*).
44   National Department of Health *Ethics in Health Research: Principles, Processes and Structures* (2015) para 3.2.6.
45   Ibid paras 3.2.4.3 & 3.2.6.
46   Ibid para 3.2.6.

17.3.6 Using the 'four principles'[47] during the review

17.3.6.1 Autonomy and respect for persons

RECs pay great attention to the consent process for the enrolment of participants in an investigation. This consent must be voluntary, informed, written, and needs to be gained before enrolment in a study except in certain situations such as where potential participants are critically ill. Informed consent means that a participant in a study must understand, appreciate and voluntarily agree to what is proposed.[48] This is frequently a stumbling block, perhaps due to language difficulties or lack of education. Cultural factors regarding who may give consent may also play a role. There are many vulnerable groups for whom special care must be taken, for example those with physical or mental reasons leading to incompetence to consent, prisoners, soldiers, subordinates to researchers, minors, orphans, and the critically ill.

For the critically ill, a suggested technique that could be used is the following:[49] if an REC feels that there is potential benefit for an ill person to participate in a study, but that person is not competent to consent, then a legally competent family member or in the absence of the family member, other legally competent person may give consent.[50] Where the other legally competent person is an experienced clinician, he or she must not be part of the research programme or involved in the patient's care. Any legally competent person who acts on behalf of a patient has to decide if participation in the research is in the best interests of the patient. Ethically, should a close relative later become available, re-consenting should be done to enable the patient to remain in a study. If an ill person recovers sufficiently to give an informed consent, re-consenting should be done for continued participation in the study and for use of the data collected (delayed or deferred consent).

Where children (under 18 years of age) are involved as research participants, consent from parents or guardians together with assent from the child are requisite.[51] If a child is enrolled in research and during the course of the research reaches the age of 18, the re-consent of the child who has become an adult will be required for the participant to remain in the research programme and parent/guardian consent will no longer be necessary.

---

47   See above Chapter 1.
48   See above Chapter 6.
49   See para 17.3.5 above.
50   See above Chapter 6.
51   National Health Act s 71(2).

17.3.6.2   Non-maleficence and beneficence

A common question is whether RECs evaluate the science of an application. Ideally, the science should be screened by a committee dedicated to this purpose prior to ethical evaluation. Commonly, however, the quality of the science in the proposed research is broadly considered by the REC. Poor-quality science is regarded as unethical. Ensuring that the science is of a high standard is important in ensuring research participants are protected against physical harms. Harms could also be of a psychological, social or economic nature. Some research may also probe sensitive issues and result in re-traumatisation or the triggering of psychological reactions. Stigma to individuals or cohorts of participants could result because of social attitude (e.g. people known to be involved in HIV research).

17.3.6.3   Justice

There is an ethical obligation to treat each person in accordance with what is right and proper. In research, this is primarily distributive justice. There should be equitable distribution of both burdens and benefits of research participation. The study should leave the participant and/or community better off or no worse off. Researchers have an obligation to justify their choice of research questions and to ensure that such questions are neither gratuitous nor result in the exploitation of study participants. The selection, recruitment, exclusion and inclusion of research participants must be just and fair, based on sound scientific and ethical principles.

Where research involves participants from vulnerable communities, added protections will be necessary to safeguard their vulnerabilities. There needs to be justification for doing research in vulnerable communities. Moreover, the research should be responsive to their particular vulnerabilities. Vulnerable communities should not be targeted for research just because of administrative and logistical ease of availability.[52]

The choice as to what is to be used in the control arm of a study needs to be fair and just. Where there is a proven intervention, it would be unethical to use a placebo unless there is compelling and justifiable reason to do so.

At the end of the research, the intervention, if proven to be effective, should be made available to at least the research participants. This is commonly termed 'post-trial access'. It would be unethical to withdraw the intervention when the study is completed – especially when beneficial effects are seen in the participants.

Research participants should be compensated for trial-related injuries. A requirement in South Africa is that there is adequate insurance cover for research

---

52   HPCSA Guidelines for Good Practice in the Healthcare Professions Booklet 13: *General Ethical Guidelines for Health Researchers* (2016) para 4.1.3.

participants.[53] The principle of justice would be violated if participants are expected to cover the costs of their study participation. Participants also need to be compensated for any 'out-of-pocket expenses' which include travel costs to the study site, time or any other related costs. While it is important to ensure that participants are compensated fairly, undue inducements should be avoided as these may influence would-be participants to engage in the research against their better judgement.

17.4 Research involving communities

Researchers should have clear plans on how research will be conducted in community settings. This includes how communities are to be consulted or involved in the research process and how, in general, they are to be kept informed. Communities, also referred to as 'collectivities' in the National Department of Health Guidelines,[54] is an expression used to distinguish some distinct groups from informal communities, commercial or social groups. According to the Guidelines, such groups are distinguished by:

(a) beliefs, social structures, values, and other features that identify them as a separate group;

(b) collective decision making that is according to tradition and beliefs;

(c) the custom of leaders expressing a collective view; and

(d) members of the community being aware of the common interests and activities of the group.

17.4.1 Group harms

Community consultation is important to avoid 'group harms' which have adverse affects on the entire group to which the research participants belong. The group is the focus of the harm. All or most members of the group are potentially harmed, even those far removed from the research itself and unrelated to research participants. Group harms can occur in all types of research. Harms include physical, psychological, economic and social (e.g. stigmatisation of groups or identifiable cohorts of participants).

---

53   National Department of Health *Ethics in Health Research: Principles, Processes and Structures* (2015) para 3.5.3.
54   Ibid para 3.2.9.

Community consultation will go a long way in assisting researchers to become more aware of:

(a) the specific vulnerability of the group;

(b) the potential for group harms and how to minimise those harms; and

(c) the potential for group benefits of the research, and how to maximise those benefits.

17.4.2 Categories of personal information

The norm in research ethics is to respect privacy and protect the confidentiality of data gathered during research, including tissue samples. In terms of the Guidelines,[55] there are six categories of personal data:

(a) Identifiable information that is reasonably expected to identify an individual alone or in combination with other information

(b) Directly identifying using direct identifiers (e.g. name, identity number)

(c) Indirectly identifying using a combination of indirect identifiers (e.g. date of birth, address, unique personal characteristics)

(d) Coded information where direct identifiers are removed and replaced by codes

(e) Anonymised information that is irrevocably stripped of direct identifiers with no code

(f) Anonymous information that never had identifiers.

Justification is necessary if research data are to be identifiable or potentially identifiable. If tissue is to be stored, research participants must be informed whether it will be identifiable, potentially identifiable or de-identified, and have the implications of such storage explained to them. For example, a consequence of de-identified storage is that participants will not be able to get back their tissue, whereas if the tissue is identifiable or potentially identifiable, their confidentiality may be partially breached.

17.4.3 The Protection of Personal Information Act (the POPI)

In South Africa, the POPI[56] has been enacted, inter alia, to promote the protection of personal information processed by private and public bodies; to introduce certain conditions for the establishment of minimum requirements

---

55   National Department of Health *Ethics in Health Research: Principles, Processes and Structures* (2015) Appendix 1.

56   Act 4 of 2013.

for the processing of personal information; to provide for the rights of persons with regard to unsolicited electronic communication and automated decision making; and to regulate the flow of personal information across the borders of the country.[57] Most of the Act is in force.

In terms of section 18 of POPI, responsible parties must take reasonable practicable steps to ensure that data subjects are made aware of at least the following:

(a) What information is being collected and from what source

(b) The name and address of the responsible party

(c) The purpose for which the information is being collected

(d) Whether or not the information is required voluntarily or mandatorily

(e) The consequences of failing to provide the information

(f) Any particular law authorising or requiring the collection of that information

(g) The fact that the responsible party may intend to transfer the information to a third country or international organisation and the level of protection which will be afforded to that information by that third country or intentional organisation

(h) Any further information which is necessary in the circumstances, to make the processing of a data subject's personal information reasonable.

These steps need to be taken prior to the information being collected unless the data subject is already aware of the information. Otherwise, it should be communicated to the data subject as soon as reasonably practicable after it has been collected.

As regards protection across national boundaries, section 72 of the POPI states that a responsible party in the Republic of South Africa may not transfer personal information about a data subject to a third party who is in a foreign country unless that country has similar laws protecting the processing of personal information of data subjects. The POPI re-affirms the current position with regard to the requirements for informed consent in that informed consent is to be obtained to process personal information.

---

57   A Dhai 'Genetics, genomics, biobanks and health databases in health research' in *Health Research Ethics: Safeguarding the Interests of Research Participants* 165–211.

17.5 Biobanks and health databases in health research

Growing prominence is being placed on the storage and sharing of human biological materials (HBMs) and data in health research. Storage is in biobanks and health databases. The WMA, in its Declaration of Taipei,[58] defines a biobank as 'a collection of biological materials and associated data'. A health database is defined as 'a system for collecting, organizing and storing health information'. Both are collections on individuals and populations and give rise to similar concerns about dignity, autonomy, privacy, confidentiality and discrimination.

The WMA's Declaration of Helsinki states as follows:[59]

> For medical research using identifiable human material or data, such as research on material or data contained in biobanks or similar repositories, physicians must seek informed consent for its collection, storage and/or re-use. There may be exceptional situations where consent would be impossible or impracticable to obtain for such research. In such situations the research may be done only after consideration and approval of a research ethics committee.

The Declaration of Taipei provides the additional ethical principles required for use of data and materials in research.[60] The Declaration of Taipei defines biological materials as referring to 'a sample obtained from an individual human being, living or deceased, which can provide biological information, including genetic information, about that individual'.[61]

In South Africa, the NHA defines tissue as 'human tissue, and includes flesh, bone, a gland, an organ, skin, bone marrow, or body fluid, but excludes blood or a gamete'. The Regulations Relating to the Use of Human Biological Material define biological material as 'material from a human being including DNA, RNA, blastomeres, polar bodies, cultured cells, embryos, gametes, progenitor stem cells, small tissue biopsies, and growth factors from the same'.[62] This latter definition is broad enough to include all human tissue. Furthermore, it specifies that HBMs may be removed or withdrawn from living persons for health research.

The NHA does not provide any stipulations on biobanks. However, the NHA's Material Transfer Agreement defines biobank as 'an institution or unit thereof that safeguards an organized collection of Human Biological Materials and associated data from different individuals, which are usually kept for an

---

58   See Chapter 2.
59   World Medical Association *Declaration of Helsinki on Ethical Principles for Medical Research Involving Human Subjects* (2008) article 2; see Chapter 2.
60   A Dhai 'Genetics, genomics, biobanks and health databases in health research' in *Health Research Ethics: Safeguarding the Interests of Research Participants* (2019) 165–211.
61   *WMA Declaration of Taipei on Ethical Considerations regarding Health Databases and Biobanks* (2016): http://www.wma.net/en/30publications/10policies/d1/index.html (accessed on 24 March 2020).
62   National Department of Health 'Notice 177: Regulations relating to human biological materials' *Government Gazette* (2012).

unlimited period of time, for the purposes of health research'.[63] It is mandatory to use the NHA's material transfer agreement template when transferring HBMs for research to other countries.

17.6 Scientific misconduct

When considering scientific misconduct, a useful starting point is to define the relevant terms. 'Honesty' means truthfulness and being transparent, 'misconduct' means improper or unprofessional behaviour, and 'research' means a systematic investigation in order to establish facts and reach new conclusions.[64]

Researchers, whether they are in health or other fields, are individuals who seek to increase knowledge through the reporting of truthful observations. However, throughout history there have been dishonest individuals who have been guilty of scientific misconduct and the same applies today.

There are examples of known or suspected cases of scientific misconduct from as far back as Ptolemy (2AD), who reported astronomical measurements not done, to that of Mendel (1865), who reported genetic results too good to be true.[65] In modern times, many have committed scientific misconduct, often at prestigious institutions. A few more examples range from manipulated results in cardiac research by Darsee (1981) at Harvard University in the USA,[66] through Bezwoda (2000) at the University of the Witwatersrand who misrepresented results in the treatment of breast cancer,[67] to Hwang Woo-Suk (2005) who falsified cloning research at the University of Seoul in South Korea.[68]

The United States Office of Research Integrity defines three types of research misconduct, although generally where scientific misconduct is effected, there is a combination of all three:[69]

(a) Fabrication – making up data or results and recording or reporting them

(b) Falsification – manipulating research materials, equipment or processes, or changing or omitting data or results such that the research is not accurately represented in the research record

---

63   National Department of Health *Material Transfer Agreement* (2018): https://www.gov.za/sites/default/files/41781_gon719.pdf (accessed on 10 April 2020).

64   See generally, W Broad and N Wade *Betrayers of the Truth: Fraud and Deceit in the Halls of Science* (1982).

65   Ibid.

66   A Kohn *False Prophets* (1988).

67   RB Weiss, RM Rifkin, FM Stewart, RL Theriault, LA Williams , AA Herman and RA Beveridge 'High-dose chemotherapy for high-risk primary breast cancer: An on-site review of the Bezwoda study' (2000) 355 *Lancet* 999–1003.

68   See Hwang Woo-Suk: http://en.wikipedia.org/wiki/hwang_woo-suk.

69   Office of Research Integrity: https://ori.hhs.gov/definition-misconduct (accessed on 10 April 2020).

(c) Plagiarism – appropriation of another person's ideas, processes, results or words without giving appropriate credit.

It is interesting that although science in general, and individual scientists in particular, are intensely sceptical about the possibility of error in observations, they seldom consider the possibility of fraud, and when they are aware of it they tend to believe that it is rare and self-correcting.[70] Research depends on personal trust, a trust that the evidence has been honestly gathered and reported.[71]

Why are scientists involved in research misconduct? One reason is that credit in science usually goes to the person who is the first to have made an original discovery and those who follow seldom get recognition. A classic example of this was the claim of Dr Robert Gallo, an American scientist, that he had discovered the HI virus when in fact it had already been found by a French researcher Dr Luc Montaigner from the Pasteur Institute in Paris, who later received the 2008 Nobel Prize in Medicine for his discovery.[72] Besides personal recognition, another reason for scientific misconduct is self-preservation by researchers who might not have been as productive as expected.

How does one prevent or control scientific misconduct? Scrupulous record keeping and periodic checks by authorities monitoring research are one method of controlling scientific misconduct, but a better method is to instil a culture of personal commitment to scientific integrity in all researchers.

Scientific misconduct is usually exposed when a presentation at a conference or an article published in a scientific journal is questioned. In the latter case, editors of scientific journals have a responsibility to investigate complaints and where necessary, to publish a retraction. An example of this action is the retraction by the *American Journal of Clinical Oncology* of an article by three cancer researchers involved in the Bezwoda affair.[73] In addition, previous publications by authors known to have committed scientific misconduct are usually carefully scrutinised and investigated.

The United States has taken the lead in the prevention and investigation of scientific misconduct combined with punishment of guilty individuals through the government Office of Research Integrity (ORI), that has jurisdiction over all persons and entities that receive federal financial support. The ORI runs education programmes to increase scientific integrity and publishes details of proven cases of scientific misconduct together with the punishments on its

---

70 AN Schechter, JB Wyngaarden, JT Edsall, J Maddox, AS Relman, M Angell and WW Stewart 'Colloquium on scientific authorship: Rights and responsibilities' (1989) 3 *FASEB J* 209–217.
71 AS Relman 'Lessons from the Darsee Affair' (1985) 308 *N Eng J Med* 1415–1417.
72 HF Judson *The Great Betrayal: Fraud in Science* (2004).
73 American Society of Clinical Oncology 'Retraction for Bezwoda et al.' (1995) 13 *J Clin Oncol* 2483–2489; (2001) 19 *J Clin Oncol* 2973.

website.[74] In the United Kingdom there is the Committee on Publication Ethics (COPE). This too has a website that offers advice and shares cases anonymously.[75] Additionally, free flowcharts are provided on the website to help individuals to deal with perceived misconduct.

It is not that easy to detect scientific misconduct. All scientific manuscripts submitted for publication in journals of repute are reviewed by peers. While this peer review can prevent the publication of poor science and can improve the presentation of a particular article, it cannot always detect fraudulent material. Sometimes warning signs may present such as variations in the numbers in the reported experiments and the absence of sufficient information to check results. Another sign is that an experiment may be reported successful using small numbers when other researchers have required very large sample sizes for similar experiments.

Conflicts of interest may be a problem when secondary interests have the potential to influence primary interests.[76] Problems arise when these interests are not declared. For example, a researcher may claim to be independent when he or she actually has shares in a company that has produced the product that the researcher will be testing. The primary interest here is ethical research, i.e. the protection of research participants. The secondary interest will be the potential financial gain to the researcher as a member of the company. Similarly, an unscrupulous member of an REC might not declare a relationship with a particular investigation and take part in the decision making by the REC.

RECs also have a monitoring role. Approvals last a specified time; for example, annual re-certifications of research projects are a necessary requirement in international and local guideline documents. Researchers are required to report on research progress to an REC and to report adverse events or violations of protocols. In the latter, an REC must decide on what remedial action is necessary. The same procedures are applied by most RECs in South Africa.

When scientific misconduct is proven, the punishments for guilty researchers may include dismissal from employment, barring from obtaining research funds, suspension or complete removal of a licence for clinical practice, and even imprisonment with or without a fine.

---

74   Office of Research Integrity: https://ori.hhs.gov/definition-misconduct (accessed on 10 April 2020).

75   Committee on Publication Ethics: http://www.publicationethics.org (accessed on 10 April 2020).

76   See above Chapter 15.

Some questions on research ethics

1. Why is the ethical and responsible conduct of research particularly important in South Africa?

2. As an REC member, you have been allocated a research protocol for ethics review. The research is funded by a company that funds activities regularly in the department that you head. What should you do and why?

References

Abdool Karim, SS & Abdool Karim, Q (eds) *HIV/AIDS in South Africa* (2005) Cape Town, Cambridge University Press

American Society of Clinical Oncology 'Retraction for Bezwoda et al' (1995) 13 *J Clin Oncol* 2483–2489; (2001) 19 *J Clin Oncol* 2973

Appelbaum, PS & Grisso, T 'Assessing patients' capacities to consent to treatment' 319 (1988) *N Engl J Med* 1635–1638

Arendse, N 'Employment, HIV and AIDS: Proposals for law reform' (1993) 9 *SA Journal on Human Rights* 89

Baruch, S, Huang, S, Prichard, D et al. *Human Germline Genetic Modification: Issues and Opinions for Policymakers* (2005) Washington DC, Genetics and Public Policy Center

Beauchamp, TL & Childress, JF *Principles of Biomedical Ethics* 3 ed (1994) New York, Oxford University Press

Beauchamp, TL & Childress, JF *Principles of Biomedical Ethics* 4 ed (1997) New York, Oxford University Press

Beauchamp, TL & Childress, JF *Principles of Biomedical Ethics* 6 ed (2009) New York, Oxford University Press

Beauchamp, TL & Childress, JF 'Respect for autonomy' in TL Beauchamp and JF Childress (eds) *Principles of Biomedical Ethics* 7 ed (2013) New York, Oxford University Press 101–149

Beecher, H *Research and the Individual Human Subject* (1970) Boston, Little Brown

Beecher, HK 'Ethics and clinical research' (1966) 274 *N Engl J Med* 1354–1360

Beltrami, EM, Williams, IT, Shapiro, & Chamberland, ME 'Risk and management of blood-borne infections in health care workers' (2000) 13 *Clinical Microbiol Review* 385–407

Berlin, I *Four Essays on Liberty* (1990) New York, Oxford University Press

Blackburn, S (ed) *Oxford Dictionary of Philosophy* (1996) New York, Oxford University Press

Bosma, HA, Delevita, DJ & Grotevant, HD (eds) *Identity Development: An Interdisciplinary Approach* (1994) Thousand Oaks, SAGE

Boyd, K, Higgs, R & Pinching, A (eds) *The New Dictionary of Medical Ethics* (1997) Hoboken NJ, Wiley-Blackwell

Brand, J, Steadman, F & Todd, C (eds) 'Mediation among the range of processes for resolving disputes' *Commercial Mediation: A User's Guide* 2 ed (2016) Claremont, Juta

British Medical Association *The Medical Profession and Human Rights* (2001) London, Zed Books

British Medical Association 'The doctor–patient relationship' in *Medical Ethics Today: The BMA's Handbook of Ethics and Law* 3 ed (2012) London, Wiley-Blackwell

Broad, W & Wade, N *Betrayers of the Truth: Fraud and Deceit in the Halls of Science* (1982) London, Ebury Press

Brody, BA 'A historical introduction to the requirement of obtaining informed consent from research participants' in Doyal, L & Tobias, JS (eds) *Informed Consent in Medical Research* (2001) London, BMJ Books

Brown University *The Nuremberg Code: Wartime Experiments on the Inmates of Nazi Concentration Camps* (2000)

Burchell, J & Milton, J *Principles of Criminal Law* 3 ed (2005) Claremont, Juta

Cahill, LS 'Genetics: Commodification, and social justice in the globalization era' (2001) 11 *Kennedy Institute of Ethics Journal* 221–238

Callicott, JB 'Non-anthropocentric value theory and environmental ethics today' (1984) 21 *Am Phil Q* 299–309 University of Illinois Press

Carstens, P & Pearmain, D *Foundational Principles of South African Medical Law* (2007) New York, Butterworths LexisNexis

Centers for Disease Control 'Recommendation for preventing transmission of human immunodeficiency virus and hepatitis B virus to patients during exposure-prone invasive procedures' 1991 40 (RRO8) *Morb Mortal Wkly Rep* 1–9

Chadwick, R 'What counts as success in genetic counselling?' (1993) 4 *Journal of Medical Ethics* 33–36

Chatman, EF 'A theory of life in the round' (1999) 5 (3) *J Am Soc Informat Sci* 207–219

Chochinov, HM, Wilson, KG, Enns, M & Lander, S 'Depression hopelessness and suicidal ideation in the terminally ill' (1998) 39(4) *Psychosomatics* 366–370

Claassen, N 'Mediation as an alternative solution to medical malpractice court claims' (2016) 9(1) *SAJBL* 7–10

Cleaton-Jones, P & Vorster, M 'Workload of a South African university-based health research ethics committee in 2003 and 2007' (2008) 1 *SAJBL* 38–43

Cook, RJ, Dickens, BM & Fathalla, MF (eds) *Reproductive Health and Human Rights* (2003) New York, Oxford University Press

Couzin, J 'FDA Drops Helsinki Rules' (2008) 390 *Science* 731

Cruess, RL, Cruess, SR & Johnston, SE 'Professionalism: An ideal to be sustained' (2000) 356 *Lancet* 156–69

Dada, MA & McQuoid-Mason, DJ *Phlebotomy Learnership Guide* (2007) Pathology Laboratory Support Services, Ampath Trust, Johannesburg

Dada, MA & McQuoid-Mason, DJ (eds) *Introduction to Medico-Legal Practice* (2001) Durban, Butterworths

De Cock, K, Mbori-Ngacha, D & Marum, E 'Shadow on the continent: Public health and HIV/AIDS in Africa in the 21st century' (2002) July *Lancet* 360

Dhai, A 'Genetics, genomics, biobanks and health databases in health research' in *Health Research Ethics: Safeguarding the Interests of Research Participants* (2019) Juta, Cape Town 165–211

Dhai, A 'Medical negligence: Alternative claims resolution an answer to the epidemic?' (2016) 9(1) *SAJBL* 2–3

Dhai, A 'Physician-assisted dying and palliative care: Understanding the two' (2015) 8(2) *SAJBL* 2–3

Dhai, A 'The Life Esidimeni tragedy: Moral pathology and an ethical crisis' (2018) 108(5) *SAMJ* 382–385

Dhai, A, Moodley, J, McQuoid-Mason, DJ & Rodeck, C 'Ethical and legal controversies in cloning for bio-medical research – A South African perspective' (2004) 94 *SAMJ* 906–907

Dible, HI *Napoleon's Surgeon* (1970) London, Heinemann Medical

Ellington, JW (trans) *Grounding for the Metaphysics of Morals* 3 ed (1993) Indianapolis, Hackett

Etzioni, A 'Introduction' in Etzioni, E (ed) *The Essential Communiatarian Reader* (1998) Lanham MD, Rowman & Littlefield

Feltz, B 'The philosophical and ethical issues of climate change' (2019) July-Sept *The UNESCO Courier* 7–9

Ferlito, B & Dhai, A 'The Life Esidimeni tragedy: Some ethical transgressions' (2018) 108(3) *SAMJ* 157

Finlay, I & George, R 'Legal physician-assisted suicide in Oregon and The Netherlands: Evidence concerning the impact on patients in vulnerable groups – another perspective on Oregon's data' (2011) 37 *Journal of Medical Ethics* 171–174

Fisk, NM & Braude, P 'Stem cells' (2001) 3 *The Obstetrician and Gynaecologist* 211–212

Friedman, M 'Feminism in ethics: Conceptions of autonomy' in Frickem, M & Hornsby, J (eds) *The Cambridge Companion to Feminism in Philosophy* (2000) Cambridge, Cambridge University Press

Ganzini, L, Goy, ER & Dobscha, K 'Prevalence of depression and anxiety in patients requesting physicians' aid in dying: A cross sectional survey' (2008) 337 *BMJ* 1682

Garg, P 'Parental attitudes attributable to the risk of death of newborns and infants in North India' (2008) 8(1) *Developing World Bioethics* 51–52 Hoboken NJ, Blackwell

Gellner, E *Relativism and the Social Sciences* (1985) Cambridge, Cambridge University Press

Gerth, HH & Wright Mills, C (eds) Max Weber *Essays in Sociology* (1984) Oxford University Press, USA

Gilligan, C *A Different Voice: Psychological Theory and Women's Development* (1982) Cambridge, Harvard University Press

Gilligan, C 'Moral Orientation and Moral Development' in Feder Kittay, E & Meyers, DT (eds) *Women and Moral Theory* (1987) Lanham MD, Rowman & Littlefield

Glover, J *Ethics of New Reproductive Technologies: The Glover Report to the European Commission* (1989) DeKalb IL, Northern Illinois University Press

Grobler, C & Dhai, A 'Social media in the healthcare context: Ethical challenges and recommendations' (2016) 9(1) *S Afr J BL* 22–25

Gyekyo, K *Tradition and Modernity Philosophical Reflections on the Africa Experience* (1997) New York, Oxford University Press

Hampshire, S, Williams, B, Nagel, T & Dworkin, R *Public and Private Morality* (1991) Cambridge, Cambridge University Press

Hassim, A, Heywood, M & Berger, J (eds) *Health and Democracy – A Guide to Human Rights, Health Law and Policy in Post-apartheid South Africa* (2007) Westlake, Siber Ink

Have, TH & Janssens, R 'Futility, limits and palliative care' in Have, TH & Clark, D (eds) *The Ethics of Palliative Care: European Perspectives* (2002) Maidenhead, Open University Press

Häyry, M *Liberal Utilitarianism and Applied Ethics* (1994) London, Routledge Hayward, T 'Anthropocentrism: A misunderstood problem' (1997) 6 *Env Val* 51

Held, V *The Ethics of Care* (2005) New York, Oxford University Press

Hoffmaster, B *Bioethics in Social Context* (1984) Philadelphia PA, Temple University Press

Holm, S 'Going to the roots of the stem cell controversy' (2002) 16 *Bioethics* 493–507

Institute of Medicine Committee on Quality of Healthcare in America *Crossing the Quality Chasm: A New Health System for the Twenty First Century* (2001) Washington DC, National Academy Press

International Dual Loyalty Working Group *Dual Loyalty and Human Rights in Health Professional Practice: Physicians for Human Rights and School of Public Health and Primary Health Care* (2002) University of Cape Town, Health Sciences Faculty

Jafari, M 'Challenges in climate change and environmental crisis: Impact of aviation industry on human, urban and natural environments' (2013) 3(3) *International Journal of Space Technology Management and Innovation* 24–46

Jones, DA 'Evidence of the adverse impact in assisted suicide and euthanasia' (2015) 351 *BMJ* H443

Jordaan, L 'The right to die with dignity: A consideration of the constitutional arguments' (2009) 72 *THRHR* 192–216, 374–393

Judson, HF *The Great Betrayal: Fraud in Science* (2004) Boston MA, Houghton Mifflin Harcourt

Juengst, ET 'Ethical issues in human gene transfer research in the development of human gene therapy' in Ashcroft, R, Dawson, A & Draper, H (eds) *Principles of Health Care Ethics* (2007) Hoboken NJ, John Wiley

Kainz Benthamite, HP *Social Utility as a Strictly Objective Norm* (1995) London, Macmillan

Kant, I *Grounding for the Metaphysics of Morals* (1785) Indianapolis, Hackett

Kant, I *Groundwork for the Metaphysics of Morals* (1785) Abbot, TK (trans) Lara Denis (ed) *Groundwork for the Metaphysics of Morals* (2005) Indianapolis, Hackett

Kant, I *Groundwork for the Metaphysics of Morals* 4 ed (1911) Indianapolis, Hackett

Kennedy, I & Grubb, A *Medical Law* 2 ed (1994) Durban, Butterworths

Kerns, TK *Jenner on Trial* (1997) Lanham MA, University Press of America

Kirby, M 'AIDS and the Law' (1993) 9 *SA Journal on Human Rights* 15–16

Kohlberg, L *Essays on Moral Development: The Philosophy of Moral Development* vol 1 (1981) New York, Harper & Row

Kohn, A *False Prophets* (1988) Hoboken NJ, Blackwell

Koniaris, LG, Zimmers, TA, Lubarsky, DA & Sheldon JP 'Inadequate anaesthesia in lethal injection for execution' (2005) 5(9468) *Lancet* 1412–1414

Lieberman, JD & Derse, AR 'HIV-positive health care workers and the obligation to disclose' (1992) 13 *Journal of Legal Medicine* 333–365

Lutz, B 'Prevention of transmission of blood-borne pathogens to patients during invasive procedure' (1991) 8(3) *AIDS Inf Exch* 2–11

Lutzenberger, J 'Science, technology, economics, ethics and environment' in Callicott, JB & da Rocha, FJR (eds) *Earth Summit Ethics* (1995) Albany, State University of New York Press

Macklin, R *Against Relativism: Cultural Diversity and the Search for Ethical Universals in Medicine* (1999) New York, Oxford University Press

Malherbe, J 'Counting the cost: The consequences of increased medical malpractice litigation in South Africa' (2013) 103(1) *SAMJ* 83–84.

Malone, K 'Environmental education researchers as environmental activists' (1999) 5 *Env Edu Res* 163–177

Martinez, R 'Losing empathy – commentary' in Kushner, TK & Thomasma, DC (eds) *Ward Ethics* (2001) New York, Cambridge University Press

Matsoso, MP & Fryatt, R 'National health insurance: The first 18 months' (2013) 103(3) *SAMJ* 156–158

McIntyre, D & Gilson, L 'Putting equity in health back onto the social policy agenda – Experience from South Africa' (2002) 54 *Social Science and Medicine* 1637–1656

McIntyre, D & Gilson, L 'Redressing disadvantage – Promoting vertical equity within South Africa' (2000) 8(3) *Health Care Analysis* 235–258

Mclean, GR & Jenkins, T 'The Steve Biko affair: A case study in medical ethics' (2003) 3(1) *Developing World Bioethics* 77–95

McQuoid-Mason, DJ 'Assisted suicide and assisted voluntary euthanasia: *Stransham-Ford* High Court case overruled by the Appeal Court – but the door is left open' (2017) 107(5) *SAMJ* 381–382

McQuoid-Mason, DJ 'Can the consent provisions in the Choice on Termination of Pregnancy Act, which do not require children to be assisted by a parent or guardian, be used for live births caesarean section in emergency situations?' (2018) 11(1) *SAJBL* 43–45

McQuoid-Mason, DJ 'Disclosing details about the medical treatment of a deceased public figure in a book: Who should have consented to the disclosures?' (2017) 107(12) *SAMJ* 1072–1074

McQuoid-Mason, DJ 'Emergency medical treatment and 'do not resuscitate' orders: When can they be used?' (2013) 103(4) *SAMJ* 223–225

McQuoid-Mason, DJ 'Establishing liability for harm caused to patients in a resource-deficient environment' (2010) 100(9) *SAMJ* 573–575

McQuoid-Mason, DJ 'Hospital-acquired infections – when are hospitals legally liable?' (2012) 102(6) *SAMJ* 353–354

McQuoid-Mason, DJ 'Is it ethically and legally justified for doctors to provide futile medical treatment if patients or their proxies are prepared to pay for it? What should doctors do?' (2017) 107(2) *SAMJ* 108–109

McQuoid-Mason, DJ 'Is there an ethical duty and legal duty on doctors to disclose their fees before treatment?' (2015) 105(3) *SAMJ* 96–97

McQuoid-Mason, DJ 'Is the mass circumcision drive in KwaZulu-Natal involving neonates and children less than 16 years of age legal? What should doctors do?' (2013) 103(5) *SAMJ* 283–284

McQuoid-Mason, DJ 'Life Esidimeni deaths: Can the former MEC for health and public health officials escape liability for the deaths of the mental health patients on the basis of obedience to "superior orders" or because the officials under them were negligent?' (2018) 11(1) *SAJBL* 5–7

McQuoid-Mason, DJ 'Living wills' (1993) January *Continuing Medical Education* 59–64

McQuoid-Mason, DJ 'Michael Jackson and the limits of patient autonomy' (2012) 5(1) *SAJBL* 11–14

McQuoid-Mason, DJ 'Public health officials and MECs should be held liable for harm caused to patients through incompetence, indifference, maladministration or negligence regarding the availability of hospital equipment' (2016) 106(7) *SAMJ* 681–683

McQuoid-Mason, DJ 'Sending patients electronic reminders of the need for urgent treatment to prevent life-threatening illnesses – some lessons to be learned and a cautionary reminder that self-representation can be dangerous (2019) 109(11) *SAMJ* 845–847

McQuoid-Mason, DJ 'State doctors, freedom of conscience and termination of pregnancy' (1997) 1(6) *Human Rights and Constitutional Law Journal of SA* 15–17

McQuoid-Mason, DJ 'Termination of pregnancy and children: Consent and confidentiality issues' (2010) 100(2) *SAMJ* 213–214

McQuoid-Mason, DJ 'Termination of pregnancy and children: Professor McQuoid-Mason replies' (2011) 101(2) *SAMJ* 212

McQuoid-Mason, DJ 'The medical profession and medical practice' in Joubert, WA & Faris, JA (eds) *The Law of South Africa* 17(2) 2 ed (2008) Butterworths, Durban

McQuoid-Mason, DJ 'UKZN Anniversary symposium on the medico-legal and ethical implications on human tissue use' (2011) 4(1) *SAJBL* 13–14

McQuoid-Mason, DJ 'When may doctors give nurses telephonic instructions? (2016) 106(8) *SAMJ* 787–788

McQuoid-Mason, DJ 'Withholding or withdrawal of treatment and palliative treatment hastening death: The real reason why doctors are not held legally liable for murder' (2014) 104(2) *SAMJ* 102–103

McQuoid-Mason, DJ 'With the clinical independence of doctors in hospitals faced with a shortage of resources: What should doctors do?' (2014) 104(11) *SAMJ* 741–742

McQuoid-Mason, DJ & Dada, MA *A-Z of Nursing Law* (2009) Claremont, Juta

McQuoid-Mason, DJ & Dada, MA 'The National Health Act with regard to tissue transplantation' (2006) 24 *CME* 2006 16–18

Mill, JS *On Liberty* (1958) London, Forgotten Books (republished 2008)

Munson, R *Intervention and Reflection: Basic Issues in Medical Ethics* 7 ed (2004) Belmont CA, Wadsworth-Thomson Learning

Nattrass, N *The Moral Economy of AIDS in South Africa* (2004) London, Cambridge University Press

Norheim, OF 'Ethical perspective: Five unacceptable trade-offs on the path to universal health coverage' (2015) 4(11) *Int J Health Policy Manag* 711–714

Norheim, OF 'Ethical priority setting for universal health coverage: Challenges in deciding upon fair distribution of health services' (2016) 14 *BMC Medicine* 14–75

Norton, B 'Ecology and opportunity: Intergenerational equity and sustainable options' in Dobson, A (ed) *Fairness and Futurity: Essays in Environmental Sustainability and Social Justice* (1999) 118–150 New York, Oxford University Press

Norton, B *Toward Unity Among Environmentalists* (1991) New York, Oxford University Press

Norton, BF 'Environmental ethics and weak anthropocentrism' in Pierce, C & Van de Veer, D (eds) *People, Penguins, and Plastic Trees* 2 ed (1995) 182–192 Belmont CA, Wadsworth

Nuffield Council on Bioethics *Human Tissue: Ethical and Legal Issues* (1995). London, KKS Printing

Orr, D *Ecological Literacy, Education and the Transition to a Post Modern World* (1992) Albany NY, State University of New York Press

Pellegrino, ED & Thomas, DC *The Good of the Patient: The Restitution of Beneficence in Medical Ethics* (1987) New York, Oxford University Press

Pellegrino, ED 'Altruism, self-interest and medical ethics' (1987) 258 *JAMA* 1939–1940

Pellegrino, ED 'Codes, virtue, and professionalism' in Sugarman, J and Sulmasy, D *Methods in Medical Ethics* 2 ed (2010) Washington DC, Georgetown University Press

Pellegrino, ED 'The interanal morality of clinical medicine: A paradigm for the ethics of the helping and healing professions' (2001) 26(6) *J Med and Phil*

Pellegrino, ED *The Virtues in Medical Practice* (1993) New York, Oxford University Press

Porco, TC, Martin, JN, Page-Shafer, KA, Cherlebois, E, Grant, RM & Osborne, DH 'Decline in HIV infectivity following the introduction of highly active antiretroviral therapy' (2004) 18(1) *AIDS* 81–88

Potter, VR *Bioethics Bridge to the Future* (1971) Upper Saddle River NJ, Prentice Hall

Potter, VR & Whitehouse, PJ 'Deep and global bioethics for a liveable third millennium' (1998) 12 *The Scientist* 9

Purdy, LM 'Assisted reproduction, prenatal testing, and sex selection' in Kuhse, H & Singer, P (eds) *A Companion to Bioethics* 2 ed (2009) Hoboken NJ, Wiley-Blackwell

Purtilo, R *Ethical Dimensions in the Health Professions* 3 ed (1999) Philadelphia, Saunders

Rachels, J *The Elements of Moral Philosophy* (2003) New York, McGraw-Hill

Reich, W 'The word "bioethics" struggle over its earliest meanings' (1995) 5 *Ken Inst Eth J* 31

Relman, AS 'Lessons from the Darsee Affair' (1985) 308 *N Eng J Med* 1415–1417

Rifkin, J *Algeny* (1993) Viking Press, New York

Robinson, P 'Prenatal screening, sex selection and cloning' in Kuhse, H & Singer, P (eds) *A Companion to Bioethics* (1998) Hoboken NJ, Wiley-Blackwell

Royal College of Physicians 'Doctors in society: Medical professionalism in a changing world' (2005) 5:S5–40 *Clin Med (London)*

Sadleir, E & De Beer, T *Don't Film Yourself Having Sex and Other Legal Advice for the Age of Social Media* (2014) Johannesburg, Penguin Books

Schechter, AN, Wyngaarden, JB, Edsall, JT, Maddox, J, Relman, AS, Angell, M & Stewart, WW 'Colloquium on scientific authorship: Rights and responsibilities' (1989) 3 *FASEB J* 209–217

Schlesinger, M 'A loss of faith: The sources of reduced political legitimacy for the American medical profession' (2002) 80 *The Milbank Quart* 185–236

Schneiderman, LJ, Jecker, NS & Jonsen, AR 'Medical futility: Its meaning and ethical implications' (1990) 112 *Annals of Internal Medicine* 949–954

Schweitzer, A *The Philosophy of Civilization* (1987) Buffalo NY, Prometheus Books

Shaffer, DR *Social and Personality Development* 5 ed (2005) Boston MA, Wadsworth Cengage Learning

Shaw, WH *Social and Personal Ethics: Classical Theories* (1993) Boston MA, Cengage Learning

Slabbert, M 'Burial or cremation – who decides?' (2016) 49(2) *De Jure* 230–241

Slabbert, M 'Combat organ trafficking – reward the donor or regulate sales?' (2008) 73(1) *KOERS* 75–99

Slabbert, M 'Ethics, justice and the sale of kidneys for transplantation purposes' (2010) 13(2) *PER* 2–31

Slabbert, M 'The law as an obstacle in solid organ donations and transplantations' (2018) 81(1) *THRHR* 70

Slabbert, M 'This is my kidney, I can do what I want with it' (2009) 3 *Obiter* 499–517

Slabbert, M & Oosthuizen, H 'Creating a market for human organs in South Africa' (2007) 28 *Obiter* 44, 304

Slabbert, M & Van der Westhuizen, C 'Death with dignity in lieu of euthanasia' (2007) 2 *SA Public Law* 366–384

Slote, MA *The Ethics of Care and Empathy* (2007) London, Routledge

Smith, KA, Harvath, TA, Goy, ER & Ganzini, L 'Predictors of pursuit of physician-assisted death' (2015) 49(3) *Journal of Pain and Symptom Management* 555–561

Soini, S 'The interface between assisted reproductive technologies and genetics: technical, social, ethical and legal issues' (2006) 14 *European Journal of Human Genetics* 588–645

Solter, D & Gearhart, J 'Putting stem cells to work' (1999) 283 *Science* 1468–1470

Spar, DL *The Baby Business: How Money, Science and Politics Drive the Commerce of Conception* (2006) Brighton MA, Harvard Business Review

Stern, W *Foundations of Ethics as a Positive Science* (1897) from *The Philosophy of Civilization* Buffalo NY, Prometheus

Strauss, SA *Doctor, Patient and the Law* 3 ed (1993) Pretoria, JL Van Schaik

Strauss, SA *Legal Handbook for Nurses and Health Personnel* 7 ed (1992) Cape Town, King Edward VII Trust

Strauss, SA & Strydom, MJ *Die Suid-Afrikaanse Geneeskundige Reg* (1967) Pretoria, JL Van Schaik

Szabo, CP, Dhai, A & Veller, M 'HIV-positive status among surgeons – an ethical dilemma' (2006) 96 *SAMJ* 1072–1075

Temkin, O & Temkin, CL (eds) *Ancient Medicine: Selected Papers of Ludwig Edelstein* (1967) Baltimore MD, Johns Hopkins University Press

Thompson, JJ *Ideology and Modern Culture* (1992) Palo Alto CA, Stanford University Press

Van Niekerk, AA & Kopelman, LM (eds) *Ethics and AIDS in Africa: The Challenge to Our Thinking* (2005) Walnut Creek CA, Left Coast Press

Van Wyk, CW & Slabbert, M 'Post-mortems, burials, anatomy' in Joubert, WA & Faris JA (eds) *The Law of South Africa* 20 Part 2 2 ed (2008)

Veach, R *Medical Ethics* (1997) Burlington MA, Jones & Bartlett

Venter, B & Slabbert, M '*S v Frederiksen* (33/2016 ZAFSHC: SACR 29 (FB) (14 September 2017): Human tissue in a freezer: a crime or not?' (2019) *De Jure* 109–114

Walters, L 'Human gene therapy: Ethics and public policy' (1991) 2 (2) *Human Gene Therapy* 115–122 New Rochelle NY, Mary Ann Liebert

Weber, M *Essays on Sociology* (1919) New York, Oxford University Press

Weiss, RB, Rifkin, RM, Stewart, FM, Theriault, RL, Williams, LA, Herman, AA & Beveridge, RA 'High-dose chemotherapy for high-risk primary breast cancer: An on-site review of the Bezwoda study' (2000) 355 *Lancet* 999–1003

Weissman, IL 'Stem cells – scientific, medical and political issues' (2002) 346 *NEJM* 1576–1579

Williams, B *Ethics and the Limits of Philosophy* (1985) Cambridge, Harvard University Press

Williams, JR *World Medical Association Medical Ethics Manual* (2005) World Medical Association

Wiredu, K 'How not to compare African thought with Western thought' in Eze, EC (ed) *African Philosophy: An Anthology* (2000) Hoboken NJ, Wiley-Blackwell

World Medical Association *Medical Ethics Manual* 3ed (2015)

Wynia, MK, Cummins, D, Flemming, D, Karjens, K, Orr, A, Sabin, J, Saphire-Bernstein, I & Witlen, R 'Improving fairness in coverage decisions: Performance expectations for quality improvement' (2004) 4(3) *American Journal of Bioethics* 87–100

Electronic sources

AIDS Law Project and the AIDS Legal Network *HIV/AIDS and the Law* 2 ed (2005). Available from: http://bibliobase.sermais.pt:8008/BiblioNET/Upload/PDF7/005049.pdf (accessed 23 June 2020)

AIDS Law Project *HIV/AIDS and the Law: A Resource Manual* 2 ed (2001) https://section27.org.za/2003/06/hivaids-and-the-law-manual/ (accessed 2 July 2020)

Association of American Medical Colleges *A Flag in the Wind: Educating for Professionalism in Medicine* (2003) http://users.clas.ufl.edu/msscha/Readings/flaginthewind_professionalism_med.pdf (accessed 2 July 2020)

Benjamin, DJ, Choi, JJ & Strickland, A *Social Identity and Preferences* (2008) Yale International Centre for Finance Working Paper No. 08-13. https://papers.ssrn.com/Sol3/papers.cfm?abstract_id=1124994n (accessed 2 July 2020)

Committee on Publication Ethics: http://www.publicationethics.org (accessed 10 April 2020)

Critical Care Society of South Africa *Allocation of scarce critical care resources during the COVID-19 public health emergency in South Africa* (2020). Available from: https://criticalcare.org.za/wp-content/uploads/2020/04/Allocation-of-Scarce-Critical-Care-Resources-During-the-COVID-19-Public-Health-Emergency-in-South-Africa.pdf (accessed 6 April 2020)

Dambisya, YM & Modipa, SI 'Capital flows in the health sector in South Africa: Implications for equity and access to health care' *Equinet Discussion Paper* 76 (2009). Available from: http://www.equinetafrica.org/bibl/docs/DIS76pppDAMBISYA.pdf (accessed 21 May 2010)

Department of Health *National Health Insurance Bill* (2018). Available from: https://www.gov.za/sites/default/files/41725_gon635s.pdf) (accessed 6 April 2020).

Department of Health *Policy on National Health Insurance* (2011). Available from: http://pmg-assets.s3-website-eu-west-1.amazonaws.com/docs/110812nhi_0.pdf (accessed 6 April 2020).

Department of Health *National Health Insurance Policy* (2017). Available from: https://cdn.mg.co.za/content/documents/2017/06/29/whitepaper-nhi-2017compressed.pdf (accessed 6 April 2020).

Dhai, A 'Informed consent' (2008) 1 *The South African Journal of Bioethics and Law* 27–30. Available from: http://www.sajbl.org.za/indexphp/sajbl/article/viewFile/5/9 (accessed 27 March 2010)

Florence Nightingale (1893) pledge. Available from: http://www.countryjoe.com/nightingale/pledge.htm (accessed 2 August 2010)

Government Gazette, 7 February 2020, No 43000. Available from: http://www.gpwonline.co.za (accessed 20 April 2020)

Health Professions Council of South Africa guidelines for good practice in the health care professions booklets. Available from: https://www.hpcsa.co.za/Uploads/Professional_Practice/Ethics_Booklet.pdf (accessed 18 June 2020)

Health Professions Council of South Africa Guidelines for Good Practice in the Health Care Professions Booklet 2 *Ethical and Professional Rules of the Health Professions Council of South Africa as Promulgated in Government Gazette R717/2006.* Available from: http://www.hpcsa.co.za (accessed 26 March 2020)

Health Professions Council of South Africa Guidelines for Good Practice in the Health Care Professions Booklet 4 *Seeking Patients' Informed Consent: The Ethical Considerations.* Available from: http://www.hpcsa.co.za (accessed 26 March 2020)

Health Professions Council of South Africa Guidelines for Good Practice in the Healthcare Professions Booklet 6: *Ethical Guidelines for Good Practice with regard to HIV* (2016) https://www.hpcsa.co.za/Uploads/Professional_Practice/Conduct%20%26%20Ethics/Booklet%206%20Gen%20Ethical%20Guidelines%20for%20Management%20of%20Patients%20with%20HIV.pdf (accessed 2 July 2020)

Health Professions Council of South Africa Guidelines for Good Practice in the Healthcare Professions Booklet 17: *Ethical Guidelines on Palliative Care* (2019) https://www.hpcsa.co.za/Uploads/Professional_Practice/Conduct%20%26%20Ethics/HPCSA%20Booklet%2017%20-%20Ethical%20Guidelines%20for%20Palliative%20Care.pdf (accessed 2 July 2020)

Health Professions Council of South Africa Guidelines for Good Practice in the Healthcare Professions Booklet 5 *Confidentiality: Protecting and Providing Information.* Available from: http://www.hpcsa.co.za (accessed 26 March 2020)

Health Professions Council of South Africa Guidelines for Good Practice in the Healthcare Professions Booklet 7: *Guidelines for the Withholding and Withdrawing of Treatment* (2016) https://www.hpcsa.co.za/Uploads/Professional_Practice/Conduct%20%26%20Ethics/Booklet%207%20Guidelines%20withholding%20and%20withdrawing%20treatment%20September%202016.pdf (accessed 1 July 2020).

Health Professions Council of South Africa Guidelines for Good Practice in the Healthcare Professions Booklet 10: *General Ethical Guidelines for Good Practice in Telemedicine* (2014). Available from: https://www.hpcsa.co.za/Uploads/Professional_Practice/Conduct%20%26%20Ethics/Booklet%2010%20Telemedicine%20September%20%202016.pdf (accessed 20 April 2020)

Health Professions Council of South Africa Guidelines for Good Practice in the Healthcare Professions Booklet 16 *Ethical Guidelines for Social Media* (2019). Available from: https://www.hpcsa.co.za/Uploads/Professional_Practice/Conduct%20%26%20Ethics/Ethical2%20Guidelines%20on%20Social%20Media.pdf (accessed 20 April 2020)

http://www.brown.edu/Courses/Bio_160/Projects2000/Ethics/THENUREMBURGCODE.html (accessed 9 July 2009)

http://www.hpcsa.co.za (accessed 20 May 2010)

http://www.sahistory.org.za/pages/people/bios/biko-s.htm (accessed 5 January 2010)

http://www.sciencemag.org/cgi/reprint/320/5877/731b.pdf (accessed 29 June 2009)

http://www.wma.net/e/policy/d1.htm (accessed 10 May 2009)

http://www.wma.org (accessed 19 May 2010)

http://www.doh.gov.za/docs/policy-fhtml (accessed 14 April 2010)

http://www.wma.net/e/policy/l4.htm (accessed 14 April 2010)

Hwang Woo-Suk. Available from: http://en.wikipedia.org/wiki/hwang_woo-suk (accessed 23 March 2010)

International Dual Loyalty Working Group *Dual Loyalty and Human Rights in Health Professional Practice: Proposed Guidelines and Institutional Mechanisms* (2002) 1–2. Available from: http://apha.confex.com/apha/132am/techprogram/paper_80265.htm (accessed 20 May 2010)

Jones, DA 'Evidence of the adverse impact in assisted suicide and euthanasia' (2015) 351 *BMJ* H443. Available from: http://www.bmj.com/content/351/bmj.h4437/rr-10 (accessed 1 November 2015)

Life Healthcare *The importance of triage* (2019). Available from: https://www.lifehealthcare.co.za/news-and-info-hub/latest-news/the-importance-of-triage-management/) (accessed 8 April 2020)

Medical Research Council of South Africa Booklet 2 *Reproductive Biology and Genetic Research: Guidelines on Ethics for Medical Research* 4 ed (2002) https://www.samrc.ac.za/sites/default/files/attachments/2016-06-29/ethicsbook2.pdf (accessed 2 July 2020)

Moseneke, DE *The Life Esidimeni arbitration report*. Available from: http://www.saflii.org/images/LifeEsidimeniArbitrationAward.pdf (accessed 11 June 2018)

Mthethwa, A 'Court orders quarantine after mother and daughter test positive for Covid-19 but refuse isolation' *Daily Maverick* 18 March 2020. Available from: https://www.dailymaverick.co.za/article/2020-03-18-court-orders-quarantine-after-mother-and-daughter-test-positive-for-covid-19-but-refuse-isolation/ (accessed 1 April 2020)

National Commission for the Protection of Human Subjects of Biomedical and Behavioural Research *The Belmont Report* (1979) https://www.hhs.gov/ohrp/regulations-and-policy/belmont-report/read-the-belmont-report/index.html (accessed 2 July 2020)

National Department of Health *Clinical Trials Guidelines* 2 ed (2006) http://www.kznhealth.gov.za/research/guideline2.pdf (accessed 2 July 2020)

National Department of Health 'Notice 177: Regulations relating to human biological materials' *Government Gazette* (2012) Regulation Gazette No. 35099. 2 March 2012, Vol 561, No 9699. https://www.greengazette.co.za/documents/regulation-gazette-35099-of-02-march-2012-vol-561-no-9699_20120302-GGR-35099.pdf (accessed 2 July 2020)

National Department of Health *Clinical Trials Guidelines* 2 ed (2006). Available from: http://www.kznhealth.gov.za/research/guideline2.pdf (accessed 10 April 2020)

National Department of Health *Material Transfer Agreement* (2018): https://www.gov. za/sites/default/files/41781_gon719.pdf (accessed 10 April 2020)

National Health Insurance Bill B-11 (2019). Available from: https://www.gov.za/ documents/national-health-insurance-bill-b-11-2019-6-aug-2019-0000 (accessed 30 March 2020)

National Patients' Rights Charter. Available from: http://www.doh.gov.za/docs/ legislation/patients rights/chartere.html (accessed 12 May 2010)

Nuremberg Tribunal *The Nuremberg Code* (1948). Available from: http://ohsr.od.nih.gov/ guidelines/nuremberg.html (accessed 9 July 2009)

Office of Human Research Protections. Available from: http://www.hhs.gov/ohrp/ (accessed 15 July 2010)

Office of Research Integrity. Available from: https://ori.hhs.gov/definition-misconduct (accessed 10 April 2020)

Office of Research Integrity *Annual Report* (2006). Available from: http://www.ori.hhs. gov (accessed 15 July 2010)

Organization of African Unity African (Banjul) Charter of Human and People's Rights (1981) https://www.achpr.org/public/Document/file/English/ban jul_charter.pdf (accessed 2 July 2020)

Organization of African Unity African Charter on the Rights and Welfare of the Child (1990) https://www.un.org/en/africa/osaa/pdf/au/afr_charter_rights_welfare_child_ africa_1990.pdf (accessed 2 July 2020)

Patients' Rights Charter. Available from: http://www.doh.gov.za/docs/legis lation/ patientsright/charter e.html (accessed 20 May 2010)

SAPA *HIV+ man loses appeal over unprotected sex*. Available from: https://www.iol.co.za/ news/hiv-man-loses-appeal-over-unprotected-sex-1561786 (accessed 29 March 2020)

Saves – the living will society. Available from: http://www.livingwill.co.za (accessed 24 April 2010)

South African Government *National Health Insurance*. Available from: https://www. gov.za/about-government/government-programmes/national-health-insurance-0 (accessed 30 March 2020)

SA Law Commission *Euthanasia and the Artificial Preservation of Life* (Working Paper 53) Project 86 (1994). Available from: https://www.justice.gov.za/salrc/reports/r_ prj86_euthen_1998nov.pdf (accessed 23 June 2020)

South African Law Reform Commission *Medico-Legal Claims* Issue Paper 33 Project 141 (2017). Available from: https://www.justice.gov.za/salrc/ipapers/ip33_prj141_ Medico-legal.pdf (accessed 3 April 2020)

South African Law Reform Commission *Medico-Legal Claims* Project 141 (2017). Available from: http://salawreform.justice.gov.za/ipapers/ip33_prj141_Medico- legal.pdf (accessed 3 April 2020)

South African Medical Association *SARS-CoV-2 (COVID-19) Guidance for Managing Ethical Issues*. Available from: https://www.samedical.org/files/covid19/doctor_ resource/SAMA_Ethics%20Guidance%20_COVID-19%20Ethics_2020%20 7%20Apr.pdf (accessed 25 April 2020)

South African Medical Research Council Guidelines on the Responsible Conduct of Research (2018). Available from: https://www.samrc.ac.za/sites/default/files/attachments/2018-06-27/ResponsibleConductResearchGuidelines.pdf (accessed 10 April 2020)

South African National Department of Health *Ethics in Health Research: Principles, Processes and Structures* (2015). Available from: https://www.ul.ac.za/research/application/downloads/DoH%202015%20Ethics%20in%20Health%20Research%20Guidelines.pdf (accessed 10 April 2020)

The Life Esidimeni disaster: The Makgoba report. Available from: http://www.politicsweb.co.za/documents/the-life-esidimeni-disaster-the-makgoba-report (accessed 1 April 2020)

Times Live. Available from: https://www.timeslive.co.za/news/south-africa/2019-07-11-da-slams-r29bn-medical-negligence-claims-against-gauteng-health/ (accessed 15 August 2019)

UNESCO *Declaration of Ethical Principles in Relation to Climate Change* (2017). Available from: https://unesdoc.unesco.org/ark:/48223/pf0000260889 (accessed 9 April 2020)

United Nations Department of Public Information *Platform for Action and Beijing Declaration: Fourth World Conference on Women, Beijing, China, 4-15 September 1995* (1995) https://www.un.org/womenwatch/daw/beijing/platform/plat2.htm (accessed 2 July 2020)

United Nations *International Covenant on Civil and Political Rights* (1966) https://treaties.un.org/doc/publication/unts/volume%20999/volume-999-i-14668-english.pdf (accessed 2 July 2020)

United Nations *International Covenant on Economic, Social and Cultural Rights* (1966) https://www.ohchr.org/EN/professionalinterest/pages/cescr.aspx (accessed 2 July 2020)

United Nations *Universal Declaration of Human Rights* (1948) https://www.un.org/en/universal-declaration-human-rights/ (accessed 2 July 2020)

United Nations Development Project *Sustainable Development Goals* (2015). Available from: http://www.undp.org/content/dam/undp/library/corporate/brochure/SDGs_Booklet_Web_En.pdf (accessed 6 April 2020)

United States Government *The President's Council on Bioethics. Human Cloning and Human Dignity: An Ethical Inquiry* (2002) 80–110. Available from: http://www.bioethics.gov (accessed 8 December 2006)

Williams, JR 'The future of medical professionalism' (2009) 2 *The South African Journal of Bioethics and Law* 48–50. Available from: http://www.sajbl.org.za/index.php/sajbl/article/viewFile/55/50 (accessed 27 July 2010)

World Health Organization Advisory Committee on Health Research. *Genomics and World Health: Report of the Advisory Committee on Health Research* (2002). https://apps.who.int/iris/handle/10665/42453 (accessed 2 July 2020)

World Health Organization *Protecting Health from Climate Change: Global Research Priorities* (2009) https://www.who.int/globalchange/publications/9789241598187/en/ (accessed 2 July 2020)

World Health Organization *Definition of palliative care*. Available from: http://www.who.int/cancer/palliative/en/ (accessed 5 April 2020)

World Health Organization *Making Fair Choices on the Path to Universal Health Coverage* (2014). Available from: http://apps.who.int/iris/bitstream/10665/112671/1/9789241507158_eng.pdf?ua=1 (accessed 1 October 2017)

World Health Organization *Rapid Scoping Review of Medical Malpractice Policies in Obstetrics* (2015). Available from: http://www.who-report_malpracticemodels_-12aug2015_final.pdf (accessed 1 April 2020)

World Health Organization *Telehealth* (2016). Available from: https://www.who.int/sustainable-development/health-sector/strategies/telehealth/en/ (accessed 20 April 2020)

World Medical Association *Declaration of Venice on Terminal Illness* (2006) 1. Available from: http://www.wma.net/e/policy/i2.htm (accessed 10 May 2009)

World Medical Association *Declaration on Professional Autonomy and Self-Regulation* (2005) 1. Available from: http://www.wma.net/e/policy/a21.htm (accessed 10 May 2009)

World Medical Association *Declaration on the Abuse of the Elderly* (2005) 1. Available from: http://www.wma.net/e/policy/a4.htm (accessed 10 May 2009)

World Medical Association *Declaration on the Rights of the Child to Healthcare* (1998) 1. Available from: http://www.wma.net/e/policy/c4.htm (accessed 10 May 2009)

World Medical Association *Declaration on the Rights of the Patient* (2005). Available from: http://www.wma.net/e/policy/l4.htm (accessed 10 May 2009)

World Medical Association *Declaration on Therapeutic Abortion* (2006). Available from: http://www.wma.net/e/policy/a1.htm (accessed 10 March 2010)

World Medical Association. Available from: http://www.wma.org (accessed 19 May 2010)

World Medical Association *International Code of Medical Ethics and the Declaration of Geneva* (2006). Available from: http://www.wma.net/e/policy/c8.htm (accessed 10 May 2009)

World Medical Association *Handbook of Medical Ethics* (2015). Available from: https://www.wma.net/wp-content/uploads/2016/11/Ethics_manual_3rd_Nov2015_en.pdf (accessed 23 April 2020)

World Medical Association 'The Physician's Pledge' *Declaration of Geneva* (1948), as amended (2017). Available from: https://www.wma.net/policies-post/wma-declaration-of-geneva/ (accessed 20 April 2020)

Index

www.ingramcontent.com/pod-product-compliance
Lightning Source LLC
Chambersburg PA
CBHW051333200326
41519CB00026B/7412